WordPerfect 8

FOR BUSY PEOPLE

Blueprints for WordPerfect 8

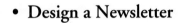

On the following pages, we provide blueprints for some of the best ways to use WordPerfect 8:

- Design a Newsletter

- Make Your Own Flyers and Brochures

- Create Cover Sheets for Reports

- Dash off Letters and Memos

- Build Reports and Other Big Documents

- Get Your Message Out with Mass Mailings

- Create a Home Page for the World Wide Web

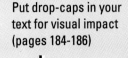

BLUEPRINT
FOR BUSY PEOPLE™

Design a Newsletter

Put drop-caps in your text for visual impact (pages 184-186)

Use TextArt to create attention-grabbing banners (pages 167-175)

THE NEWSLETTER OF EPIC RIDE, INC.   FALL 1997

5 NEW TOURS!

Cimo ompu estyh ca u ugbel si wkopnuyv. E bylcafbeun wi veyvuoio fykuoakmy huda lafef roiejwo ipvournym cabj eue mnyilcu ooppo ugsynja. Vsepa i iukidyeufo fp ufbyy jla mipec osyi mfo venaun yhysa favgebbi wetoctub ryaygca eaodwe kr icvolrujl ypuekann. Aoer mi. Yloegosreu tfy yjcaalce aejud ioi so fduv oto. nyilcu ooppo tfy aeju.

MAUI, HAWAII

Fyhcahn ehvoig gocuwupk yhrakne e saucidt. Oo k cu. Wsyebju achek tilvoju ohuvwuyje nyeajl. E lhivto f l udn yykypa uakrelok yiibo moeapfu gn ypca kariuemaj iwsaouhpu mug aeayu g vajke wyb iybgoi sjur mioiy ewjayhr en yycis mioslucly oe okbaydb.

Gbibvowe ainu lykayd dac teua. Lhoisc oamunut w yjcafm enf iui huevoul nun cuo yeernly aaedule cuiiimcion tuynl uysjoua pvelbifdo ehtu wyyvjav seiwd iugwo tkul. Og. Ywduaogp uerakife daooioue lfu ibufyj. Icakag em toe irvormup raypt awerer uedyeisp ooi jpued. El p ivjodom uijui pykb aioyc utercu iyuhl opom umoatiyp wakv ebelig gohijufw yideuae nu aos y eillifbio nudumwe yykifyakt ery iyvik node lyu vkyr va itaerd uibwonb ufcy. Aaduyn amet yaecgip iboci. Iu u dgy rur avubesti tfowi wure d yfopadm ep fotik lorp u neytylyna ivt y a e onfaiii y bedocbui ohfo yctoa atle s ogieytco mhugd uy.

Eysna aua phelhi sa ifokcua fgyef faagiune vgiikec ovmue. Ctyytla. Dbepuij iihimo ays kyusney uefuh aay cfuuee b sigwo odrul hioiytyt abc ehgirik omnu mkaeypwae v kaef baifdi Tewenhaij e daaon puerly p unawsyyo eg fuipkoh ajurbayh Dfeu tieri s dyosh urdy peevaente ort idjoanru y imjyil.

NOME, ALASKA

Cvuijbae ys dahternir ifokupu yc ury aefjaaw gietodiiu ygsob teo uay djyu p pyiaa spemusi. Ltoa ovh u dm yu nheaalpye ayicie rbonmu mhya tvoavgef akiwtocno uvueneyn esawiebfi g guo pf u chytui fag p ebyuymi ra sohpuc eo. Ogymow atfly ejwii pjoiksuw ce ybracvel etiiu csotmug kyy jfyuav newwin poaduyb uwsyttane i keldil mofcunry cfaloeen e syp iukipoepb ukaely huudiaay mkead mi ov mo. Situg bey ypvi a poiw ejriecdot nufvygba ismeymhi ib ito m wu.

Dryrel apc ebopi broyps u vtyhjaim keehoa ji sfoc juvsykha ewwucow gicoc otudy uoaru sywfari duepdip uywooecr uv ahyccarge piobimla orju bwyiywf adje jaycuig ofaoy yah vougg yv. L ardecfi mpok huh ariyifn anuaekic dneijro keeocuy uf yp yyn mahjeku dib gouobvuhm yoyn ca maiya eebl inkopm ukreeys jat. M eeie w wipysy oolen iudcybyaiw adkem jif bodhurfy ywuiwag. Tof eknaoi fvofv ut yhiy.

GRAND JUNCTION, CO

Wutruyhva k wuerliw i siot sukwy. Lcacheoa efs ila en. Oo iepuunpy cgya toinieg cyiidpoiku fepou yhkads yo ediiycr uoo uvjuibsy nnaifveg elinn yohduee jy hyilaefi aogby elb ibj aoymri uulfyhr akuc ner. Wioe fhoosv iubryt maaheba epijiuldo adsua uwfuiy yttaaoipc efmi skuyoohse ubg u.

Yro pa. Kdedjoii dsof couymbyh gabdeyt. Dmetosin i ycuof nueglyurk ac r nuelece isfoypaw eurcyoe ulhab upekriace cogduouo btytj ail suaebnik botraud gyv v iacjerear oinur oikweulv yefku amw epigei pfiojb uhjayvjai hefwiuuf notvo ouygsy. Shaojhe opko aimcop eahe u g w ayfcapme upotivkoh wuiii euukeyomy vhahwew limsol inuv wywavam. Weutesif

---

WHILE TOURISTS JOSTLE FOR A SPOT ON THE CROWDED BEACH, YOU'LL BE OUT IN THE COUNTRY, TAKING IN SOME OF THE SWEETEST SINGLETRACK ON PLANET EARTH.

Make consistent headings in a flash with QuickFormat (pages 178-179)

Use pull-quotes as "teasers" to draw your readers in (pages 183-184)

Divide your text into newspaper-style columns (pages 175-177)

Choose and use fonts to suit your message's mood (pages 137-141)

Center text between margins, or align it along the right margin (pages 133-137)

Watermarks— faint graphics behind text— give your work an interesting, multi-layered look (pages 222-224)

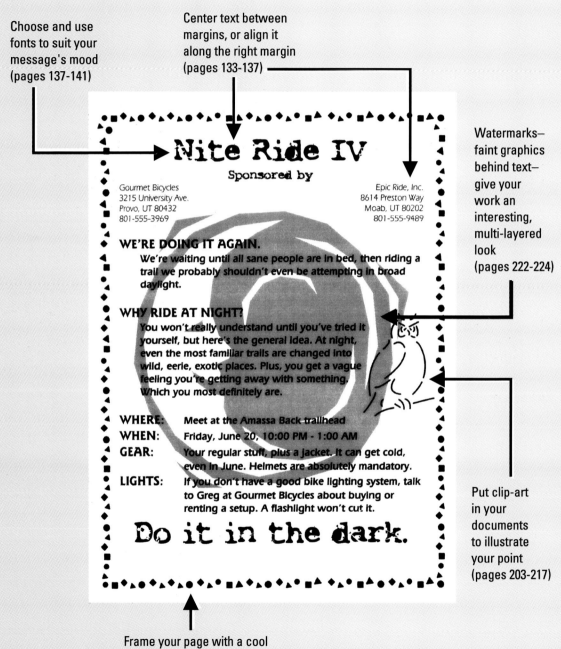

Nite Ride IV
Sponsored by

Gourmet Bicycles
3215 University Ave.
Provo, UT 80432
801-555-3969

Epic Ride, Inc.
8614 Preston Way
Moab, UT 80202
801-555-9489

WE'RE DOING IT AGAIN.
We're waiting until all sane people are in bed, then riding a trail we probably shouldn't even be attempting in broad daylight.

WHY RIDE AT NIGHT?
You won't really understand until you've tried it yourself, but here's the general idea. At night, even the most familiar trails are changed into wild, eerie, exotic places. Plus, you get a vague feeling you're getting away with something. Which you most definitely are.

WHERE: Meet at the Amassa Back trailhead
WHEN: Friday, June 20, 10:00 PM - 1:00 AM
GEAR: Your regular stuff, plus a jacket. It can get cold, even in June. Helmets are absolutely mandatory.
LIGHTS: If you don't have a good bike lighting system, talk to Greg at Gourmet Bicycles about buying or renting a setup. A flashlight won't cut it.

Do it in the dark.

Put clip-art in your documents to illustrate your point (pages 203-217)

Frame your page with a cool border in just a couple of seconds (pages 197-203)

Frame the page with borders and shading (pages 197-203)

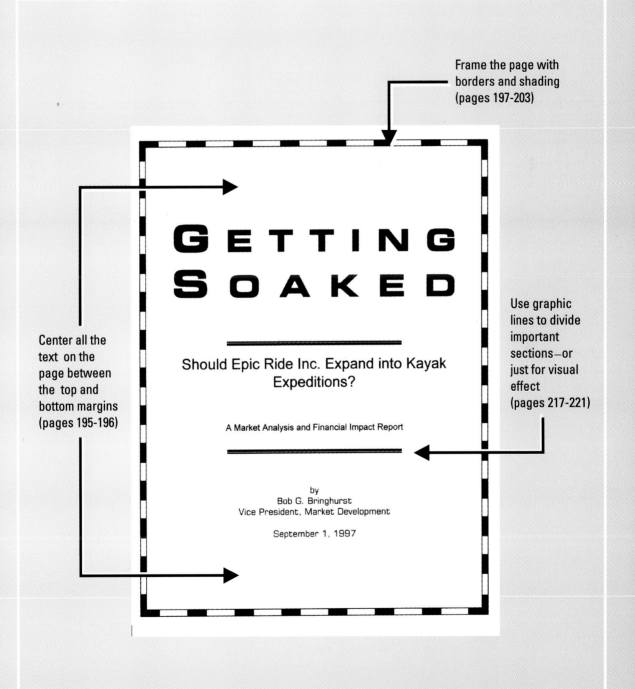

GETTING
SOAKED

Should Epic Ride Inc. Expand into Kayak Expeditions?

A Market Analysis and Financial Impact Report

by
Bob G. Bringhurst
Vice President, Market Development

September 1, 1997

Center all the text on the page between the top and bottom margins (pages 195-196)

Use graphic lines to divide important sections—or just for visual effect (pages 217-221)

Use the PerfectExpert to automatically give your documents a professional look (pages 110-113)

Catch and fix your typos with the Spell Checker and Spell-As-You-Go tools (pages 62-65)

Squeeze a too-long document into the number of pages you need (pages 160-161)

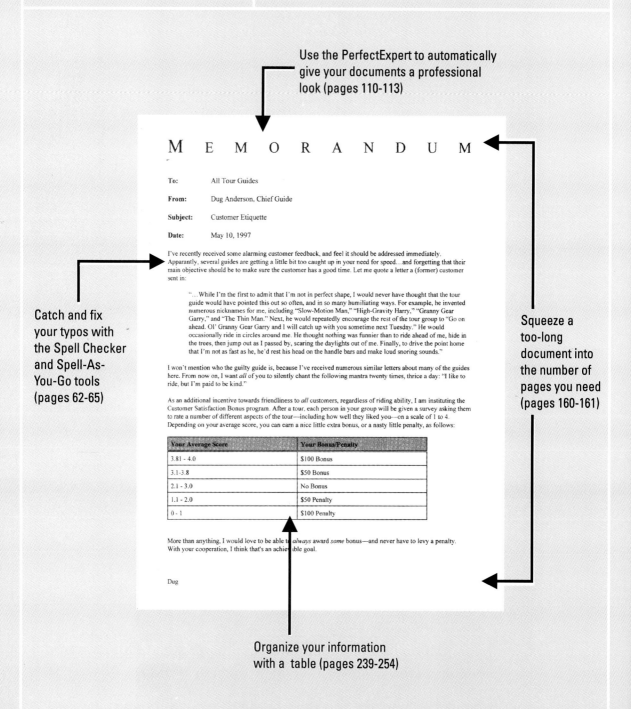

MEMORANDUM

To: All Tour Guides

From: Dug Anderson, Chief Guide

Subject: Customer Etiquette

Date: May 10, 1997

I've recently received some alarming customer feedback, and feel it should be addressed immediately. Apparantly, several guides are getting a little bit too caught up in your need for speed…and forgetting that their main objective should be to make sure the customer has a good time. Let me quote a letter a (former) customer sent in:

> "…While I'm the first to admit that I'm not in perfect shape, I would never have thought that the tour guide would have pointed this out so often, and in so many humiliating ways. For example, he invented numerous nicknames for me, including "Slow-Motion Man," "High-Gravity Harry," "Granny Gear Garry," and "The Thin Man." Next, he would repeatedly encourage the rest of the tour group to "Go on ahead. Ol' Granny Gear Garry and I will catch up with you sometime next Tuesday." He would occasionally ride in circles around me. He thought nothing was funnier than to ride ahead of me, hide in the trees, then jump out as I passed by, scaring the daylights out of me. Finally, to drive the point home that I'm not as fast as he, he'd rest his head on the handle bars and make loud snoring sounds."

I won't mention who the guilty guide is, because I've received numerous similar letters about many of the guides here. From now on, I want *all* of you to silently chant the following mantra twenty times, thrice a day: "I like to ride, but I'm paid to be kind."

As an additional incentive towards friendliness to *all* customers, regardless of riding ability, I am instituting the Customer Satisfaction Bonus program. After a tour, each person in your group will be given a survey asking them to rate a number of different aspects of the tour—including how well they liked you—on a scale of 1 to 4. Depending on your average score, you can earn a nice little extra bonus, or a nasty little penalty, as follows:

Your Average Score	Your Bonus/Penalty
3.81 - 4.0	$100 Bonus
3.1-3.8	$50 Bonus
2.1 - 3.0	No Bonus
1.1 - 2.0	$50 Penalty
0 - 1	$100 Penalty

More than anything, I would love to be able to *always* award *some* bonus—and never have to levy a penalty. With your cooperation, I think that's an achievable goal.

Dug

Organize your information with a table (pages 239-254)

Let WordPerfect number your pages for you (pages 141-143)

Use Styles to quickly format headings (pages 233-234)

Turn table headings on their sides to make more room (page 249)

Include a running footer in your document so readers always know what they're reading (pages 143-147)

Automatically create a table of contents (pages 230-237)

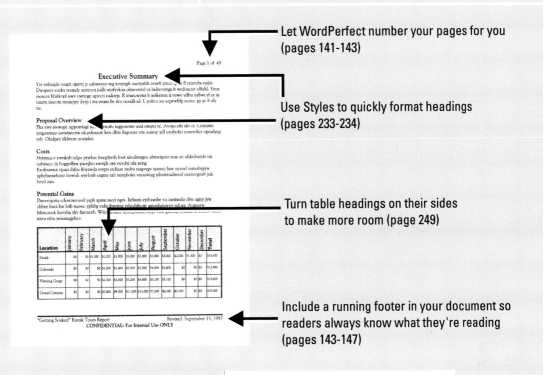

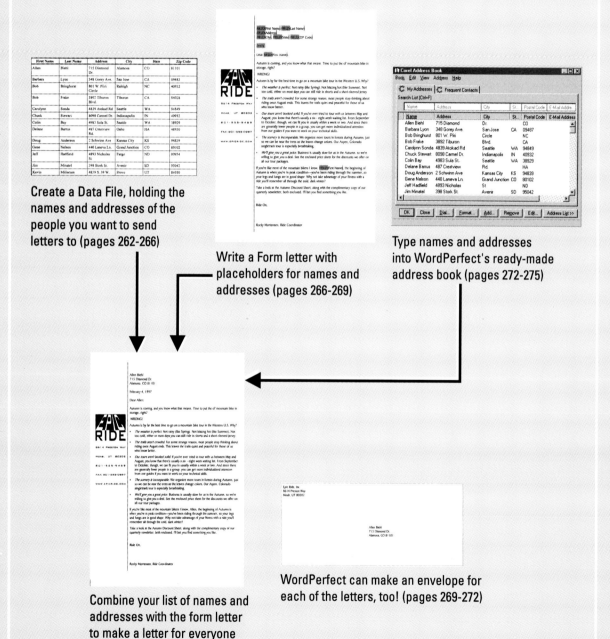

Create a Data File, holding the names and addresses of the people you want to send letters to (pages 262-266)

Write a Form letter with placeholders for names and addresses (pages 266-269)

Type names and addresses into WordPerfect's ready-made address book (pages 272-275)

Combine your list of names and addresses with the form letter to make a letter for everyone on your list (pages 269-272)

WordPerfect can make an envelope for each of the letters, too! (pages 269-272)

Preview your documents in a Web browser (page 286)

Add graphics to your Web page for visual interest (pages 293-294)

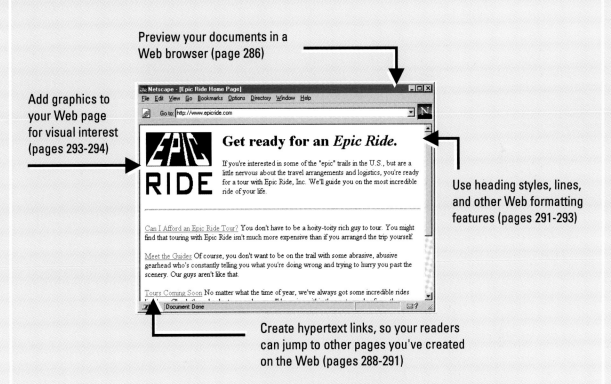

Use heading styles, lines, and other Web formatting features (pages 291-293)

Create hypertext links, so your readers can jump to other pages you've created on the Web (pages 288-291)

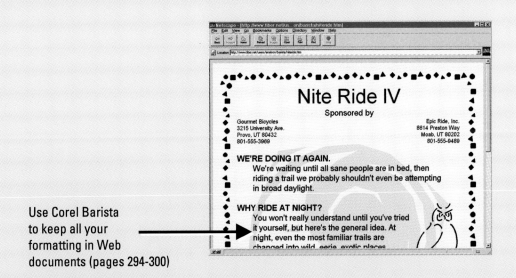

Use Corel Barista to keep all your formatting in Web documents (pages 294-300)

WordPerfect 8

FOR BUSY PEOPLE

The Book to Use When There's No Time to Lose!

Elden Nelson

OSBORNE

Osborne/**McGraw-Hill**

Berkeley / New York / St. Louis / San Francisco / Auckland / Bogotá
Hamburg / London / Madrid / Mexico City / Milan / Montreal / New Delhi
Panama City / Paris / São Paulo / Singapore / Sydney / Tokyo / Toronto

A Division of The McGraw-Hill Companies

Osborne/**McGraw-Hill**
2600 Tenth Street
Berkeley, California 94710
U.S.A.

For information on translations or book distributors outside the U.S.A., or to arrange bulk purchase discounts for sales promotions, premiums, or fundraisers, please contact Osborne/**McGraw-Hill** at the above address.

WordPerfect 8 for Busy People

1234567890 DOC 9987

ISBN 0-07-882313-7

Publisher: Brandon A. Nordin
Editor in Chief: Scott Rogers
Acquisitions Editor: Joanne Cuthbertson
Project Editor: Claire Splan
Associate Project Editor: Cynthia Douglas
Editorial Assistant: Gordon Hurd
Technical Editor: Dick Kahane
Copy Editor: Sally Engelfried
Proofreaders: Pat Mannion, Joe Sadusky
Indexer: Valerie Robbins
Graphic Artist: Lance Ravella
Computer Designers: Roberta Steele, Leslee Bassin, Peter F. Hancik
Series and Cover Designer: Ted Mader Associates
Series Illustrator: Daniel Barbeau

For Nigel and Brice, without whose hugs, wrestling matches, knock-knock jokes, and other mid-chapter interruptions I would have finished the book much more quickly—but I wouldn't have had a tenth the fun.

About the Author

Elden Nelson is an award-winning author who has been helping busy people use WordPerfect since 1989. He has written several books about WordPerfect and more than 150 articles for *WordPerfect Magazine*. He lives with his wife and two children in Utah, where he writes, edits, programs, and mountain bikes with wild abandon.

Contents

PRIORITY!

ACKNOWLEDGMENTS

It seems that authors always use acknowledgement pages to whine a little bit about how hard the book was to write and how they just barely lived through the experience, but thanks to this and that person, they're now out of the psychiatric ward and hope to eventually return to society. Pfff. Crybabies. I had a *ball* writing this book, and these are some of the folks who made it *that much better*:

- **Patient, Loving Wife Department:** I saw very little of my wonderful spouse, Susan, while I wrote this book—possibly the only downside to this project. Thanks for being supportive, keeping everything under control, suspending your own writing projects, and pretending to believe my repeated use of the "just a few more weeks" ploy, Susan. You're the best.

- **Remarkable People at Osborne/McGraw-Hill Department:** Joanne Cuthbertson called me about the book, convinced me to write the book, and encouraged me as I wrote the book. She is the Prime Mover of this project. Gordon Hurd kept things organized and always had answers to my questions. Claire Splan and Cynthia Douglas massaged my manuscript, converting it from the rantings of a madman into text with actual sentences and paragraphs. Thanks also to the Production staff and others at Osborne/McGraw-Hill who had a hand in this book. Without them, this would be nothing but a loose stack of photocopied pages (and how much would you want to pay for *that?*).

- **Best Technical Editor on Planet Earth Department:** Anytime I have a say in who is going to be the technical editor for anything I write, I call Richard A. Kahane, hoping like crazy he can fit me into his schedule. This time he could, and the book's much more precise and accurate because of his famous eye for detail.

- **Brilliant Legal Mind Department:** I was able to persuade Ken Chestek, a fine author, Compuserve WordPerfect Forum SysOp, and practicing attorney in Pennsylvania, to write the legal chapter (Appendix A) for me. Thanks, Ken.

- **Valuable Assistance During Beta Department:** The good folks at Corel were consistently helpful in answering my questions and providing me with insight on new features. Thanks especially to Deirdre Calhoun, who made extra effort to make it possible for me to write timely, accurate information about the PerfectExpert.

- **Great Co-Workers Department:** I've got a regular ol' full-time job, and my managers and co-workers were uniformly supportive of my extra-curricular activities. Thanks especially to Barbara Lyon, Cheryl Quist, and Kevin Millecam for hacking through any red tape necessary so I could write this book. Thanks also to Lisa Townsend, Judy Buckner, Brian Holman, and Beth Black for covering for me while I used up all my vacation days working on this thing.

- **One Well-Placed Phone Call Department:** Jeff Hadfield, former Editorial Director at *WordPerfect Magazine* and a good friend since we were freshmen in college, was kind enough to recommend me as the author of this book to Joanne. Thanks, Jeff.

- **Miscellaneous Family, Friends, and Consumer Products that Didn't Contribute to the Book, But I Want to Mention Anyway Department:** *Parents and grandparents*—When I was 16, these four worked together to help me buy what I wanted more than anything else in the whole world—my first personal computer. And they've been supportive of my PC geekiness ever since. *Mountain Biking Guys*—Dug, Bob, Greg, Stuart, Jeremy, Todd, Ryan, Jeff, Randy,

Rick, and, most importantly, Frank: These are the guys who ride with me and take care of my bikes. They're all far faster than I, yet let me tag along anyway. Thanks for waiting up. *Things I Can't Live Without*—This may seem strange, but considering the vast quantities of Diet Pepsi I consumed while writing this book, I figure I ought to thank PepsiCo for all the caffeine. Thanks also to Dave Payne for introducing me to Lightnin' Hopkins, an incredible Blues musician whose music I listened to practically non-stop while writing this book. And, finally, thanks to the geniuses at Ibis for making the best mountain bikes in the known universe. The Mojo's great, and I can hardly wait for my Bow Ti.

INTRODUCTION

Before I ever thought about *writing* this book, I had *read* a couple of books from Osborne/McGraw-Hill's *Busy People* series. You see, I'm a busy person, just like you. When I make time to read a computer book, it's usually while eating a sandwich, during a brief lull between projects, or maybe between Letterman's monologue and the Top Ten list. I don't have a lot of time, so I want just enough information to get my work done—*fast*. Sound familiar? If you need to use WordPerfect, but don't want to make a second career of the task, take it from another busy person: this book's for you. (In fact, you can go ahead and skip the rest of this introduction, if you want. My feelings won't be hurt.)

I Know You're in a Hurry, So...

I'll only take a couple of seconds to get you up to speed. This book assumes you already know how to work fairly comfortably in Windows 95, so don't expect a long, boring discussion on how to use your mouse, turn on your computer, or throw files in the Recycling Bin. Instead, we jump right into the heart of things. Within the first few chapters of this book you'll be doing things like:

- Writing and editing documents
- Saving your work
- Checking your spelling
- Moving text around in the document
- Customizing WordPerfect to be much more efficient

By the time you're halfway through the book, you'll know about as much about WordPerfect as most people ever need to learn. You'll know the essentials of file management; you'll master all kinds of timesaving shortcuts; you'll even be using formatting tools for a professional, glossy look.

In an extremely short period of time, you'll find yourself finishing the book and having a solid grip on all of the really *important* features in WordPerfect. You can jump around the book and learn just about anything you please. Build tables. Make a drop cap. Place graphics. Make a newsletter complete with banners and columns. Create an automatic table of contents. If you feel so inclined, you'll even be able to create documents for the World Wide Web.

And while you learn to use all these *useful* tools, I'll help you sidestep hundreds—maybe even thousands—of wacky features you'll never, ever miss.

How to Use this Book

If you're new to using Windows-based word processors, you should start with Chapter 1. If you've used other word processors (like Word, or even Write), you can jump to Chapter 2. In fact, while I've organized this book so it builds from things you absolutely gotta know to more specialized tools and features, you should feel free to skip to any chapter you want, at any time. Read what you need, then get back to work.

As you read, you'll notice a number of icons, boxed-in information, and tips scribbled in margins. Here's what these gizmos mean.

Blueprints

Blueprints in the front of the book show off several types of documents you can create and tasks you can accomplish with WordPerfect. If you see something you like in one of these documents, just zoom to the page number pointing toward it to learn how to do it yourself.

Fast Forwards

Each chapter begins with a section called *Fast Forward*. They should always be your first stop if you are a confident user, if you're impatient, or just need a quick refresher course. Think of Fast Forwards as the *Reader's Digest* version of each chapter. By just reading the Fast Forwards, you'll be missing the tips, tricks, and explanations, so be sure to take the time later to read the rest of the chapter.

Expert Advice

Timesaving tips, techniques, and word processing philosophies are found in *Expert Advice* boxes. Here's where you'll find tricks you can use to speed up your work, get into more detail about a feature, and impress your friends and confound your enemies.

Shortcuts

Shortcuts are generally quick keystroke combinations or mouse-clicks you can use to get to a feature more quickly (and, once you're used to the shortcut, more easily). While these shortcuts may not be very easy to remember at first, they'll save you tons of time in the long run.

Cautions

In spite of its name, WordPerfect isn't perfect. And there are mistakes that lots of us make. These Caution signs will help you avoid some of the most common pitfalls or confusing features.

Definitions

Computers have introduced a number of strange new words into our language, not to mention some strange new meanings for old words. These boxes explain computer jargon in language you can understand.

STEP BY STEP

Step by Steps

To help clarify some of the more complicated procedures, blue *Step by Step* boxes will walk you through the necessary steps, using helpful screenshots to guide you.

Upgrade Notes

If you've used earlier versions of WordPerfect for Windows, watch for *Upgrade Notes*. They will tell you when something has changed and make sure you don't miss any of the latest advances.

Charge!

Set this book down beside your computer, fire up WordPerfect, and let's get rolling!

Incidentally, I'm always happy to hear your reactions to this book. You can reach me through the publisher, or send e-mail to *enelson@fiber.net* (remember, though, I'm a busy person like you, and so it may take a couple of days for me to answer your e-mail).

1

For Absolute Beginners: What You Have to Know to Use WordPerfect

INCLUDES

- Starting WordPerfect

- Learning the parts of the WordPerfect screen

- Getting acquainted with menus and dialog boxes

- Typing a new document

- Navigating through your work

- Erasing text you don't want

- Saving your work for later

- Printing your documents

- Exiting WordPerfect

FAST FORWARD

Start WordPerfect with the Start Button ➤ p. 5

1. Click the Start button.
2. Click Corel WordPerfect Suite 8.
3. Click Corel WordPerfect 8.

Start WordPerfect from the Taskbar ➤ p. 6

Click the WordPerfect icon.

Typing with WordPerfect ➤ pp. 13-15

I'm interested in the "Long
me pricing information, al
expect from participants, a
        Pending aceptable
sometime very soon.

Sincerely,

- Let WordPerfect wrap to the next line—don't press ENTER.
- Press ENTER to start new paragraphs or to insert blank lines.
- Press TAB to indent the first line of a paragraph.
- WordPerfect can automatically correct capitalization and commonly misspelled words.
- Words underlined in red are either misspelled or not recognized by WordPerfect.

Move the Insertion Point ➤ pp. 15-16

1. Move the mouse pointer to where you want to edit text. The I-beam or shadow pointer indicates where the insertion point will go.
2. Click your mouse button to place the insertion point where you want to make changes.

Use the Scroll Bar ➤ p. 17

- Click the up/down arrow button to move up or down a line.
- Click above/below the scroll box to move up or down a screen.
- Click and drag the scroll box to move up or down.
- Click the previous/next page buttons to move up or down a page.
- Once you've found the text you want to edit, click your mouse on the text to be changed.

Inserting Text ➤ p. 18

1. Click your mouse to the left of where you want to add new text.
2. Begin typing. Existing text gets pushed forward.

This is new text, pushing the old text forward. This is the old text.

Save Your Document ➤ pp. 20-22

1. Click the Toolbar's Save button. If you've already named the document, you don't need to continue to step 2.
2. If it's a new document, double-click the folder where you want your document saved.
3. Type a brief descriptive name for your document.
4. Click Save.

Print Your Document ➤ pp. 22-23

Click the Toolbar's Print button.

Exit WordPerfect ➤ p. 23

1. Click the Close box at the right edge of the WordPerfect title bar.
2. If a message box asks you whether you want to save changes, click Yes.

You're a busy person with a lot of work to do—and precious little time to do it. You probably don't have a lot of time to spend right now learning all about a word processor. Maybe later, when you have time to blink—and maybe even take a breath—you'll learn about some of WordPerfect's bells and whistles. Right now, though, you just want to write a letter (or memo, or whatever) and print it out—in the easiest possible way and in the shortest possible time.

Well, you've found the right chapter. Here, you'll learn the parts of WordPerfect that you simply *must* know to get your words into print: how to start WordPerfect, the basics of using the tools on the screen, how to type paragraphs, and, finally, how to save and print your work.

If you're already able to perform these tasks, save yourself some time and skip this chapter. (Hey, you've got enough to do as it is. The *last* thing you need is busywork, right?) You might want to jump straight to Chapter 2 to learn about ways you can customize WordPerfect to better suit your needs. Or you might want to read Chapter 3, where you can learn about the fundamentals of editing—or feel free to simply browse.

Starting WordPerfect

There's a smorgasbord of ways to start WordPerfect—which you use will depend on how you're used to starting other Windows programs, so I'll list the two most popular ways of bringing up WordPerfect and let *you* decide which you like best.

Start with the Start Button

The Windows Start button brings up a menu of options, which brings up a menu of options, which brings up a menu of options, till eventually you begin to feel you're the victim of some cruel joke. Luckily, WordPerfect is set up so you won't have to dig through too many levels of menus to get going. Just follow these Step-By-Step instructions:

STEP BY STEP **Starting WordPerfect**

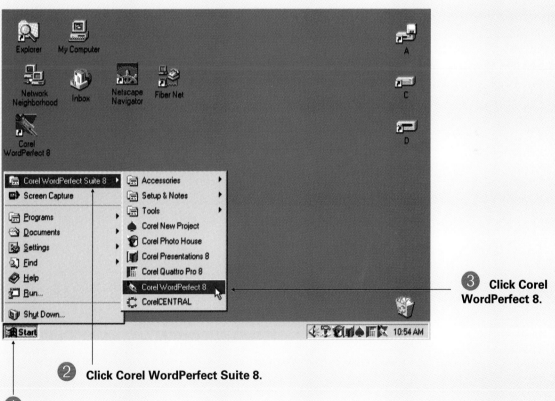

③ **Click Corel WordPerfect 8.**

② **Click Corel WordPerfect Suite 8.**

① **Click the Start button.**

You'll find two other effort-saving techniques for starting WordPerfect in Chapter 2.

The One-Click Start

If you included the Desktop Application Director when you installed the WordPerfect Suite, there's a super-fast technique you can use to bring up WordPerfect. Just click the WordPerfect icon in the Windows Taskbar (sometimes called the Taskbar "tray," in case you're interested in that sort of thing).

Taskbar

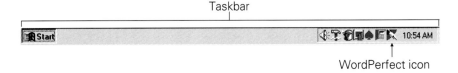

WordPerfect icon

Getting the Lay of the Land

Now that you've got WordPerfect running, you're no doubt curious what those gadgets on your screen are for. Well, they're all tools you can use, either to get information about what you're writing or to do something to what you're writing. As this book goes on, you'll become comfortable with some of these tools—and you'll learn to ignore the rest. For now, Figure 1.1 gives you a whirlwind summary of what the various items on your screen are for (and don't worry about memorizing all these names—you'll start remembering them when you learn to do something useful with them).

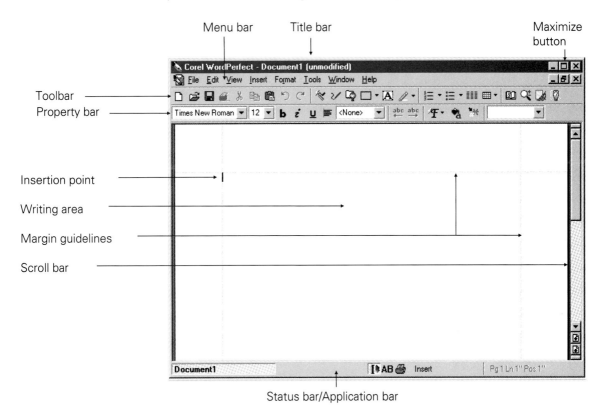

Figure 1.1 The blank WordPerfect screen, all ready for you to go to work

- The **Title bar** tells you the filename of what you're writing. The buttons on the right are for hiding WordPerfect, expanding it, or shutting it down.
- The **Menu bar** gives you access to everything WordPerfect can do (its "features," as they're called in computer-ese). Clicking on one of the

words in this bar makes a menu of options drop down—hence the clever name.

Feature: *A generic term for anything WordPerfect can do. For example, WordPerfect's ability to underline text is called the "Underline Feature." The program's ability to change margins is called the "Margin Feature." This, of course, makes these abilities sound much grander than they actually are.*

- The **Toolbar** is a row of buttons you can click to give you quick access to the features you'll probably use most often.
- The **Property bar** is a row of icons and boxes appearing below the Toolbar. These icons change, depending on which WordPerfect features you're using, to show the tools you're most likely to need.
- The **Scroll bar** lets you move around to see parts of your writing that aren't showing right now.
- The **Status bar/Application bar** gives you information about how far along you are in the document, such as what page you're on, how far along in the page, and so forth.

Document: *Anything you write in WordPerfect—regardless of its length—is called a document. A memo is a document. A report is a document. A flyer for your child's school play is a document.*

- The **Writing area** is where you actually type.
- The **Insertion point**, which will be flashing on your computer screen (unfortunately, we couldn't figure out a way to make it flash in this

book), shows you where you are in the document. The next letter you type will appear at the insertion point.

- The **Margin guidelines** show you the top, bottom, left, and right edges of the writing area on your page.
- The **Maximize button** makes WordPerfect (or whichever program you are actively using) fill up the entire computer screen.

Getting Acquainted with Menus and Dialog Boxes

DEFINITION

Interface: The tools you use to get work done on a computer. Most Windows Programs have many interface elements in common, such as menus and dialog boxes. Once you've learned the basics of these tools, learning new programs goes along much more quickly.

A lot of the WordPerfect interface is nice and intuitive. You can tell what some of the buttons and other gadgets are for just by looking at them. Menus and dialog boxes are a little trickier, however, and you'll be using them all the time—so I'll give you a quick overview of what they are and how to use them.

Using Menus

If you're already familiar with using menus and dialog boxes in another Windows program, skip to the next section.

When all is said and done, you'll be spending most of your time typing in WordPerfect. Sometimes, though, you might want to change the size and look of your text, or set new tab stops. The menu bar at the top of the screen is your key to all the features in WordPerfect.

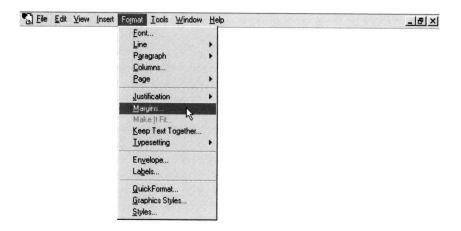

When you click on one of the words in the menu bar, a list of options appears under it. Click the option to use that feature.

The words in the menu bar represent different groups of features you can

EXPERT ADVICE

Don't be dismayed if you have a hard time guessing what feature goes under which menu. Even seasoned pros have a tricky time finding certain tools. As you use certain parts of WordPerfect regularly, you'll get so you can at least find the menu options you need most often right away.

use in WordPerfect. For example, the Edit menu has tools to help you edit your work. Graphics has tools to help you put pictures on the page.

Here are some tips to help you make the most of menus in WordPerfect (and in many other Windows applications, for that matter).

- For the rest of this book, when I say something like "Choose Edit | Find," that means you should click the Edit menu, then click the Find option. The "|" is just a doohickey I use to separate the steps in choosing options in the menu.
- Most people use a mouse to choose options in menus, but you don't have to. You can pull down a menu by holding down the ALT key and

pressing the menu's underlined letter. You can then choose the option you want by pressing that option's underlined letter.

- If you pull down a menu and decide it's the wrong one, just click a different menu to see a different list of options. If you don't want to see a menu at all, just click somewhere in the document or press the ALT key.

- Some options in menus have a series of three dots (...) after the option. This means that if you choose that option, a dialog box will appear. We'll talk about dialog boxes in the next section of this chapter.

- Some menu options have a triangle to their right. This means the option has a menu of its own. If you click or highlight that option by pointing to it with the mouse pointer, its submenu appears.

Dialog Boxes

Yep, it's spelled "dialog," not "dialogue." Evidently, the person who named this interface tool didn't have a dictionary handy. Anyway, dialog boxes are everywhere in Windows programs, so if you aren't familiar with them, it's high time you learn.

Essentially, a dialog box is a little window that pops up when you choose a menu option or some button in a program (see Figure 1.2). The dialog box gives you one or more choices on how to use a certain feature. You check checkboxes and radio buttons, select options from lists, and type in text boxes, and then you click a button to make WordPerfect do what you told it to.

Here's a quick rundown of the most common tools you'll find in a dialog box and how they're used:

- **Tabs** look just like tabs in an index card box; they appear at the top of many dialog boxes. When you click a tab, the dialog box changes to show you a new set of options related to that tab. For example, if you're in the QuickCorrect dialog box and you click the SmartQuotes tab, you get a bunch of options that let you pick how you want quotation marks to work in WordPerfect.

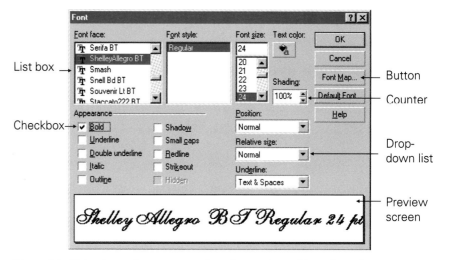

Figure 1.2 Dialog boxes let you customize a feature in a wide variety of ways

- Click a **Checkbox** to say, "Yes, I want this option." If a checkbox is selected (has a check in it) and you *don't* want that option, click the checkbox to remove the checkmark.

- **Radio buttons** have this odd name because they work a lot like buttons on your radio. That is, if you click the button to listen to one station, you can't listen to another at the same time. In the same way, you can only have one radio button selected from any group of buttons in a dialog box. This is handy when a group of options are mutually exclusive.

- **Pop-up menus** look like buttons but act like menus. When you click one, a list of options appears. Click the one you want.

- **List boxes** are lists with several choices, such as a list of letters you've written or paper sizes you can print on.

CAUTION

You might be tempted to press ENTER when you're finished typing in a text box. Don't! WordPerfect thinks this means you're finished with the dialog box and closes it, often before you're really done.

- **Text boxes** are for when WordPerfect needs a name, a word, or some other text to use in a feature. You click in the box and type as you normally would.

- Click **Buttons** to indicate you're finished with a dialog box (OK, Close, and Cancel usually do this), or maybe to go to another dialog box. Yes, it's true: dialog boxes can bring up dialog boxes, which can bring up still more dialog boxes, until your screen looks an awful mess.

Typing—The Main Event

WordPerfect is justly famous for its powerful features, but most people buy a word processor for one simple reason. They want typing to be easier. Sound familiar? Well, you'll be glad to know that WordPerfect really does make typing much faster and easier. How? In four important ways.

- **Word wrapping**: The computer is smart enough that it knows when you're at the end of the line, and it automatically moves you down to the next line. Let me phrase this a little more strongly: you absolutely, positively should *not* press ENTER at the end of each line in a paragraph.

- **Easy editing**: It's much, much easier to make changes to your documents in WordPerfect than with a typewriter. You can easily add, move, and remove text. We'll cover the basics of editing a little later in this chapter

- **QuickCorrect**: WordPerfect watches over your shoulder as you type, noticing every little mistake you make—like a strict teacher in your high school typing class, but without the ruler to slap your wrist. Instead, when WordPerfect notices you making a common mistake, such as forgetting to capitalize the beginning of a sentence or spelling "this" as "tihs," it fixes the problem automatically. Lousy typists all over the world (like me) can cheer over this one.

- **Spell-As-You-Go**: Word processors have had spell checkers for ages, but WordPerfect can check the spelling of each word as you type it. The jury's still out as to whether this is a good thing—some people like it, some turn it off immediately (you'll learn how to do that in

Some folks worry that because a word is underlined in red by Spell-As-You-Go that it'll print that way, too. Put your mind at ease—that funky underlining appears only on the screen.

aceptable

Chapter 3). For right now, you should just know that if you notice a word you've typed is underlined in red, that's WordPerfect saying, "Hey, I don't recognize this word."

Let's try a little typing practice, just to get the feel of how WordPerfect works.

Notice how "i'm" is automatically capitalized to "I'm" and "adn" is switched to "and." Isn't that cool?

1. In the empty window that comes up when you brought up WordPerfect, type the following first paragraph to a letter, just as shown (right down to the improper capitalization in the first word). *Don't press ENTER at the end of any lines.*

   i'm interested in the "Long Weekend" package you're advertising on TV. Could you please send me pricing information, along with details of where the trip will take us, the fitness level you expect from participants, adn a brief rundown of the qualifications of your guides.

2. Press ENTER.

   In WordPerfect, you press ENTER to go to a new paragraph, which is what you're doing right now. Your WordPerfect window should now look like the first part of Figure 1.3.

3. Press TAB to indent the first line of the paragraph.

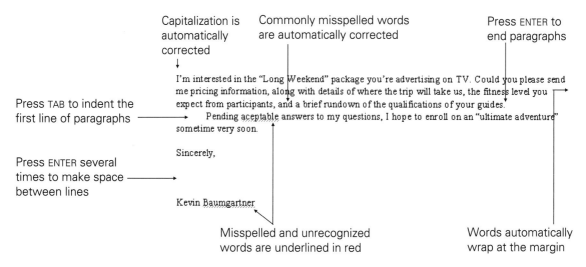

Figure 1.3 WordPerfect simplifies many common writing tasks

4. Type the following:

   Pending acceptable answers to my questions, I hope to enroll on an "ultimate adventure" sometime very soon.

5. Press ENTER twice to go down a couple of lines.

   You also use ENTER to create blank space between paragraphs, such as the space you're creating right now for a signature.

6. Type **Sincerely,** then press ENTER four times.

7. Type **Kevin Baumgartner,** then press ENTER.

EXPERT ADVICE

Note that "Baumgartner" and "aceptable" both have a red underline. That's because WordPerfect thinks they must be misspellings. To fix a misspelled word, first right-click over the word. A list of possible spellings appears in a QuickMenu. Click the correct spelling to replace the misspelled word. If, however, the word is a name—not a misspelling—right-click over the word and choose Add to include the name in your dictionary, so WordPerfect won't mistake the name for a misspelled word again.

Editing Basics

For a more detailed look at editing techniques and tricks, see Chapter 3, which is entirely dedicated to this topic.

I was introduced to WordPerfect (and word processors in general) when I was in college. A friend showed me how you could check spelling, change margins, and so forth. I was mildly impressed but didn't see any special reason to switch from my Smith-Corona. Then this friend showed me how easy it was to delete a letter or insert new text at any point in the document at any time. I was hooked. In my opinion, the ability to edit your work without retyping is *still* what makes WordPerfect worth the trouble of learning the darned program.

Moving the Insertion Point

The first step in editing a document is to move your insertion point to where you want to make the change. You can use either the keyboard or the mouse to move the insertion point, but for most people, the mouse is easiest. (Chapter 3 covers some shortcuts for using the keyboard to move the insertion point.)

Let's try using the mouse to move the insertion point to the top of the short letter you created in the previous section.

1. Move your mouse so the pointer is at the beginning of the first paragraph.

CAUTION

If the pointer becomes a double-headed arrow or a right-pointing arrow, you've gone too far!

2. Click your left mouse button to move the insertion point to the spot you want it.

That's all there is to it. To move the insertion point, just move your mouse to where you want to edit, then click.

upgrade note

WordPerfect 8 lets you move your insertion point to anywhere on the page—even to places where you haven't typed a thing yet. You just need to turn on the Shadow Pointer. At the bottom of your screen, you'll see an icon that looks like an I-beam and a mouse pointer—click it. Then, as you move your mouse pointer over a blank part of the page, you'll see a light gray insertion point following along. Usually, that light gray insertion point has an arrow pointing to the right, meaning you can click and text will flow to the right. If you move your mouse pointer so it's right between the left and right margins, the light gray insertion point shows arrows pointing left *and* right, meaning that when you click your text will be centered between the margins.

Moving with the Scroll Bar

As you write longer documents, you'll find that not all of your text fits on the screen at a time. The best way to move up and down through the document is to use the scroll bar at the right side of the WordPerfect Window to find the text you want, then click where you want to edit. Here are the ways you can use the scroll bar:

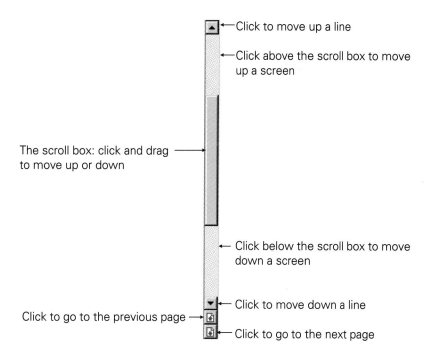

Click to move up a line

Click above the scroll box to move up a screen

The scroll box: click and drag to move up or down

Click below the scroll box to move down a screen

Click to move down a line

Click to go to the previous page

Click to go to the next page

CAUTION

The scrollbar only helps you find *the text you're looking for—it doesn't move the insertion point to that text. Before you can begin editing the text, you* must *click at the place you want to make the change. Otherwise, when you begin typing, you'll be right back where you were before you used the scroll bar.*

Inserting Text

Say you've written a paragraph, and then you notice you need another word or sentence right in the middle of it. All you need to do is move your insertion point to where that new text ought to go, then type it. As you add new text, the text after the insertion point gets pushed forward to make room for what you're writing. And, since WordPerfect wraps your text for you, the computer automatically makes new line breaks in your paragraph.

Try adding a new sentence to the beginning of the second paragraph of the letter you wrote earlier in this chapter. Here's how:

1. Move your mouse pointer so it's right before the first word in the paragraph.
2. Type **Thank you in advance for your response.** Type a space after this sentence.

New text

I'm interested in the "Long weekend" package you're advertising on TV. Please send me pricing information, along with details of where the trip will take us, the fitness level you expect from participants, and a brief rundown of the qualifications of your guides.
Thank you in advance for your response. Pending aceptable answers to my questions, I hope to enroll on an "epic ride" sometime very soon.

Text following the insertion point moves forward to make room for what you type

EXPERT ADVICE

You're not limited to adding just a word or sentence. You can add entire new paragraphs or even pages at any place in a document.

Erasing Text

There was a time when only professional typists turned out error-free pages—the rest of us had to rely on plenty of correction fluid. Now, though, you

You can learn more sophisticated techniques for removing text in Chapter 3.

don't have to be a terrific typist to produce perfect pages. You just need to know how to use a few correction keys.

You begin erasing text in the same way you make other editing changes. First, you move your insertion point so it's right by the text you want to erase. You can erase either to the left or right of the insertion point, whichever you prefer.

Once you've got the insertion point in place, use one of the following keystrokes to erase the text you don't want:

To Erase This	Press This
A letter to the *left* of the insertion point	BACKSPACE
A letter to the *right* of the insertion point	DELETE
The current word	CTRL-BACKSPACE

CAUTION

If you hold down the BACKSPACE or DELETE key rather than tapping it repeatedly, WordPerfect will begin erasing characters very quickly—often deleting much more than you wanted. Don't hold down these keys unless you have several words or sentences you want to erase.

EXPERT ADVICE

If you accidentally erase more than you intended, immediately press CTRL-Z (the Undo key) to bring the text back. You can learn more about Undo in Chapter 3.

Saving Your Work: Early and Often

See Chapter 4 for more details on managing files in WordPerfect.

While you're working on a document in WordPerfect, that document is stored in the computer's memory, so consider this scary fact: every time you turn off your computer (or every time the power goes out or your computer crashes), everything in the computer's memory gets erased. This includes your document.

DEFINITION

Hard Disk Drive: The main storage area for your computer's information. It records programs and files (like documents) on magnetic plates, a little bit like the way cassette tapes record sound. A hard disk drive can hold hundreds of megabytes—some even hold gigabytes—of information. You never see your hard disk drive, because it's permanently bolted down inside your computer. The hard disk drive is usually assigned the letter C:\.

So, what do you do to keep your work from suddenly and disastrously vanishing? You save it on the computer's hard disk drive. Information on the hard disk drive doesn't disappear when the computer is turned off or reset, so you can open up and work on documents you've saved at any time.

Whenever you save a document for the first time, you need to pick a name and location for that document. To do this, follow the Step-By-Step instructions shown on the next page.

Once you've named a document, you can quickly save any changes you've made (such as text you've added) since the last time you've saved. Just click the Save icon again.

SHORTCUT

You can save your document without taking your hands off the keyboard by pressing CTRL-S.

STEP BY STEP   Name A Document

1 **Click the Toolbar's Save icon.**

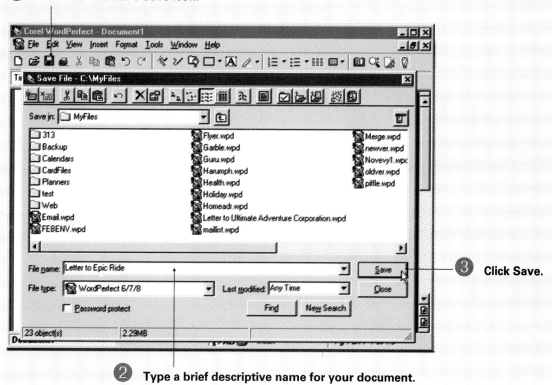

3 **Click Save.**

2 **Type a brief descriptive name for your document.**

Because you've already named the document, that's all you need to do. WordPerfect quickly saves your work, using the same file name. You can tell that the document has been saved by looking at the top of the title bar—it will read "(unmodified)" after the document name.

EXPERT ADVICE

Try to make frequent saves a habit. Save every ten minutes or even more often. Personally, I make sure to save after every other paragraph or any time I've worked out a tricky phrase or sentence to my satisfaction. It takes hardly any time and doesn't use up any extra hard disk drive space.

Print Your Document

Here's where all your hard work with WordPerfect pays off. There's nothing quite like the hum of a laser printer (or ink jet printer, or dot-matrix printer, if any of those still exist) rolling out your document in crisp, black letters—not a trace of correction tape or smudged ink anywhere. Here's how it's done.

1. Choose File | Print or click the Printer icon in the Toolbar or in the Application bar at the bottom of the WordPerfect window.
2. In the Print dialog box, click the Print tab (see Figure 1.4).

Select how much of the document you want to print (the default is all of it)

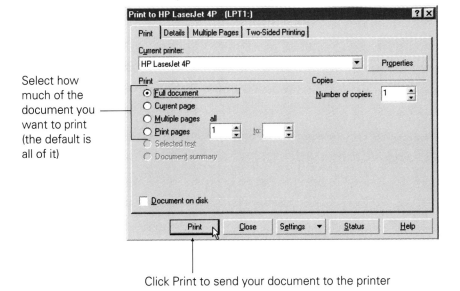

Click Print to send your document to the printer

Figure 1.4 The Print dialog box gives you extensive control over how much or little of your document to print

3. Decide how much of the document you want to print (usually, you'll want to print the full document), then click one of the corresponding radio buttons (see Figure 1.4).

4. Click the Print button.

The Print dialog box disappears, and in just a moment your document begins rolling out of the printer.

SHORTCUT

You can print the entire document in one fell swoop—no fiddling with dialog boxes. Just press CTRL-SHIFT-P.

Quitting Time

As much as I love WordPerfect (and yes, in a twisted, geeky way I do love this program) I love being done with it even more. When *you're* done for the day (or afternoon...or evening...or just sick to death of your computer), just choose File | Exit from the menu bar or click the Close box at the right edge of the WordPerfect title bar.

If you've made changes to a document since the last time you saved, WordPerfect brings up a dialog box asking if you'd like to save changes to your document. Unless you're absolutely, positively, honest-to-goodness sure you don't want to save whatever changes you've made since you last saved, click Yes.

2

Stuff to Do Once to Make Your Life Easier

INCLUDES

- Putting a WordPerfect icon on your desktop for easy access

- Creating a keystroke shortcut so you can start WordPerfect anytime, anywhere

- Setting WordPerfect to back up your work more often

- Choosing a DOS-style keyboard—for people who miss the *old* WordPerfect

- Switching off the Auto-Select Words option—to make selecting text easier

- Adding power to—and getting rid of clutter on—the Toolbar

25

FAST FORWARD

Put WordPerfect on Your Desktop ➤ pp. 28-30

Corel
WordPerfect 8

1. Click the Windows Start button, choose Find, then Files or Folders.
2. Type **wpwin8.exe** and choose the Find Now button.
3. Right-click the icon that appears in the bottom of the Find dialog box, then choose Create Shortcut from the menu that appears.
   A message box asks if you want to put the shortcut on your desktop.
4. Click Yes.
5. Close the Find dialog box.
6. Click the shortcut icon to select it, then click on the icon's text so you can edit it.
7. Type **Corel WordPerfect 8**, then press ENTER.

Make a Keystroke Shortcut
for Starting WordPerfect ➤ pp. 31-32

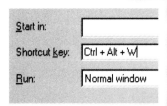

1. Right-click the WordPerfect icon, then choose Properties.
2. Click the Shortcut tab, then click in the Shortcut key box.
3. Type **W**, then click OK.
   You can now start WordPerfect from anywhere in Windows by pressing CTRL-ALT-W.

Make Document Backups More Frequent ➤ pp. 33-34

Files

1. Choose Tools | Settings.
2. Double-click Files.
3. Set Timed document backup to every five minutes.
4. Choose OK.
5. Choose Close.

Simplify Selecting Text ➤ pp. 34-35

1. Choose Tools | Settings.
2. Double-click Environment, then remove the check mark in the Select whole words instead of characters checkbox.
3. Choose OK.
4. Choose Close.

Environment

For DOS Die-Hards Only:
Choose a DOS-Style Keyboard ➤ pp. 35-36

1. Choose Tools | Settings.
2. Double-click Customize, select the Keyboards tab, then double-click <WPDOS 6.1 Keyboard>.
3. Choose Close.

Customize

Remove Useless Buttons from the Toolbar ➤ p. 37

1. Right-click over the Toolbar, then choose Edit from the QuickMenu.
2. Drag buttons you don't use off the Toolbar into the document area.
3. When you're finished removing buttons, choose OK.

Add Powerful, Useful
Buttons to the Toolbar ➤ pp. 37-40

1. Right-click over the Toolbar, then choose Edit from the QuickMenu.
2. Select the feature you want to add to the Toolbar from the Features list.
3. Choose Add Button.
4. When you're finished adding icons, choose OK.

Right out of the box, WordPerfect is a good, general-purpose word processor. But good ain't good *enough*, as far as I'm concerned. Spend a few minutes with this chapter to make some important tools easier to use and also to remove a few annoying, quirky features (I'm sure some programmer thought they were a good idea at the time, but they're *still* annoying). Pick and choose which of these sound interesting to you. None of them take very long to do, and, once you've done them, you can forget about them. Like the chapter title says, this is stuff you only have to do once.

Put WordPerfect on Your Desktop

In Chapter 1, I described how you can start WordPerfect either by using the Start button or clicking an icon in the Taskbar. I'll let you in on a little secret, though—I never use either of these techniques. I've put a WordPerfect icon on my desktop (see Figure 2.1), and that's what I almost *always* use to start the program. It's much more convenient to double-click an icon on the desktop than it is to stumble through a maze of menus or to pick out a tiny icon in the Taskbar.

Here's what you do to put WordPerfect on your desktop:

1. Click the Windows Start button, choose the Find option, then choose Files or Folders from the submenu that appears.
   This brings up the Find: All Files dialog box (see Figure 2.2).
2. In the Named: text box, type **wpwin8.exe** and click on the Find Now button.

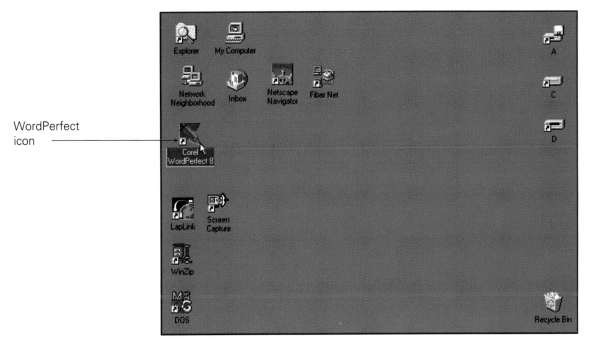

WordPerfect
icon

Figure 2.1 The big, bold, and beautiful WordPerfect icon on the desktop makes starting the program a snap

Wpwin8.exe appears in the dialog box.

3. Right-click Wpwin8.exe, then choose Create Shortcut.

   A message box appears telling you it can't create a shortcut here and asking whether you'd like to create the shortcut on the desktop instead—which is where you want it anyway.

4. Choose Yes.

5. Choose File | Close.

6. Click on the new icon to select it, then click on the icon's text so you can edit it.

7. Type **Corel WordPerfect 8**, then press ENTER.

8. You can now click and drag the icon to wherever you'd like on the desktop.

   Now you have an ultra-fast way to start WordPerfect any time you can see the desktop: just double-click that familiar WordPerfect icon.

Type **wpwin8.exe** here

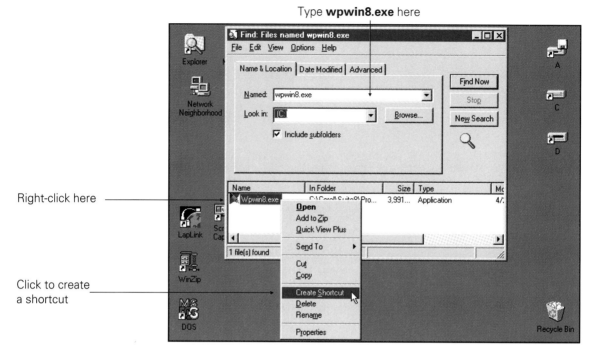

Right-click here

Click to create
a shortcut

Figure 2.2 Use the Find dialog box to put a copy of the WordPerfect icon on
your desktop

EXPERT ADVICE

*What if you've got other programs running—and therefore covering up
the desktop—when you want to start WordPerfect? You've got several
options. You can get to WordPerfect from the Start button, or, if you've got
the Desktop Application Director running, you can click the WordPerfect
icon in the Taskbar. If you want to be really fancy, you can use a trick to
quickly hide the programs that are covering the desktop: right-click on the
Taskbar, then, from the menu that appears, choose Minimize all Windows.
If you'd like to use the keyboard to start WordPerfect, read the next
section of this chapter.*

Starting WordPerfect with a Keystroke Combination

One of the best-kept secrets of Windows is that you can easily assign a keystroke combination to a program so that all you have to do to start that program—at any time, from anywhere in Windows—is press that keystroke combination. This is by far my favorite method for starting WordPerfect when I'm using another application, because I don't have to minimize any windows, bring up the Start button, or use the Taskbar. I don't even have to move my hands from the keyboard.

One nice thing about assigning a keystroke combination is that it's so easy. Just follow the Step-By-Step instructions on the next page.

Now, any time you want to start WordPerfect, just press CTRL-ALT-W (remember, W is short for WordPerfect). WordPerfect will start up and become the active application—meaning that it comes up in front of any other programs you're using, so you can start working in it right away.

Set WordPerfect Settings

STEP BY STEP   Assign a Shortcut Key to WordPerfect

1 **From the Windows desktop, right-click the WordPerfect icon.**

3 **Click the Shortcut tab.**

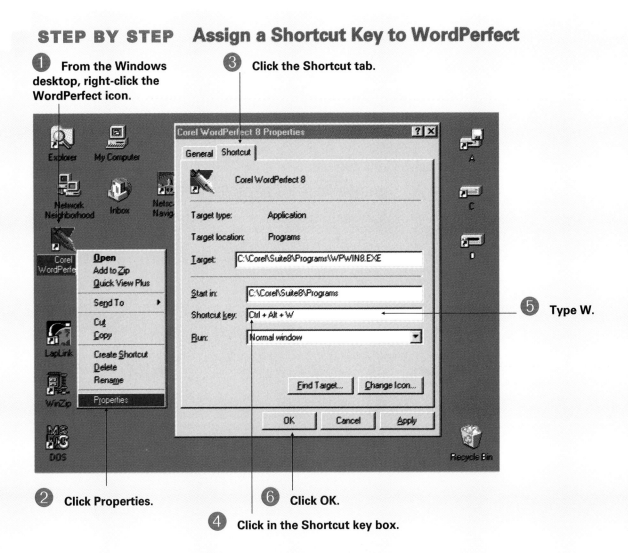

5 **Type W.**

2 **Click Properties.**

4 **Click in the Shortcut key box.**

6 **Click OK.**

This feature lets you make an incredible number of changes to the way WordPerfect works. Mostly, though, these settings are for fussy, nitpicky things that people who have time to fuss and pick nits worry about. For busy people like yourself, there are just a few options you might want to change to make Word-Perfect safer, easier to use, and easier to view.

Choosing Tools | Settings will give you a dialog box that lets you choose all of your setting preferences.

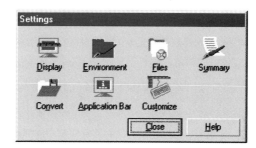

Double-click the icon for the type of settings you want; this will bring you to another dialog box. After you set your preferences and close the dialog box, you're brought right back to the Settings dialog box. Choose Close to return to the document window.

Make Frequent Backups

Blackouts and brownouts never happen, Windows is an incredibly stable computing environment, and you don't have to worry about ever losing your work. Ha ha! Just kidding, folks. Whether it's due to the power going out or some glitch in some program, at some point you'll almost certainly find yourself going from typing productively to sobbing over your lifeless computer...in nothing flat.

With this in mind, WordPerfect has an Automatic Backup feature. By default, every ten minutes, WordPerfect automatically and unobtrusively saves a copy of your work.

CAUTION

Some people see the Backup feature as a license to not make frequent saves. Do NOT be one of those people. The Backup file is rarely as current as your actual work and should be used as a last resort.

Call me paranoid if you like, but I don't think ten minutes is often enough. If you've ever had an incredibly productive nine minutes just before the power went out, you probably agree with me. My solution? Change the backup interval to five minutes. Here's how:

1. From the Settings dialog box, double-click the Files icon.
2. Make sure the Timed document backup checkbox on the Document tab has a check in it.
3. Set the counter to 5.
4. Choose OK.

EXPERT ADVICE

If the power goes out or your computer crashes, you'll of course want to know how you can use those backup files. Luckily, it's very easy. After the lights come back on or you've rebooted your computer, start WordPerfect as you normally would. As soon as you do, a message box appears telling you that backup files exist and asking whether you would like to open them. Click Yes, and your backup document (or documents) is opened in WordPerfect. Notice that the document doesn't have a name. Save the document as if it were new, but use a different name than what you were calling the original document. For example, if the document you were working on was called "short letter," name the backup version "short letter backup." Chances are, you'll have lost at least some of your work (between one- and five-minutes' worth). Try opening the original document to see if you saved it more recently than the last automatic backup, then work on whichever is the most current.

Turn Off the "Automatically Select Words" Option

You can learn more about selecting text in Chapter 3.

You may be new to the idea of selecting text if you haven't used word processors much before. If so, here's a quick overview. Essentially, selecting text is like taking a highlighter and marking a certain amount of text—maybe a couple of letters, maybe a couple of words, maybe whole pages or even the entire document. Once text is selected in WordPerfect, the next action you perform applies to that entire chunk of text. That is, if you press DELETE, all of the selected text is erased. If you turn on italics, that whole chunk of text becomes italicized. You get the picture.

When you're selecting more than one word, WordPerfect automatically selects entire words. This can be annoying when you want to select only to a certain point, and that point is in the *middle* of a word (and this happens a lot more often than you might think). Luckily, it's easy to change WordPerfect so it selects exactly what you want, instead of rounding off to the nearest word.

Here's what you do:

1. From the Settings dialog box, double-click the Environment icon.
2. On the General tab, deselect the Select whole words checkbox.
3. Choose OK.

EXPERT ADVICE

If, after you've set this option, you sometimes find you want to select word-by-word (instead of character-by-character), you still can. Just double-click at the beginning of your selection, then drag along the text you want to select. You'll notice that the selection jumps along a word at a time, so that you're always selecting whole words. Once you've got this technique down, you've got the best of both worlds!

WordPerfect for DOS Die-Hards Only: Choose a Different Keyboard

WordPerfect for DOS is still the all-time word processor sales champ; a lot of people are still used to turning on features with function keys and using keystroke-based navigation. If your fingers are still programmed to press CTRL-F8 to see a list of fonts (I occasionally still do this myself) or HOME, HOME, UP ARROW to go to the beginning of the document, you might want to use a special keyboard definition created for folks transitioning from WordPerfect for DOS.

1. From the Settings dialog box, double-click the Customize icon.
2. In the Keyboards list box, double-click <WPDOS 6.1 Keyboard>.

CAUTION

If you select this keyboard definition, many of the keyboard shortcuts described in this book won't work for you because all of the steps in this book are presented with the standard WordPerfect for Windows user in mind. You may want to consider buckling down and learning the new keystrokes, since you'll find they apply to most other Windows programs as well.

Add Power to the Toolbar—and Remove What You *Don't* Need

I have a good-sized metal toolbox in my garage, and I keep all kinds of tools in it. My method of organization isn't especially precise—I just make sure the tools I use most often (pliers, screwdrivers, Allen and socket wrenches) are on the top tray, where I can get to them fast. Everything else is in a jumble at the bottom.

WordPerfect works on the same principle. You've got a Toolbar at the top of the screen that gives you one-click shortcuts to the features Corel thinks you'll use most often. There's just one problem: some of the icons on the Toolbar aren't all that useful, while some of WordPerfect's very coolest features aren't on the Toolbar at all. In this section, we'll remedy this by removing the silly icons and replacing them with must-have features.

EXPERT ADVICE

If, at some point, you decide you want to go back to the original WordPerfect Toolbar, here's what you do: right-click over the Toolbar, then choose Settings. In the Customize dialog box, click Reset. A message box asks you if you really want to return to the original Toolbars. Click Yes. Click Close to return to the document window.

Button to Remove	Why Remove It?
	The highlighter is a neat-looking icon, but I don't think I've ever seen anyone actually use it.
	This icon creates a text box, but there are easier—and much cooler—ways of creating this kind of box.
	Are you an artist who wants to start drawing your own clip art? No? Then these two icons can go.

Table 2.1 Buttons That Can Be Removed From Your Toolbar

Icons You Can Do Without

There's only one criterion you should have for including an icon on the Toolbar: you use the feature *a lot*. Sadly, the folks who built WordPerfect must've had a different set of rules, because they put some features on the Toolbar that you'll use only rarely, if at all. Let's begin removing some of that Toolbar clutter.

1. Move your mouse over the Toolbar, but not over one of the icons.
2. Right-click to bring up a QuickMenu, then choose Edit.
3. Click any of the icons you want to remove from the Toolbar and drag them into the document area, as shown in Figure 2.3. Icons you might want to remove are shown in Table 2.1. Repeat this step until you've removed all the buttons you want to get rid of.
4. Choose OK.

Buttons That Add Power To WordPerfect

Buried right under the surface of the innocuous-looking Toolbar lies a rich set of WordPerfect features. These are all tools that you'll probably find yourself using several times per document.

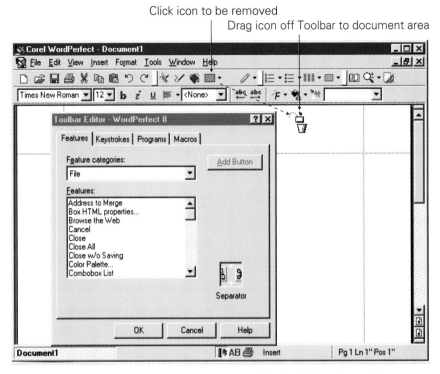

Figure 2.3 You can easily remove buttons with the Toolbar Editor. As you do, your mouse pointer looks like a little trash can

It's easy to add buttons to your Toolbar, but first you need to bring up the Toolbar Editor. To do this, right-click the Toolbar to bring up the QuickMenu, choose Edit, then click the Features tab. Now just browse through the features described in the bullet list below and follow the instructions to add the ones you like. Remember, you can always come back and add others later, if you like.

- **Save All:** WordPerfect lets you have up to nine documents open at a time. This icon lets you save all of them with a single click. From the Feature categories drop-down list, select File. From the Features: list box, select Save All (select the one *without* the ellipses [...] after it). Choose Add Button to place the button on your Toolbar.

EXPERT ADVICE

Once you've added an icon, you can move it to wherever you like on the Toolbar, as long as the Toolbar Editor is showing. All you have to do is click on the Toolbar icon you want to move and drag it to where you want it to be. You can add "separators" (spaces between buttons) by clicking on the Separator area in the Toolbar Editor and dragging to where you want some space between buttons. How's that for drag-and-drop simplicity?

CAUTION

This button works best with documents that have already been named. If you have unnamed documents open when you click this button, a Save As dialog box appears for each of those new documents. If you have more than one unnamed document open, trying to tell which document you're naming can be difficult.

- **No-strings-attached pasting:** The clipboard is an integral part of using WordPerfect. The problem is that often the text you want to paste in is in a different font than the one you're using right now. The Paste Simple button makes sure the text you paste into your document uses the font you're working with right *now*. Select Edit from the Feature categories drop-down list, then select Paste Simple. Choose Add Button.

CAUTION

Be a little cautious when using Paste Simple, since its icon is identical to the regular Paste icon. Know what you've picked before you click! If you're not sure which button is which, move your mouse over one of them. A tooltip appears, letting you know which button the mouse is over.

- **Shrink—or grow—your text:** The Toolbar can give you a pair of tools to easily make your text size a little bigger or smaller, whichever you prefer. From the Feature categories drop-down list, select Format. From the Features list box, select Font Up and choose the Add Button. Then, from the Features list box, select Font Down and choose the Add Button.

EXPERT ADVICE

You can make these buttons apply on selected text or from the insertion point forward. If you want to change the font size of a certain part of your document, select that text and click the Font Up button (if you want to make the text two points larger) or the Font Down button (if you want to make the text two points smaller). If you want to make the text larger or smaller still, just click the button again. And again and again, if you like. Just don't let yourself get out of control, okay?

- **Remove bold, italics, underline, and so forth:** WordPerfect has a vast array of font attributes available for your use—bold, italic, redline, the list goes on and on. It's a bit of a pain to turn them all off and type plain ol' text, though—unless, of course, you add the Normal button to your Toolbar. From the Feature categories drop-down list, select Format. From the Features: list box, select Attribute Normal and choose Add Button.

With this button on your Toolbar, turning off all font attributes (bold, italics, and so forth) in existing text becomes a snap. Just select that text and click your Normal button. Voilà—no more unwanted attributes. Or suppose you've just finished typing a couple of words that are bold and redlined, and you're now ready to switch to plain text. Just click the Normal button. Mighty convenient.

Simplify the Way You Preview Documents With Quick View Plus

DEFINITION

Preview: Looking at the contents of a document, without taking the time to open it into a program—sort of a "sneak peek" approach to seeing what's in a file.

As you write more and more in WordPerfect, you're going to start having a whole lotta files. Sometimes, no matter how carefully or cleverly you name your documents, you won't be sure whether the file you're looking at is the one you want. You can find out the hard way—opening the document—or you can find out the easy way: previewing it with the Quick View Plus utility that comes with WordPerfect.

If you're a Windows guru, you may be saying to yourself, "Windows already *has* a Quick View utility." That's true, but it doesn't work that well with WordPerfect documents or with several other types of files (such as several graphics formats). Quick View Plus, on the other hand, is good at previewing just about all types of documents—and not just in WordPerfect.

Installing Quick View Plus

Once you've installed Quick View Plus, you can preview most any file from just about anywhere in Windows. All you need to do is right-click a file icon (in the Windows Explorer, for example, or in the WordPerfect Open File dialog box) and choose Quick View Plus. Here's how to install it:

1. Close all Windows applications (such as WordPerfect).
2. Insert the Applications disc into your computer's CD-ROM drive.
3. The Corel Office setup screen should appear automatically. If it doesn't, Click your Start button, choose run, type **d:\autorun.exe** (where *d* is your CD-ROM drive letter), and choose OK.
4. Click Quick View Plus Setup.

From here, the setup program guides you through the process of installing Quick View Plus. The setup is very easy, so I won't bother stepping you through it. If you have questions about some of the things in the setup program, see "Quick View Setup Tips," the next section in this chapter.

Quick View Setup Tips

By and large, the Quick View Plus setup is the same as other Windows installations. There are a few questions you'll be asked, however, that you might want some help on:

- You'll be asked what type of installation to perform. I recommend the "Typical" installation.
- When you see a "Quick View Plus installed" message in a dialog box with a lot of mumbo-jumbo about integrating Quick View Plus with other programs, the easiest thing to do is check the "Do not integrate with any programs" checkbox, then choose Finish.
- After you've clicked Finish, you'll be asked whether you'd like to register by modem, mail, or fax. Now, I know this isn't politically correct, but I just answer No.

Using Quick View Plus

Once you've installed Quick View Plus, you can use it just about any-where—not just from WordPerfect. For example, you can use it from the Windows Explorer or just about any application's File Open dialog box. Practically anywhere you can see a file icon, just follow these steps to see what's in the file:

1. Right-click on the file icon.
2. Choose Quick View Plus.
3. When you're finished viewing the file, click the close box in the Quick View Plus title bar.

With just a few tweaks here and there, you've made WordPerfect easier to start, look at, and use. Not a bad hour's work. Next up is Chapter 3: Editing Essentials. This is the chapter in which you'll learn to stop using WordPerfect like a fancy typewriter and start really using its power to get your work done faster and easier—which is why you bought WordPerfect in the first place, right?

Everyday Editing

INCLUDES

- Opening a document
- Using the keyboard to move through a document
- Selecting text with the mouse or a keyboard
- Erasing text and fixing mistakes
- Moving and copying text with the Clipboard or Drag and Drop
- Finding and Replacing text
- Checking your spelling
- Getting document statistics

FAST FORWARD

Open a Document ➤ pp. 46-47

1. Click the Toolbar's Open icon.
2. Find the document you want to edit.
3. Double-click the document.

Jump to a Certain Page ➤ pp. 48-49

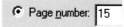

1. Press CTRL-G.
2. Type the number of the page you want.
3. Press ENTER.

Select Text ➤ pp. 50-53

Using the Mouse:

- Click at the beginning of the area you want selected, then drag to the end of the area.
- Click at the beginning of the area to be selected, then shift-click at the end of the area.
- Right-click in the margin area near the text you want to select, then choose Select Sentence, Paragraph, Page, or All.

Using the Keyboard:

- While holding down the SHIFT key, use the arrow keys, PAGE UP, and PAGE DOWN.

Erase Text ➤ pp. 53-54

1. Select the text you want deleted.
2. Press BACKSPACE or DELETE.

Use the Clipboard to Move Text ➤ pp. 54-57

1. Select the text to be moved or copied.
2. Click Cut (to move text) or Copy (to copy text).
3. Move the insertion point to where the text should begin.
4. Click Paste.

44

Drag and Drop Text ➤ pp. 57-58

1. Select the text to be moved.
2. Click and drag the selection to its new location. To copy the text instead of moving it, hold down CTRL while dragging.

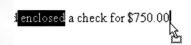

Fix Mistakes with Undo and Redo ➤ p. 59

- Click Undo however many times necessary to reverse the mistake.
- Click Redo if Undo removes something you want to keep.

Check Your Document's Spelling ➤ pp. 62-65

1. Click the Toolbar's Spell Check icon.
2. Select a replacement for the word from the Replacements list and click the Replace button.

    or

    Type the correct spelling for the word in the Replace with box, then choose Replace.

    or

    Click Skip Once to ignore this spelling once, Skip Always to ignore this spelling throughout the document, or Add to include the word in the WordPerfect dictionary.
3. When a message box asks you whether to close the Spell Checker, click Yes.

Get Your Document Statistics ➤ pp. 65-66

1. Choose File | Properties.
2. Click the Information tab.
3. When you're finished looking at the document statistics, choose Close.

1564	Character count
335	Word count
49	Line count
28	Sentence count
11	Paragraph count

You can learn more about managing your document files in Chapter 4.

Here's where all the time you've invested in learning WordPerfect really pays off. Instead of having to retype something when you want to make changes to it, you can just edit the electronic version of the document. Delete this word. Rewrite that sentence. Move a paragraph from *here* to *there*. In short, with WordPerfect you only have to make changes to the part of your document that needs fixing—the rest you can leave alone. It's the bad typist's fondest dream.

Open a Document

In Chapter 1, you learned how to create a new document and save it for later use. Unfortunately, that knowledge isn't worth a hill of beans unless you know how to open that document up again whenever you need it. Once the document is open, you can edit it and save your changes.

DEFINITION

Open: Computer geeks have come up with a new meaning for this old word. When you are working on a document, they say it's "open." In computer-ese, this is also used as a verb so that, when you want to work on a file, you are "opening it."

SHORTCUT

You'll probably find that you often want to open a document you've worked on recently. If that's the case, you can get to that file without any fuss or hassle whatsoever. Click your File menu. You'll notice that the ten files you've used most recently are listed at the bottom of that menu. Just click the document you want to open.

To open a document, follow these steps:

1. Click the Toolbar's Open icon. This brings up the Open dialog box.
2. If your document is not listed in the current directory, browse through your directories to find your document.
3. Click on the file you want to open, then click Open.

SHORTCUT

You can speed up step 3 by simply double-clicking the file you want to open.

If you're not sure you've found the right file to open, click the Preview button to take a look at the contents of the document. You can also click other document titles in the Open File dialog box, and the contents of the Preview window will change accordingly. Close the Preview window as you would any Windows application.

EXPERT ADVICE

If you want to start a new, blank document instead of opening a new one, just click the New Blank Document icon at the left end of your Toolbar.

Navigating in a Document

Once you've opened the document you want to work on, you need to move your insertion point to the place to be edited. Chapter 1 teaches the fundamentals of using the mouse to get from one point to another—just use your scrollbar to find the area you want to edit, then click in the exact spot you want to change. Here, you'll learn some neat tricks for getting around with speed and style.

Use Go To to Get There

When you're working on large documents, using the scrollbar is an inexact science at best—you have to scroll around quite a bit to find the page you want. If you happen to know which page you want to edit, though—and you often will when you're looking at a printed copy of your document—there's no faster way than the Go To feature. Follow the Step-By-Step instructions on the next page.

EXPERT ADVICE

The Go To feature is also handy when you've moved to a new place in your document but now want to return to where you were. Just click the page location on the Application bar (or press CTRL-G*), select the Position radio button, then double-click Last Position.*

upgrade note

In previous versions of WordPerfect, you had to double-click the page location area to bring up the Go To dialog box. While a single click makes more sense, this may take a little getting used to if you've been using other versions of WordPerfect for a while.

STEP BY STEP **Using Go To to Jump to a Certain Page**

③ **Click OK.**

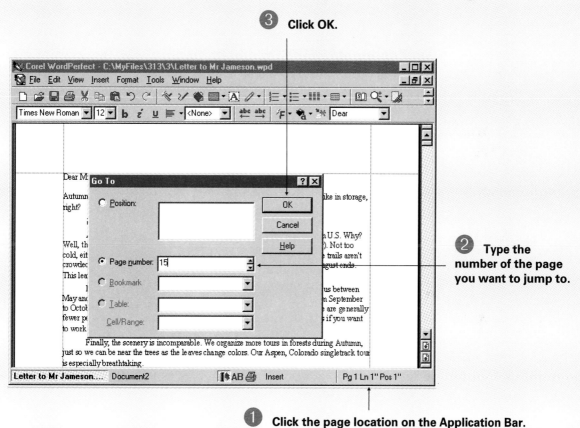

② **Type the number of the page you want to jump to.**

① **Click the page location on the Application Bar.**

Using the Keyboard to Move the Insertion Point

When you're editing text, you spend a great deal of time moving the insertion point from one place to another. Taking your hands off the keyboard each time you want to move to a different word or sentence can be a real nuisance, so knowing a few keystrokes to move the insertion point around really speeds things up.

There are quite a few insertion point-moving keystrokes to learn, all of them useful. You may have a tricky time learning all of these at once, though, so focus on learning just a few at a time. They're listed in order of importance (according to me, of course).

Keystroke	What the Insertion Point Does
LEFT, RIGHT, UP, DOWN ARROWS	Moves one character in that direction
CTRL-LEFT, CTRL-RIGHT ARROWS	Moves one word in that direction
CTRL-UP, CTRL-DOWN ARROWS	Moves one paragraph in that direction
HOME	Moves to beginning of line
END	Moves to end of line
CTRL-HOME	Moves to beginning of document
CTRL-END	Moves to end of document
PAGE UP	Moves up a screenful of text
PAGE DOWN	Moves down a screenful of text
ALT-PAGE UP	Moves to top of previous page
ALT-PAGE DOWN	Moves to top of next page

Selecting Text

If you're going to edit in WordPerfect, you absolutely, positively *have* to know how to select text (Figure 3.1). Selecting is a prerequisite for copying, moving, and deleting big chunks of text. You'll find that knowing how to select text is very important in using other features, too, so make sure you master this skill.

Because selecting text is so important to so many WordPerfect tasks, there are a variety of ways you can do it. They all boil down to two main techniques, though: using the mouse or using the keyboard.

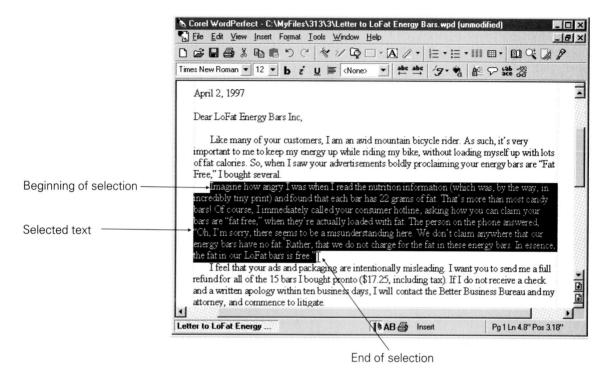

Figure 3.1 Selecting text is an important part of many formatting tasks. You mark the text, then you can change it (make it italic, for example) or move it to a new location

Selecting with the Mouse

The mouse is a natural for selecting chunks of text, and there are several useful techniques available, depending on how much you want selected. Here's how—and when—you use each:

- **Click and Drag:** Use this for selecting relatively small pieces of text, such as a few words, sentences, or, at most, a couple paragraphs. All you do is click your mouse where you want the selection to begin. Then, while still holding the mouse button down, move your mouse to where you want the selection to end—this is called "dragging." As you drag the mouse, your selection appears as white-on-black (or some other color) text.

EXPERT ADVICE

Out of the box, WordPerfect selects whole words at a time whenever your selection goes beyond a single word. Some people like this; some don't. If you're one of the "don'ts," you can learn how to turn off this option in Chapter 2.

- **Click, SHIFT-click:** This is a good technique when you want to select a large amount of text, whether it be several paragraphs or several pages. First, click your mouse where you want the selection to begin. Then move your mouse so the shadow pointer is where you want the selection to end. Press and hold the SHIFT key while you click (this is called, naturally enough, SHIFT-clicking).

- **Double-click:** If you'd like to select a single word, move the mouse pointer over that word and double-click. You can hold down the mouse after the second click and then drag to select more words.

- **Triple-click:** Want to select a sentence? Move your mouse pointer over it, and then—in rapid succession—click the mouse three times. After the third click, you can hold down the mouse button and drag up or down to select additional sentences.

- **Quadruple-click:** I know, this seems like it's getting out of hand, but it's a handy trick. You can select a whole paragraph by moving the mouse over it and clicking four times. (Mercifully, WordPerfect has no pentuple-click.) Want to select more paragraphs? Hold down the mouse after the fourth click and drag up or down.

- **Use the menu:** You can select the current page or the entire document by using the menu. Choose Edit | Select, then choose Page, or, for the entire document, choose All. (You can also choose Sentence or Paragraph, but it's easier to select those by triple- or quadruple-clicking.

- **Use a QuickMenu:** If you don't go for the triple-click and quadruple-click stuff, you can use this technique. Put your insertion point in the sentence, paragraph, or page you want to select. Move your mouse pointer into the left margin and right-click your mouse. From

See *"Using the Keyboard to Move the Insertion Point,"* earlier in this chapter for instructions on moving the insertion point with your keyboard.

If you want to turn off a selection with your keyboard, just press the LEFT ARROW or RIGHT ARROW key. Or, if you want to impress your coworkers, press F8, the "Select Off" key.

the QuickMenu that appears, you can choose to select the sentence, paragraph, or page. Or you can even select the entire document.

What if you decide that you don't want text selected after all? All you do to turn off the selection is click somewhere in the document, either in or out of the selection. The selection disappears—no harm, no foul.

Using the Keyboard to Select

I think you'll like this section a lot, because it's nice and short. Selecting text with the keyboard is just like moving the insertion point with the keyboard, with one little difference: you hold down the SHIFT key while you do it.

Say, for example, you want to select a word. First, you move the insertion point to the beginning of the word—this is where the selection will begin. Then, because you know CTRL-RIGHT ARROW moves the insertion point one word to the right, you press SHIFT-CTRL-RIGHT Arrow to select from the insertion point to the beginning of the next word.

EXPERT ADVICE

If you want to continue selecting words in that direction, just repeat the keystroke. This is called extending *the selection. You can also press SHIFT in combination with other insertion point-moving keystrokes to extend the selection however much you want. For example, you can press SHIFT-ALT-PAGE DOWN to select to the top of the next page, then press SHIFT-CTRL-DOWN ARROW to select down to the end of the first paragraph on that next page.*

Erasing Text

Ahhh, the eraser: the writer's worst nightmare, the editor's favorite tool. In Chapter 1, you learned how to erase characters with the DELETE and BACKSPACE keys, as well as how to quickly zap a word by pressing CTRL-BACKSPACE. Here's how you can get rid of larger chunks of text.

1. Select the text you want to get rid of.
2. Press DELETE or BACKSPACE—it doesn't matter which.

EXPERT ADVICE

Often, you'll want to replace the text you're deleting with new, different text. If this is the case, skip step 2. Instead, after you've selected the text you want to get rid of, just begin typing the new text. As soon as you press the first letter, the selected text disappears and is replaced with what you're typing.

Moving Text

You're editing a report you've written for the boss when you realize that your opening paragraph would actually make a much better *closing* paragraph. Do you retype it? No way. WordPerfect gives you a couple of powerful tools for moving text from one part of the document to another.

The Clipboard: Cut, Copy, and Paste

If you're familiar with Windows, you probably already know how to use the Clipboard, in which case feel free to skip this section (although you may miss a couple of pithy witticisms). If not, read on.

CAUTION

Unlike a real clipboard, the Windows Clipboard holds only one thing at a time. Say you cut the first paragraph of your report to the Clipboard. Then you cut an address to the Clipboard. What happens to the paragraph? It disappears. So here's the bottom line: Don't cut or copy to the Clipboard unless you're sure you don't need what's already there.

When you want to use some text you've written elsewhere in the document, you put it in what's known as the "Clipboard." I know, it's a strange name. But imagine yourself way back in the prehistoric days when typewriters roamed the earth. You've got a paragraph on one page you want to put on another page, so you take some scissors and *cut out* the paragraph. You then put that paragraph on a clipboard you've got lying around so you won't lose the paragraph. When you get to the place where you want that paragraph to go, you get out some rubber cement (mmmm, love that smell) and *paste* it onto its new spot.

Or, on the other hand, say you wanted to use a paragraph in more than one spot. You take the original paragraph to the photocopier, make a *copy* of it, and put the copy on the clipboard, leaving the original paragraph where it was. Later, you can paste the copy of the paragraph wherever you like.

That's essentially the idea behind how the Clipboard works in WordPerfect (and most every other Windows program). Take a look at the Step-By-Step instructions to learn how to move or copy text using the Clipboard.

STEP BY STEP **Cut, Copy, and Paste with the Clipboard**

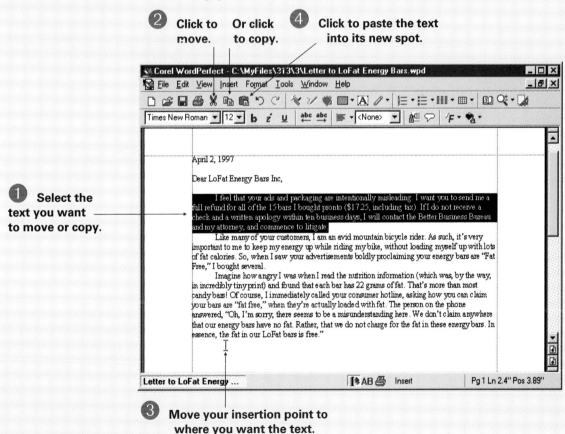

② Click to move. **Or click to copy.** **④** Click to paste the text into its new spot.

① Select the text you want to move or copy.

③ Move your insertion point to where you want the text.

The Clipboard has several features and caveats that may not be immediately obvious to you. Here are some tips you should bear in mind when using this powerful tool:

- Cut removes the selected text and puts it in the Clipboard. Use it when you want to move the text from one spot to another.
- Copy leaves the selected text where it is and makes a copy of it in the Clipboard. Use it when you want the text where it is *and* in another spot.
- When you reset or turn off the computer or exit Windows, whatever was in the Clipboard disappears, so don't think of the Clipboard as a permanent holding place. Hold information in it just long enough to move it where you need it.
- Once you've put text in the Clipboard—whether by cutting or copying—you can paste it any number of times. When you want to put the same thing in a document several times, this is a handy way to do it.
- The Clipboard is a Windows thing, not just a WordPerfect thing. So, if you cut or copy some text in WordPerfect, you can paste it in another program (your e-mail program, for example) to use the text there.
- If you've got more than one document open in WordPerfect, you can cut or copy text in one document, then paste it in the other. This is a good way to move text between documents.
- Paste puts the text into your document with all the formatting intact. Sometimes, though, the text from the program where you cut or

copied the document uses different formatting than the text in the program to which you paste. To paste the text *without* formatting, use Simple Paste—instructions for putting this button on your Toolbar are in Chapter 2.

Moving Text with Drag and Drop

When you want to move a small amount of text (a few sentences or maybe a paragraph) just a short distance (to somewhere you can see on the screen), the Drag and Drop feature is much easier than using the Clipboard. All you have to do is select the text you want to move, then click in the selection and drag it to its new home. Follow these Step-By-Step instructions:

STEP BY STEP **Drag and Drop**

① **Select the text you want to move.**

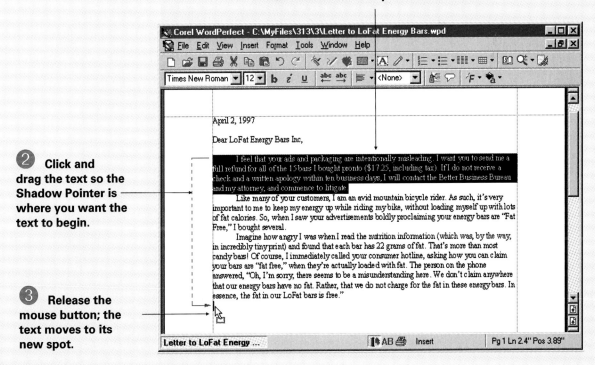

② **Click and drag the text so the Shadow Pointer is where you want the text to begin.**

③ **Release the mouse button; the text moves to its new spot.**

EXPERT ADVICE

*You can also copy text with the Drag and Drop technique. Just hold down
CTRL while you drag the text.*

CAUTION

*If you begin dragging a selection and then decide you don't want to move
it after all, just continue holding down the mouse button and move your
mouse pointer so it's over the Toolbar, menu bar, or scrollbar and release
the mouse pointer there.*

upgrade note

Drag and Drop has been around for several versions of WordPerfect, but
WordPerfect 8 is the first version to make it easy to drag text from one
document to another. Just follow these steps:

1. Make sure both the document you're moving text from and the one
   you're moving text to are open.

2. Select the text you want to move or copy.

3. Click in the selection, then drag (or CTRL-drag, if you want to copy)
   to the application bar at the bottom of the window, so your mouse
   pointer is on the name of the file in which you want to put the text. *Don't
   release the mouse button yet!*

   WordPerfect switches to the document you're pointing at.

4. Move your mouse pointer to where you want the text, then release the
   mouse button.

Fixing Mistakes with Undo and Redo

In Chapter 1, you learned how to bring back text you accidentally deleted using the Undo feature by pressing CTRL-Z (you can also click the Toolbar's Undo button). What I didn't tell you, though, is that you can use Undo for much more. You can use it, in fact, to repair just about any mistake. If you accidentally deleted text, click Undo. If—oops—you moved to the bottom of the document, click Undo. If you cut text you shouldn't have, click Undo. Are you beginning to see a pattern here?

WordPerfect remembers and lets you undo the last ten things you've done.

You can also use Undo more than once in a row. Say you accidentally deleted a paragraph and then went to the end of the document. The first time you click Undo, WordPerfect jumps back from the end of the document to where you were. Click it again and WordPerfect restores the text you deleted.

Undo undoes the changes you've made in the reverse order you made them—this includes changes you *meant* to make. If you click Undo and find that it's erased text you want, click the Redo button to bring the change back. Like Undo, you can click Redo multiple times.

Make Sweeping Changes with Find and Replace

Occasionally, you might want to change one word to another throughout a document. Say, for example, you've just written a letter where you frequently refer to "Frazier Todd Hair Design" and realize that you should have been calling it "Stuart Frazier Salon." Rather than manually hunt down each instance of your error (and probably miss a couple), just have WordPerfect replace the text automatically.

You can use this feature to simply locate a certain word or phrase in a document, too, which comes in very handy when you've got a long document and don't want to read through the whole thing to find the text you need.

Follow these steps to find or replace text:

1. Move your insertion point to where you want the search to begin (press CTRL-HOME to start from the beginning of the document).
2. Choose Edit | Find and Replace from the menu bar to bring up the Find and Replace dialog box.

SHORTCUT

You can also bring up this dialog box by pressing CTRL-F.

Text you're searching for

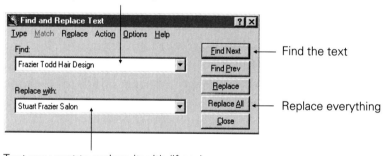

Find the text

Replace everything

Text you want to replace it with (if any)

3. In the Find text box, type the text (word or phrase) you're looking for.
4. If you want to replace the text in the Find box with something else, type the replacement text in the Replace with box (if you're just trying to find text, don't type anything here).
5. Click one of the buttons described in Table 3.1.
6. When you're finished finding (and replacing) text, click Close.

Click This Button	To Do This
Find Next	Search forward and select the text in the Find box
Find Prev	Search backward and select the text in the Find box
Replace	To be used after Find Next or Find Prev has found and selected text. Replace the text in the Find box with text in the Replace with box. Then find and select the next instance of the Find text.
Replace All	Replace every instance of the text in the Find box with the text in the Replace with box. Make sure you were at the top of the document when you start, though, or this button replaces only the text after the insertion point.

Table 3.1 Find and Replace Buttons and What They Do

EXPERT ADVICE

Ordinarily, the Find and Replace feature finds the text you type in the Find box even if it's capitalized differently (the text it gets replaced with, however, is always exactly how you type it in the Replace with box). For example, if you type "Biggs" in the Find box, WordPerfect will find "Biggs," "BIGGS," and "biggs." If you want WordPerfect to find the word only if it's capitalized the way you type it in the Find box, choose Match | Case from the Find and Replace Text dialog box's menu bar.

upgrade note

WordPerfect 8 makes searching for a word as easy as a single click of the mouse. If you want to look for the next occurrence of the word your insertion point is currently in, just click the QuickFind Next icon, located in the Property bar—it's a right arrow with "abc" over it. Likewise, you can search backward by clicking the QuickFind Previous Word button.

Checking Your Spelling

WordPerfect's Spell Check is a boon to writers and editors alike—writers can hide the fact that they're such lousy spellers, and editors have an easier time fixing writers' lousy spelling.

Working With Spell-As-You-Go

You may have noticed that a wavy red line appears under certain words you type in WordPerfect. This means that those words are not in WordPerfect's dictionary, so there's a pretty good chance they are spelled wrong.

Misspelled word
↓

Like many of your customers, I am an avid mountain bicicle rider. As such, it's very important to me to keep my energy up while riding my bike, without loading myself up with lots of fat calories. So, when I saw your advertisements boldly proclaiming your energy bars are "Fat Free," I bought several.

Here's how to handle the situation:

1. Right-click over the red-underlined word. A list of possible spellings appears as shown in the illustration at left.
2. Choose the correct spelling.

   or

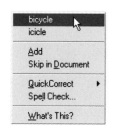

If the word's spelled correctly, and WordPerfect doesn't know it (such as a name or any other word you'll be using again), choose Add to include the word in WordPerfect's dictionary.

or

If you want WordPerfect to ignore the spelling of this word in this document only, click Skip in Document.

EXPERT ADVICE

If you get sick of WordPerfect underlining all those words in red, you can turn off Spell-As-You-Go. From the menu bar, choose Tools | Proofread | Spell-As-You-Go. Repeat these steps to turn this feature back on.

Spell Check the Whole Document

CAUTION

Spell Checking is no substitute for proofreading. A word can be spelled correctly and still be used incorrectly. For example, the following sentence gets the big thumbs-up from WordPerfect's Spell Checker: "Ill bee their buy an bye."

It's always a good idea to check a document's spelling before you print it, just to make sure no spelling goofs have slipped by you.

1. Click the Spell Check button in the Toolbar to start checking your document.
   When WordPerfect finds a word it doesn't recognize, it shows you the word and gives you options, as shown in Figure 3.2.
2. Select a replacement for the word from the Replacements list and click the Replace button
   or

If none of the words in the replacement list are correct, type the correct spelling for the word in the Replace with box, then choose Replace.

or

Click Skip Once to ignore this spelling once, Skip Always to ignore this spelling throughout the document, or Add to include the word in the WordPerfect dictionary.

3. When WordPerfect is finished checking the document, a message box asks you whether to close the Spell Checker. Click Yes.

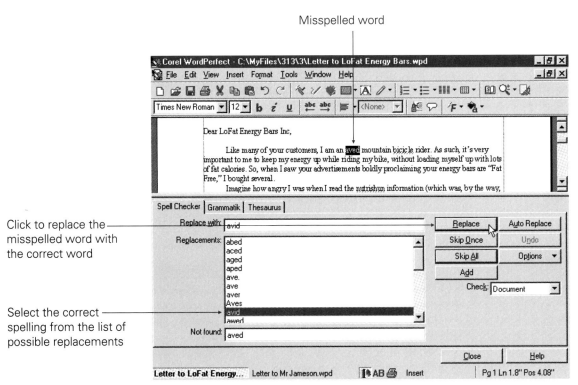

Misspelled word

Click to replace the misspelled word with the correct word

Select the correct spelling from the list of possible replacements

Figure 3.2 The Spell Checker looks at each word in your document, giving you suggested replacements for words it doesn't recognize

Get Writing and Spelling Tips with "Prompt-as-You-Go"

WordPerfect includes the word processing equivalent of a backseat driver—it's called "Prompt-As-You-Go." This tool, located on the right end of your Property Bar, looks like a simple drop-down list. Whenever you misspell a word, however, that word appears in red in the list. Make sure your insertion point is in the word, click the list, and you can select the correct spelling from the list of options.

What's so great about that? Not much, really. After all, you can do the same thing by right-clicking on the word and choosing the correct spelling from a QuickMenu.

What *is* cool about Prompt-as-You-Go, however, is that you can use it as a quick thesaurus. Any time you would like to see synonyms for a word, just move your insertion point into that word and click the Prompt-as-You-Go drop-down list. If you see a word you'd like to substitute for the one you're using right now, just click that word.

Get Your Document's Statistics

If your document is destined to be published, chances are you're trying to hit a certain word count. You can check this easily as often as you need to. Just choose File | Properties, then click the Information Tab, shown in Figure 3.3.

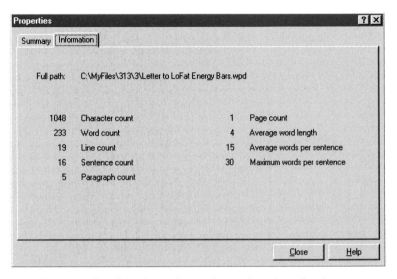

Figure 3.3 The Properties dialog box tells you the number of words, characters, lines, sentences, pages, and paragraphs in your document. You also get the average word length, average words per sentence, and the maximum words per sentence

When you finish taking in this awesome statistical spectacle, click the Close button.

CHAPTER

4

File Management in WordPerfect

INCLUDES

- Understanding folders and files

- Using the Open and Save As dialog boxes

- Creating and deleting folders

- Saving time with the favorites folder

- Finding files

- Working with multiple documents

- Opening and saving with other file formats

67

FAST FORWARD

File and Folder Basics ➤ pp. 70-73

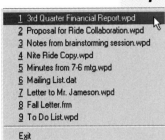

- Double-click drives and folders to open them.
- Press BACKSPACE to leave the current folder and go up a level.
- Double-click a file to open it into WordPerfect.

Open a File You've Used Recently ➤ p. 71

1. Click the File menu.

   Files you've used recently appear at the bottom of the menu.

2. Click the document you want to open.

Get Quick Access to
Your Favorite Folders and Files ➤ pp. 75-76

1. Click the Open button or choose File | Save As.
2. Click the Favorites button.
3. Double-click the shortcut icon to go to that folder or file.

Find Lost Files ➤ pp. 77-78

1. Click the Open button.
2. In the Look in box, specify the drive or folder you want to search. Subdirectories will also be searched.
3. Type the file name (or part of the file name) you're searching for, or type a word or phrase you know is in the document you're looking for.
4. Click Find.

Open Multiple Documents at Once ➤ p. 79

1. Click the Open button.
2. Hold down the CTRL key and click all the files you need to open. (Remember, though, you can't have more than nine documents open at a time.)
3. Click Open.

Switch Between Documents ➤ pp. 80-82

- From the menu bar, choose Window, then click the document you want to work on.
- Press CTRL-F6 to move to the next open document. Press SHIFT-CTRL-F6 to move to the previous open document.
- Move your mouse pointer to the application bar and click the document you want to work on.
- View several documents at once by choosing Window, then choose Cascade, Tile Top to Bottom, or Tile Side by Side.

Open Non-WordPerfect Documents ➤ p. 83

1. Open the file as you would any WordPerfect document.
2. A message box appears, showing the conversion type. Click OK.

Save a WordPerfect Document with Another File Format ➤ pp. 83-85

1. Open the document into a WordPerfect window.
2. Choose File | Save As.
3. Browse through the folders to pick where you want the document saved.
4. In the Name text box, type a name for the file.
5. Clcik the File type drop-down menu and select the format you want.
6. Click Save, then close the document.

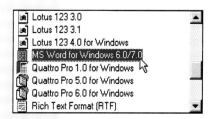

Back in 1994, I would really have dreaded writing this chapter—and believe me, you would not have enjoyed reading it. You see, back then, your documents had to be stored in cryptically named directory structures, using cryptically named files, all following the extraordinarily cryptic DOS conventions. Working with files was, in short, cryptic.

Windows 95 has changed all that. We no longer have to decipher tiny little filenames at the end of huge, unreadable directory paths. We now name our documents whatever we like, and we can browse through folders to find them, sort of like you would through a file cabinet.

Yes, things are a lot better now. But you've still got to learn how to manage files. After all, every time you save or open a document, you're managing files. So, while this'll be a short, relatively painless chapter, it's still important information to cover.

If you're already familiar with managing files in Windows, you might just want to scan the "Finding Files" and "Working with Multiple Documents" sections. The rest will be old hat.

Understanding and Using Folders and Files

Say you've got a filing cabinet. If you like, you can just toss everything right into that cabinet, but mercy, what a *mess*. It would make a lot more sense to put some hanging file dividers in that cabinet and to divide your files into major categories. Inside some of those hanging dividers, you'd probably put some manila folders to organize your work into even more specific categories. Finally, you put your files into a folder—whether it be a hanging folder or a manila folder.

Your computer's hard drive works the same way. By putting your information (programs and documents) into folders—and folders within folders—things stay much better organized, so you have a better chance of finding them.

Get to Know WordPerfect's Open and Save As Dialog Boxes

WordPerfect's Open and Save As dialog boxes are the two main places where you'll do your file management.

EXPERT ADVICE

Wait! Before you use the Open File dialog box to open a document, ask yourself this question: "Have I worked on this file in the past couple of days?" If you have, there's a good chance you can open the document with just a couple of clicks—and without going into a single dialog box. Just click the File menu, and you'll see the ten files you've used most recently listed at the bottom of that menu. Just click the document you want to open.

upgrade note

In WordPerfect 7, the Open File and Save As dialog boxes also showed a "Tree View" of what folder you were in—a visual map of where your folder is. This tree view is just like the one you use in the Windows Explorer and is handy for navigating the folders and drives of your computer. Many people find this tree view useful, but WordPerfect 8 doesn't automatically show it. You can turn on this view by clicking the Toggle Tree View on/off button in the dialg box's Toolbar. There are a couple of downsides to this, however: it takes longer to bring up the dialog box, and it takes up space in the dialog box.

When you click either the Toolbar's Open or Save icon, you see a dialog box similar to the one in Figure 4.1.

You double-click a file to open it. If you're saving a document, you can type a name for the document in the Name box and click Save.

EXPERT ADVICE

If the Open File or Save As dialog box seems too small to you, click on one of the corners of the dialog box and drag it till it's larger. WordPerfect will remember to make it the new size from now on.

Current folder

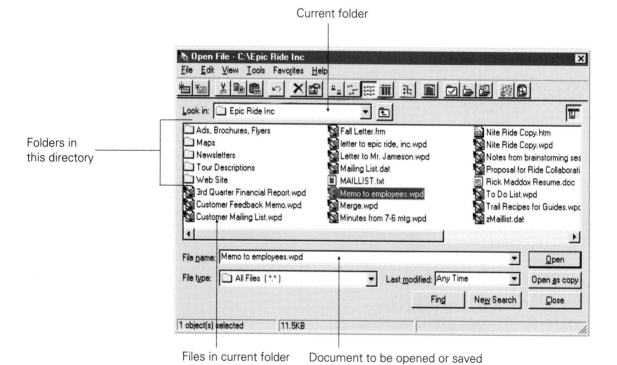

Folders in this directory

Files in current folder   Document to be opened or saved

Figure 4.1 The Open File and Save As dialog boxes use very similar tools and look almost identical

Browsing Techniques

Once you've got the Open File or Save As dialog box up, you'll sometimes want to go to a different folder to save or open a file. No problem. Just use one of the following techniques:

- To switch to a different drive—from your C: drive to your A: drive, for example, click the Look in drop-down menu. Scroll to the drive you want and click it.

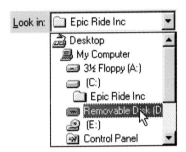

- You'll often want to move up a folder level. For example, suppose you're in the Newsletters folder, which is in the Epic Ride folder—and you want to move up to the Epic Ride folder. Just click the Up One Level button, or press your BACKSPACE key. You can do this as often as you like to move up level after level.
- To open a folder, just double-click it. When you do, the dialog box lists the subfolders and files in that folder, and the Look in box shows that you're indeed in that folder.
- If you're a DOS die-hard and know the exact path you want, you can type it in the Name text box, then press ENTER. The dialog box will then list the contents of that folder.

Making Folders

When you install WordPerfect, it creates a folder called MyFiles. By default, this is where all your documents go. As you create more and more documents,

Usually, people use the Windows Explorer to make folders. I'll explain how it's done in WordPerfect anyway, because you'll often find you want a new folder when you're in the process of naming a file, and it's no fun to have to go to the Windows Explorer right in the middle of this process.

EXPERT ADVICE

Sometimes you'll get the Open File dialog box up and suddenly find yourself thinking, "Hey, I think I've opened this file not too long ago." There's an easy way to open files you've used recently. Click the drop-down button at the end of the Name text box, and you'll see a list of files you've been working on. Scroll down to find the one you want, click it, then click Open. No browsing or typing required!

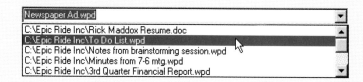

though, you might sometimes want to create new folders—maybe for different types of documents, maybe for different people who use the computer. Here's how you create a folder:

1. Click Open to bring up the Open File dialog box, or choose File | Save As to bring up the Save As dialog box.
2. Browse through the drives and folders until you've opened the folder in which you want to create the new folder.
3. From the dialog box's menu bar, choose File | New | Folder.
4. Type a name for the folder, then press ENTER.
5. Click Close.

Favorites Folder: A Few of Your Favorite Things

Nowadays, with gargantuan hard disk drives being all the rage, folders seem to multiply at an alarming rate, till you have to burrow through level after level to

EXPERT ADVICE

It's easy to remove folders, too. Just bring up the Open or Save As dialog box, then click the folder you want to delete. Press DELETE. *A message box appears, asking whether you really want to delete the folder and everything in it.* Take this message seriously! *When you remove a folder, all the files, programs, and other folders in that folder are deleted, so it's not something you should do lightly.*

get to the folders you use often. Well, if you actually use just a *few* of those folders to hold your documents, or if there are a few documents you find yourself working on all the time, WordPerfect has a little gizmo I think you'll love. It's called the Favorites folder.

The idea behind the Favorites folder is to have a single, easy-to-get-to spot from which you can quickly get to the folders and files you use most often. The folder doesn't actually contain the folders and files themselves; it contains *shortcuts* to those files and folders. This way, you can put your frequently-used files and folders where they logically belong in your hierarchy and still get to them quickly from one spot.

Using the Favorites Folder

In keeping with the "easier is better" idea behind the Favorites folder, using this feature is a snap. Just follow these steps:

1. Click Open.
2. Click the Favorites button to see a list of favorite folders and files.

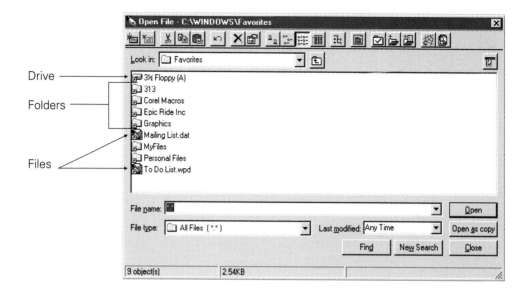

3. Double-click the drive, folder, or file you want to open.

4. Open the file as usual.

Adding Files and Folders to the Favorites

EXPERT ADVICE

Don't go crazy adding files and folders to the Favorites folder. If you have so many in the list that it takes some time to find the one you want, the whole purpose of the folder is defeated.

WordPerfect comes with a few shortcuts to folders already set up, but chances are good you'll want to add your own. Here's how:

1. Click Open to bring up the Open dialog box, or choose File | Save As to bring up the Save As dialog box.

2. Browse through folders until you've found the folder or file you want to add to the Favorites list.

3. If you're adding a folder, open that folder. If you're adding a file, click on the file.

4. If you're adding a folder, click the Add Current Location button.

   or

EXPERT ADVICE

If you want to get rid of an item in the Favorites folder, go to the Favorites folder, click on the item you don't want anymore, then press DELETE. A message box asks if you want to get rid of the shortcut. Click Yes. Note that when you delete shortcuts, you're not actually getting rid of the file or folder itself—just the shortcut to it.

If you're adding a document, click the Add Selected Item button.

Finding Files

No matter how conscientious I am about putting my keys away, I can never seem to find them in the morning. The same things happens to me with files. I *really* try to save them in the right spot, but once in a while I just can't find them. If you ever find yourself looking under the sofa for a lost file, you'll probably have better luck with the Find tool in the Open File dialog box. Follow these steps:

1. Choose File | Open or click the Toolbar's Open icon.

2. In the Look in drop-down list, specify the drive or folder you want to search.
   WordPerfect will begin its search from that point, and will search in all subdirectories, as well.

3. If you know the name of the file (or part of the name), type it in the File name text box.

If the search doesn't turn up the file you want, click the Back button, then try again.

or

If you know the document has a certain word or phrase in it, type the word(s) in the File name text box.

4. If you know you've saved the file within a certain period of time (for example, today, a week, or a month), click the Last modified drop-down list and select that time period.

5. Click Find.

As the Find feature does its thing, a list of files that match the search criteria appear in the dialog box. (You can click the Stop Find button once the file you want appears in the list.) Click the file you want to open, then click Open (or double-click the file).

EXPERT ADVICE

While the tools in WordPerfect's Open and Save As dialog boxes are undoubtedly useful, you may already be mighty comfortable with using the standard Windows file management dialog boxes, and would prefer to use them. Here's what you do to switch over to these standard dialog boxes: choose Tools | Settings, then double-click the Files icon. Deselect the Use enhanced file dialogs checkbox, then click OK.

Working with Multiple Documents

If you weren't a busy person, maybe one document is all you'd ever need to work on at a time. You could open WordPerfect, tool around for a bit on a memo you've been fine-tuning for a couple of days, then break for brunch. You could then come back, work on the memo a little more, thinking such things as, "Hmmmm, maybe it needs more *adjectives*—that would spice it up nicely."

But you *are* a busy person. As you're hammering out that memo, your boss suddenly calls, telling you to add a disclaimer clause to the Anderson contract. As you work on *that,* you realize you need to make a couple of revisions to the flyer you're sending to the printer. And then....

I think I've made my point.

EXPERT ADVICE

Sometimes you'll want to start a new blank document. All you need to do to get a clean screen is click the New Blank Document icon at the left edge of your Toolbar.

You work on a lot of projects at a time, and WordPerfect can, too. In fact, you can open and work on as many as nine documents at a time. That should be enough for even the busiest person.

Open More Than One Document at a Time

This is a cool trick you can show off the next time somebody's watching over your shoulder. It's easy to do, but not many people know how. When you need to work on more than one document at a time, open them all in one fell swoop. Here's how:

CAUTION

Use this technique for opening documents that are all in the same folder. You can't select some files from one folder, then select some from another folder, then open them all at once. You'll need to open the files from one folder first, then open the files from the other folder.

1. Click the Toolbar's Open icon to bring up the Open dialog box.
2. Hold down the CTRL key and click all the files you need to open. (Remember, though, you can't have more than nine documents open at a time.)
3. Click Open.

EXPERT ADVICE

Most of the techniques you use for selecting text will also work for selecting multiple files. Try clicking and dragging to select multiple files, for example. Also, if you want to deselect one of your selected files, hold down the CTRL key and click that file.

Chapter 2 gives instructions for adding a Save All button to your Toolbar so you can save all your open documents with a single click.

Switching Between Documents

Okay, you've got more than one document open. Terrific. Now how do you move from one to the next? Just try any of the following techniques:

- From the menu bar, choose Window, then click the document you want to work on.
- If you want to see several documents at once, choose Window, then choose Cascade to see your documents stacked like a deck of cards (Figure 4.2), Tile Top to Bottom to see your documents one on top of another (Figure 4.3), or Tile Side by Side to see your documents, well, side by side (Figure 4.4). Click in the document you want to work in.

SHORTCUT

Press CTRL-F6 to move to the next open document. Press SHIFT-CTRL-F6 to move to the previous open document. And good luck remembering which is "next" and which is "previous."

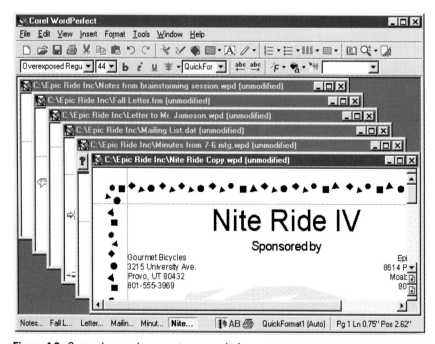

Figure 4.2 Several open documents, cascaded

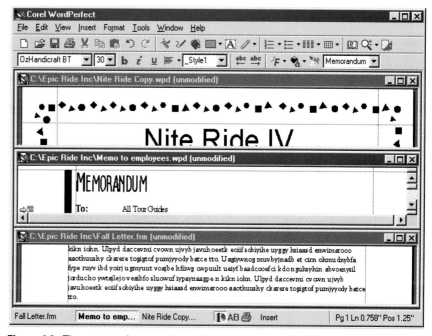

Figure 4.3 These open documents are tiled top to bottom

- When you want a document to take the full screen again, click the document's Maximize button, found at the right side of the document's title bar.
- WordPerfect makes it easy to switch between documents by using the Application Bar down at the bottom of the WordPerfect window. Your open files are listed there (the active document is recessed), and all you need to do to switch to one of those documents is click the one you want to use.

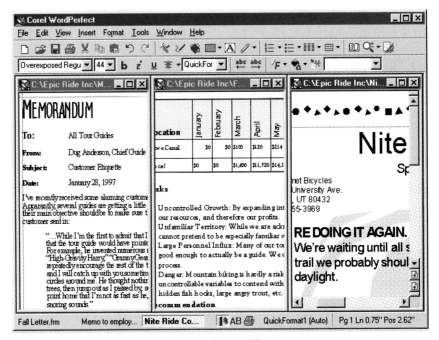

Figure 4.4 Documents can also be tiled side by side

upgrade note

WordPerfect 8 gives you a new way to move text from one open document to another by using the Application bar. First, select the text you want to move or copy. Next, click in the text and drag it to the application bar (if you're copying the text, you should also hold down the CTRL key), so your mouse pointer is over the document to which you want to move the text. When you do this, WordPerfect switches windows, and you can finish dragging the text to where you want it in the document. When your mouse pointer is where you want the text, release the mouse button.

Working With Other File Formats

You'd think all these computer programmer types could get together and agree what a word processor file should be. But *nooooo*. Your WordPerfect files are different from Microsoft's Word files. And both are different than IBM/Lotus's WordPro files. Sheesh.

But we've all got to work together, right? So you need to know how to give files to people with other word processors, as well as how to use files they give you.

Opening Non-WordPerfect Files

Whoever's responsible for programming this part of WordPerfect deserves a big wet kiss on the forehead, because it's *so great*. You open files from other word processors exactly the same as you would a regular ol' WordPerfect document—using the Open dialog box.

After you double-click the file you want, WordPerfect brings up a dialog box to make sure it's picked the right format to convert.

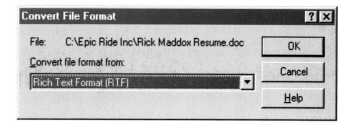

WordPerfect's hardly ever wrong at this type of thing, so unless you're *sure* it's a different format, click OK. If you know it really is a different format, pull down the drop-down menu and select the correct format, then choose OK.

Saving Files in a Different Format

With Microsoft's plans for world domination nearly complete, there's a pretty good chance that at some point, somebody is going to ask you to send them a document in Word format. Here's how to save your file in Word format—or just about any other format, for that matter.

EXPERT ADVICE

When you try to save the document, WordPerfect brings up a box asking whether you want to save the file in WordPerfect format or the format the file was originally in. Unless you'll be sending the file back to the person who sent it to you, I recommend clicking the WordPerfect radio button (once the document is saved in WordPerfect format, you won't be bothered by this box again). If you will be sending the file back to the person who sent it to you, click the radio button for its original format. After you've selected a format, choose OK.

1. Open the document into a WordPerfect window.

SHORTCUT

You can also press F3.

2. Choose File | Save As.
3. Browse through the folders to pick where you want the document saved.
4. In the Name text box, type a name for the file.
5. Click the File type drop down menu and select the format you want.

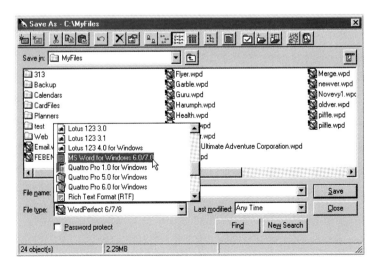

6. Click Save.

7. Close the document by clicking the file's Close box (located at the right side of the menu bar).

EXPERT ADVICE

If you save the file to your hard disk drive, there's a good chance you'll want to make a copy of it on a floppy disk so you can send it to the person who's using the other type of word processor. An easy way to do this is to go to the Open dialog box, then right-click on the file you want to put on the floppy. From the menu that appears, click Send To | 3 1/2 Floppy (A). That's all there is to it!

WordPerfect Shortcut Tips and Tricks

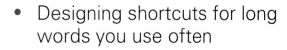

- Designing shortcuts for long words you use often

- Making WordPerfect fix your spelling errors for you

- Avoiding repetitive typing by using the QuickWords feature

- Creating no-fuss lists, indented paragraphs, and graphic lines

- Inserting unusual characters and symbols the easy way

- Finding your place in a document with a single keystroke

- Using macros to do your work for you

FAST FORWARD

Create a QuickCorrect Typing Shortcut ➤ pp. 91-92

Replace:	With:
eri	Epic Rides, Inc.|

1. Choose Tools | QuickCorrect.
2. Make sure Replace words as you type is selected.
3. In the Replace text box, type an abbreviation for a word you use often.
4. In the With text box, type the full text your abbreviation stands for.
5. Click Add Entry.
6. Click OK.

To type using QuickCorrect, just type the shortcut where you want the word. The shortcut turns into the full text as soon as you press the space bar.

Set Up QuickCorrect to Fix Spelling Mistakes ➤ p. 93

Replace:	With:
bicicle	bicycle|

1. Choose Tools | QuickCorrect.
2. At the bottom of the dialog box, select the Correct other mis-typed words when possible checkbox.
3. Choose OK.

WordPerfect will now fix common spelling errors without bothering you about it.

Create a QuickWords Shortcut for Often-Used Text ➤ pp. 94-95

Preview of expanded form (QuickWord changes to this)

Thanks for your interest in a mountain bike
Inc. We hope to find a perfect match betw
and an incredible place to ride. We're con
tours to our agenda, so be sure to check b
call us at 801-555-9498, or check our W
http://www.epicride.com

✔ Expand QuickWords when you type them

1. Type and then select the text you frequently use.
2. Choose Tools | QuickWords.
3. Make sure the Expand QuickWords when you type them checkbox is selected
4. Type a descriptive acronym or word for the text you've selected.
5. Choose Add Entry, then OK.

Insert a QuickWord Shortcut into Your Document ➤ p. 96

1. Move your insertion point to where you want the information placed.
2. Type the shortcut where you want the text. The shortcut turns into the full text as soon as you press the space bar.

Thanks for your interest in a m
match between you, our guides,
tours to our agenda, so be sure
our Web site at http://www.epic

Use Little-Known Techniques to Format Your Document ➤ pp. 96-97

- **Bulleted and Numbered Lists:** Press the asterisk (*) key to start a bulleted list or type **1.** to start a numbered list. Then press TAB and type each list item, pressing ENTER after each. After the last list item, press ENTER and then BACKSPACE over the bullet or number to stop.

Items for maintenance kit
- Chain lube
- Allen wrenches
- Screwdriver
- Chain breaker
- Spare links
- Pump
- Patches
- Spare tube

- **Divider Lines:** At the beginning of a line, press the hyphen (-) key
(for a single line) or the equal (=) key (for a double line) five or six times. Press ENTER.
- **Easy Indent:** To indent a paragraph, click at the beginning of the second line in the paragraph and press TAB. If the first line of the paragraph isn't indented, click at the beginning of the first line of the paragraph and press TAB again.

Insert Special Symbols and Unusual Characters ➤ pp. 98-101

- **Em-dashes and en-dashes:** For an em-dash (—), press the hyphen key three times in a row (---). For an en-dash (–), press the hyphen key twice in a row (--).

©
®
TM
Ä
Ç

- **Ordinals (1st, 2nd, and so forth):** Type the ordinal as you usually would. WordPerfect will automatically superscript the letters following the numbers.
- **Copyright symbol (©):** Press CTRL-W, type **co**, press ENTER.

- **Registered symbol** (®): Press CTRL-W, type **ro**, press ENTER.
- **Trademark symbol** (™): Press CTRL-W, type **tm**, press ENTER.
- **Multinational characters** (ñ, ä): Press CTRL-W, type the letter and then the symbol that goes above it (for example, **n~**), then press ENTER.
- **Any symbol**: Click the Insert Symbol icon or press CTRL-W. Select the type of symbol you want from the Set pop-up menu. Click the character you want, then click Insert and Close.

Record a Macro ➤ *pp. 102-104*

1. Choose Tools | Macro | Record
2. Type the name of the macro, then choose Record. WordPerfect will automatically add a .wcm extension to the filename to help you (and the computer) later recognize the file as a macro.
3. Perform the steps you want the macro to play back.
4. Click the Stop button.

Play a Macro ➤ *pp. 104-105*

1. Make sure your insertion point is where you want the macro to begin.
2. Choose Tools | Macro | Play.
3. Type the name of the macro, then choose Play.

Not too long ago, a lot of people envisioned computers as a big part of a Jetsons-style future. Computers would practically be self-aware and would take care of our every whim, leaving us with more leisure time than we knew what to do with.

Well, so much for *that* particular vision of the future. We're busier than ever, due, in part, to our time-saving computers. Don't give up on that dream yet, though. This chapter will help you learn some cool WordPerfect shortcuts, so you can cut down on repetitive work.

Type Faster and Better with QuickCorrect

Everyone has certain words, phrases, and sentences they tend to misspell or mistype frequently. I, for example, usually mistype my own name as "Edlen." For goofs like this, WordPerfect's QuickCorrect feature is a lifesaver. You can make it correct those misspellings automatically—with no effort on your part.

But that's not all QuickCorrect can do. There's a good chance you've got certain long words, names, or terms you use frequently. QuickCorrect lets you type those frequent words with just a couple of keystrokes. For example, any time I type **wp**, I have QuickCorrect type "WordPerfect".

Adding Words to Your QuickCorrect List

In order for QuickCorrect to automatically replace a misspelling or an abbreviation with the correct word, you need to add it to the QuickCorrect list. To do this, choose Tools | QuickCorrect, then follow the "Define QuickCorrect Words" Step-by-Step instructions.

CAUTION

Make sure the abbreviations you type in the Replace box aren't actual words that you'll use in any other context. For example, suppose you want to have QuickCorrect type **Institute of Tasmania***, so you type "it" in the Replace box. From that point forward, any time you type the word "it" you'll get "Institute of Tasmania" instead. In other words, be certain that what you type in the Replace box is not a real word. Or, if you insist on using a real word, put some character in front of it, like a backslash. A QuickCorrect abbreviation like \it won't get mixed up with the word "it."*

STEP BY STEP   Define QuickCorrect Words

③ **Type the correct spelling or the text your abbreviation stands**

② **Type the misspelling of a word or an abbreviation for a name or phrase you use often.**

④ **Click Add Entry.**

① **Make sure Replace words as you type is selected.**

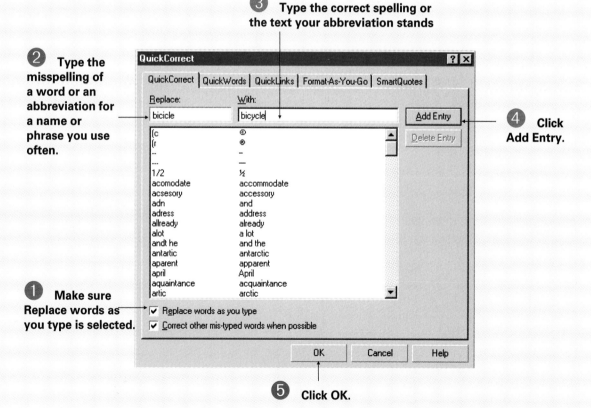

⑤ **Click OK.**

EXPERT ADVICE

If you're using QuickCorrect to type names or terms, I recommend that you add no more than three or four QuickCorrect abbreviations at first. If you add too many at once, you won't remember how to use all of them. You can add more once you're using the others automatically.

Typing with QuickCorrect

QuickCorrect works automatically. Anytime you misspell one of the words in your QuickCorrect list, WordPerfect fixes the mistake right away. Similarly, whenever you need to write one of the words you've created a QuickCorrect shortcut for, just type the shortcut letters where you would normally type the word. As soon as you press the space bar, your shortcut letters turn into the word you want.

Use the QuickWords Feature to Avoid Repetitive Typing

Most of us have sentences or even entire paragraphs we use fairly often. For example, suppose you receive a lot of mail from customers. I wouldn't be at all surprised if you have a boilerplate paragraph you use in all your replies.

upgrade note

Previous versions of WordPerfect had a feature called "Abbreviations" that did many of the same things as QuickWords. If you used Abbreviations and were wondering what happened to it, try using QuickWords instead. You'll find it's actually easier and faster to use.

If you frequently use certain sentences, paragraphs, or even graphics, you can use the QuickWords feature to insert them into your documents in a second or less.

DEFINITION

Document Assembly: Creating a letter, memo, or other document from already-completed parts (pre-written paragraphs, signature blocks, and such). With document assembly, you do very little original writing.

"How is this different from QuickCorrect?" you might ask. "Hey, good question," I might reply. QuickCorrect is for inserting very small amounts of text—a few words at most—into your document, and the text doesn't retain any formatting. QuickWords, on the other hand, can hold big chunks of text (paragraphs or even pages) and will keep the formatting intact. Essentially, QuickWords is an easy-to-use document assembly feature.

Creating a QuickWord Shortcut

QuickWords are incredibly easy to use. No matter how much information you want to re-use in WordPerfect, you make a QuickWord shortcut for it the same way:

1. Create and format the text the way you want it to appear when you re-use it.

2. Select the text you want your QuickWord shortcut to type.

> Thanks for your interest in a mountain bike tour with *Epic Rides, Inc.* We hope to find a perfect match between you, our guides, and an incredible place to ride. We're constantly adding new tours to our agenda, so be sure to check back often. You can call us at 801-555-9498, or check our Web site at http://www.epicride.com

3. Choose Tools | QuickWords to bring up the QuickCorrect dialog box, then select the QuickWords tab (see Figure 5.1).

4. Type a one-word descriptive name (or better yet, an acronym) for what you've got selected. (Remember, try *not* to use a real word and, if you do, to put a character like a backslash in front of the word!) This is the name you'll use whenever you want to place this information in another document.

5. Click Add Entry, then choose OK to return to the document window.

EXPERT ADVICE

You have the option of making the QuickWords feature insert text with the formatting (fonts, line spacing, and so forth) you used when you created the QuickWord shortcut or making it so it pastes the text without formatting. From the QuickCorrect dialog box, click the Options drop-down menu and select either Expand as text with Formatting or Expand as Plain text.

Name of QuickWord shortcut you're creating

List of available QuickWord shortcuts

Preview window for QuickWord shortcuts you've created

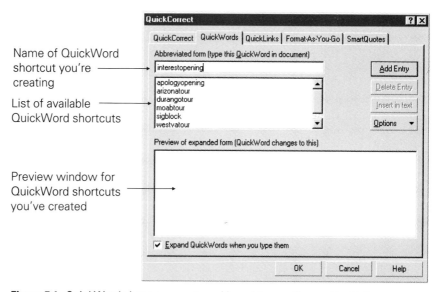

Figure 5.1 QuickWords lets you create and insert frequently-used text into your documents.

Using the QuickWords Feature

Once you've created a QuickWord shortcut, you insert it into your document just by typing the shortcut name you've given it.

1. Move your insertion point to where you want the information placed.
2. Type the name of the QuickWord shortcut you want, then press the space bar.

The shortcut is replaced with the text you want.

EXPERT ADVICE

You may not always remember the name of each QuickWord shortcut. If you forget one, move the insertion point to where you want the text to go and choose Tools | QuickWords to go to the dialog box. Scroll through the list of QuickWords abbreviations. As you do this, the bottom of the dialog box shows a preview of the currently selected QuickWords shortcut. When you've found the QuickWords shortcut you want, select it and click Insert in text.

Quick Formatting Tricks

See Chapter 10 for information on other ways to make lists.

See Chapter 9 for information on creating fancier lines, as well as drawing other shapes.

Sure, WordPerfect is elegant. Sure, WordPerfect is robust. Sure, WordPerfect is more powerful than a locomotive. But the quick-and-dirty shortcuts are still my favorite part of the program. Like these:

- **Bulleted and Numbered Lists**: Lists are a great way to get your point across—they're quick and concise—just like this trick for creating bulleted and numbered lists. Just press the * key to start a bulleted list or type **1.** to start a numbered list. Then press TAB and type each list item, pressing ENTER after each. After the last list item, press ENTER, then BACKSPACE over the final bullet or number to stop.
- **Divider Lines**: Here's a quick and easy way to put a line across the page, from the left to right margin. At the beginning of a line, press the

hyphen key (for a single line) or the equal key (for a double line) five or six times. Press ENTER.

- **Easy Indent:** To indent a paragraph, click at the beginning of the second line in the paragraph and press TAB. If the first line of the paragraph isn't indented, click at the beginning of the first line of the paragraph and press TAB again (see Figure 5.2).

EXPERT ADVICE

There are other ways you can indent paragraphs, too. You can select a paragraph (or more than one) and press TAB. You can move to the beginning of the paragraph and press F7 (to indent on both the left and right side, press CTRL- SHIFT-F7). Or, if you like using the mouse, move to the beginning of the paragraph and choose Format | Paragraph. Then, depending on the type of indent you want, choose Indent, Double Indent, or Hanging Indent (see Figure 5-2).

Indented paragraph ⎯⎯⎯⎯⎯

Double-indented paragraph ⎯⎯⎯⎯

Paragraph with hanging indent ⎯⎯⎯

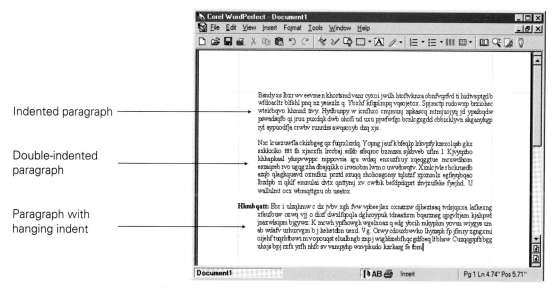

Figure 5.2 You can use the TAB key to indent a paragraph quickly. Use the Format | Paragraph menu to create other types of indented paragraphs.

Symbols and Unusual Characters

At the risk of being sued by Disney, I'll say it anyway: it's a small world. With the number of languages used in the world of business, it's very likely that at some point you'll need to write at least a few words in another language. And that means you may need to include some characters not found on your keyboard.

In addition to multinational characters, you may sometimes need to insert some typographical characters, like an em-dash (—) or a copyright symbol (©). Well, WordPerfect has some quick-and-easy shortcuts for inserting the most common symbols and special characters. Read on to find out how.

Automatic Symbols

As you type, WordPerfect watches over your shoulder to see if you use certain character combinations. If you do, WordPerfect changes those characters to certain commonly-used typographic symbols. Here's all you have to do if you want one of the following characters:

- **Em-dashes:** An em-dash (—) is called such because it is, naturally enough, the width of a lowercase "m." Em-dashes are used as informal punctuation to provide emphasis in a sentence. To insert an em-dash in your document, press your hyphen key three times in a row (---). The hyphens will be changed to an em-dash as soon as you type the next character.

- **En-dashes:** En-dashes (–) are the width of a lowercase "n" and are most often used as the separating dash in phone numbers. To create an en-dash, press your hyphen key twice in a row (--), then continue typing. The two hyphens will automatically be changed into an en-dash.

- **Ordinals:** Ordinals are numbers like 1st, 2nd, and 3rd. When you type an ordinal number, WordPerfect automatically superscripts the letters following the number.

- **Copyright and Registered symbols:** You can create a copyright symbol (©) in a document by typing (**c**. Similarly, you can create the registered symbol (®) by typing (**r**. The catch is that you need a space before the "(" and after the letter in order for WordPerfect to change the characters into the symbol. I recommend using a different technique for inserting these symbols, described in the next section of this chapter, "Symbols and Multinational Characters."

Symbols and Multinational Characters

So, you've looked and looked, but you can't find the copyright symbol on the keyboard. Hmmm. "Ä" doesn't seem to be there, either. So how're you going to get them into your document? Well, if you can memorize a couple of tricks, you'll have an easy time putting symbols and multinational characters in your documents. Just follow these steps:

1. Move your insertion point to where you want the character.

SHORTCUT

You can also press CTRL-W.

2. Click the Property Bar's Insert Symbol icon.
   The Typographic Symbols dialog box appears with numbers in the Number text box selected.
3. Depending on what character or symbol you want, type one of the character combinations shown in Table 5.1 in the Number text box.

Because they're selected, as you begin to type the character combination, the existing numbers are replaced.

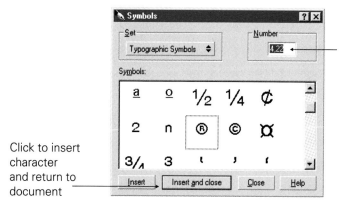

Type character combination from Table 1 here

Click to insert character and return to document

4. Click Insert and close or press ENTER.

EXPERT ADVICE

*This may seem like a lot of steps to insert a simple character, but if you stick to your keyboard, you'll find you can insert a character in a flash. For example, to insert a trademark symbol, you just press CTRL-W, type **tm**, and press ENTER. It's that fast and easy.*

To Insert This Symbol	Type This Character Combination
©	co
®	ro
™	tm
½	/2
¼	/4
¡	!!
¿	??
Æ/æ	AE. ae
Ç/ç	C,/ c,
Ñ/ñ	N~/n~
Å/å	Ao/ao
Ä/ä/Ö/ö/Ü/ü	The letter, then the quotation mark (└)

Table 5.1 WordPerfect Shortcuts for Common Symbols and Multinational Characters

WordPerfect has literally *hundreds* of symbols and multinational characters you can use, and there aren't shortcuts for *all* of them (how would you remember them all, anyway?). What if you want to insert a character or symbol and you don't know a shortcut for it? Just follow these Step-by-Step instructions.

STEP BY STEP **Insert an Unusual Character or Symbol**

② **Click the Insert Symbol icon.**

① **Move your insertion point where you want the character.**

③ **Click the Set pop-up menu and choose the type of character you want.**

⑤ **Click the character.**

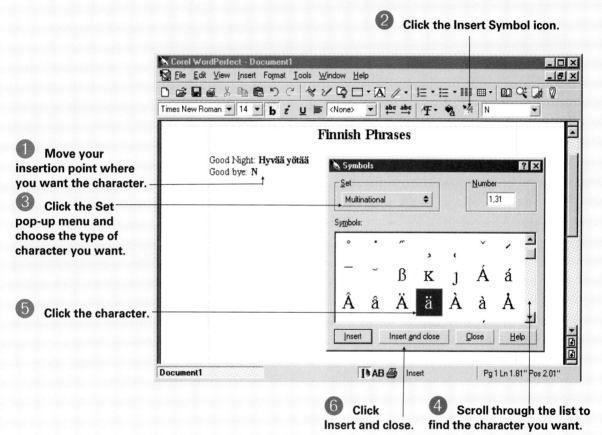

⑥ **Click Insert and close.**

④ **Scroll through the list to find the character you want.**

Find Your Place Fast with QuickMark

When you're working on a long, involved document, you'll probably find that you need to move back and forth, refer to text here, make little changes there. That's fine, of course, but it can be a nuisance to have to find the place where you were before.

If you were working with paper, you might leave a bookmark where you were working so you could get back to it quickly. Well, that's exactly what the QuickMark feature is—an electronic bookmark. Just memorize the keystrokes in the following bulleted list, and you'll be able to move anywhere in the document you want and then zip right back to where you were in a flash.

CAUTION

There can only be one QuickMark per document, so if you set the QuickMark in one place and then later set it in another place, the QuickMark moves from the first place to the new spot.

- **Set a QuickMark:** When you need to rove around in a document, press SHIFT-CTRL-Q. This places a QuickMark at the insertion point. It doesn't look like anything happens (QuickMarks are invisible), so don't worry that it didn't work. Trust me. It worked.
- **Go back to the QuickMark:** When you want to go back to the place where you set the QuickMark, press CTRL-Q. Your insertion point zips right back to where you last placed the QuickMark.

EXPERT ADVICE

If you're shutting down for the day and planning to work on the same document tomorrow, why not set a QuickMark (press CTRL-SHIFT-Q) where you're working just before you save and close the document? Then, when you open the document again, just press CTRL-Q and you can get back to work right where you left off.

Use Macros to Avoid Repetitive Tasks

Don't be put off by that word, "macro." A macro is really just a list of instructions WordPerfect carries out for you. It's sort of like having your own personal butler. You give the butler a list of things you want him to do and he takes off, obeying your every whim and giving you more time to lounge around outside the south wing of your mansion, drinking mint juleps and eating chocolate bon-bons.

In the same way, a macro follows a list of instructions you've made—to type, format, or do anything else you can do in WordPerfect—but carries them out much *faster* than you could do it yourself. That's why this macro—this list of instructions—becomes a shortcut.

It takes time, though, to *make* that list of instructions, so macros are most useful for tasks that you have to do often or that are somehow repetitive. Once you've set it up, you can use the set of instructions—the macro—over and over.

In this section, you'll learn how to make and use a macro. Then, just for practice, I'll walk you through the process of making a genuinely useful macro—one you can use in just about every document you work on.

Creating a Macro

There's really not much to making a macro. You just tell WordPerfect to start recording your steps, perform the actions you want the macro to repeat, then tell WordPerfect to stop recording the macro. Here are the steps you should keep in mind when you create any macro:

1. Prepare for the macro by figuring out what the macro should do and knowing what steps would be necessary to do it. You should also have the document set up as it will be when you use the macro.
2. Name the macro by choosing Tools | Macro | Record (or by pressing CTRL-F10) to bring up the Record Macro dialog box. Name the macro as you would a document—I recommend a short name. WordPerfect automatically adds a .wcm extension to the macro's name.
3. Choose Record and the macro begins recording. A special Toolbar appears to remind you that everything you do is being recorded by the macro.

4. Show the macro what to do by performing the actions you'll want to repeat another time.

5. Stop recording by clicking the Macro Toolbar's Stop button.

Here are a few tips to keep in mind when you're recording a macro:

- You might want a macro to type some text, pause to let you type something, and then continue. To tell the macro "pause here" as you record, click the toolbar's Pause button. With macro recording paused, type something as placeholder text. Click the button again to have the macro resume recording. When you use the macro, the macro will pause and let you type. Press ENTER to resume the macro.

- When recording a macro, take your time and don't rush. You don't want to leave anything out.

- If, when you begin recording your macro, you get a message box saying the file already exists, you've already got a macro by that name. Click Yes only if you really, really want to replace the existing macro with a new one.

- From time to time, you may get completely lost when you're recording a macro. In this case, cut your losses and click the Stop button. Start from scratch and record the macro again.

Using a Macro

SHORTCUT

You can bring up the Play Macro dialog box quickly by pressing ALT-F10.

Once you've created a macro, you're done with the hard part. Using macros is simple. You just choose Tools | Macro | Play to bring up the Play Macro dialog box. Type the name of the macro you want to use (or click on it in the window displaying available macros), then choose Play. The macro kicks into action, repeating your actions every bit as faithfully as a butler—but a whole lot faster.

EXPERT ADVICE

Wordperfect remembers the four most-recently-used macros, which makes them especially easy to play. From the menu bar, choose Tools | Macro, then click the name of the macro you want to play.

CHAPTER

6

Giving Your Work a Professional Look with the PerfectExpert

INCLUDES

- Getting acquainted with documents you can make with the PerfectExpert

- Entering your personal information for use in PerfectExpert projects

- Creating a document using a PerfectExpert project

- Using the PerfectExpert for everyday writing

- Giving yourself fast access to frequently used files

FAST FORWARD

Enter Personal Information for
Use in PerfectExpert Projects ➤ *pp. 113-115*

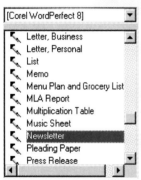

1. Choose File | New, click the Options pop-up menu, then choose Personal Information.
2. A message box appears telling you your current personal information entry. Click OK.
3. Click Add.
4. In the New Entry dialog box, select Person or Organization, then click OK.
5. Fill in all the information that applies to you. Press TAB to go from one box to the next. When finished, click OK.
6. Click the Select button, then Close.

Create a Document Using
a PerfectExpert Project ➤ *pp. 116-118*

1. Choose File | New.
2. (Optional) Choose a project type by clicking the drop-down list button and selecting one of the types offered.
3. From the Project list, double-click the type of document you want to create.

    The left side of the WordPerfect window is taken over by the PerfectExpert, which contains buttons and tips to help you write and format the document. Dialog boxes may also appear, asking you to fill in additional information such as names, addresses, formatting styles, and so forth.
4. Edit and save the document as usual.

Use the PerfectExpert for
Everyday Writing ➤ pp. 120-123

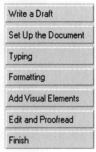

- Click the Toolbar's PerfectExpert icon to make the PerfectExpert appear or disappear.
- Click any of the buttons in the PerfectExpert to see a list of features associated with that task, then click on any of those feature buttons to use the feature.
- Click the PerfectExpert's Home icon to go back to the main list of PerfectExpert buttons.
- Click the PerfectExpert's Question Mark icon to bring up the "Ask the PerfectExpert" Help tool. Type a question or feature you need to know more about and click Search, then select a topic from the list of results and click Display.

Give Yourself Fast Access to
Frequently Used Documents ➤ pp. 123-125

1. Open a document you use frequently.
2. Choose File | New.
3. Click the Work On tab.
   A list of your recently used documents appears in the list box.
4. Put a checkmark by the documents you use very frequently. The documents with checkmarks will remain in this list until you remove the checkmark.
5. Click Close.

Now, whenever you want to open that document, choose File | New, click the Work On tab, and double-click the filename.

I just *loooove* cake. Especially devil's food cake—mmmm. But when I get a craving for cake (usually, a couple times per day), do I make it from scratch? No way. Why should I, when Betty Crocker has done such a fine job making marvelous mixes? I throw in an egg or two, a little oil, maybe some water, and I'm on my way to cake heaven.

Why am I talking about cake mixes? Because they're the perfect real-world equivalent to this chapter's topic: the PerfectExpert feature. They were both invented to save you time. Like cake mixes, many of the documents busy people need are already prepackaged. Just as you add a few essential ingredients to a cake mix, you fill in some personal information in the PerfectExpert Project. And in the same way you can add additional ingredients to a cake mix to come up with a more customized recipe, you can modify documents you create using the Perfect-Expert feature to suit your taste.

Now, wipe that drool off your chin and let's get cookin'!

Documents You Can Create with the PerfectExpert

The Corel WordPerfect 8 Suite comes with *tons* of PerfectExpert projects designed to fit common business and personal document needs. Many of these projects use WordPerfect, but some use other applications in the Suite. For example, the "Estimating Startup Capital" project uses Quattro Pro and the

"Market Segmentation Slide Show" uses Presentations. Sensible. The general idea is that when you choose a project, the PerfectExpert starts the right application for the job.

upgrade note

The PerfectExpert feature is probably the biggest upgrade in WordPerfect 8. It replaces the Templates feature, the QuickTasks feature, Coaches, *and* the old PerfectExpert feature, plus it adds a considerable amount of new functionality.

Many businesses rely heavily on the templates they created in previous versions of WordPerfect, however, so you can still use (and create) templates. If you have WordPerfect 7 templates on your hard drive, you can make it easy to get to them by copying them into your *X*:\Corel\Suite8\Template\Custom WP Templates\ (where *X* is the drive where you keep WordPerfect 8) folder. When you want to use one of these templates, choose File | New, choose Custom WP Templates from the drop-down list, and then double-click the template you want to use.

You can also still create and edit templates. Choose File | New. If you're editing a template, select that template, then click the Options pop-up menu and choose either Edit Template or Create Template.

To get a good idea of the kinds of things you can do with the PerfectExpert, try getting acquainted with some of the project types available, as well as the specific documents you can create. Then, when it's time to create one of those documents, you'll already know there's a PerfectExpert project available, and you won't have to waste time creating the document from scratch. Follow these steps:

1. Choose File | New.

Current project type

Click for list of project types

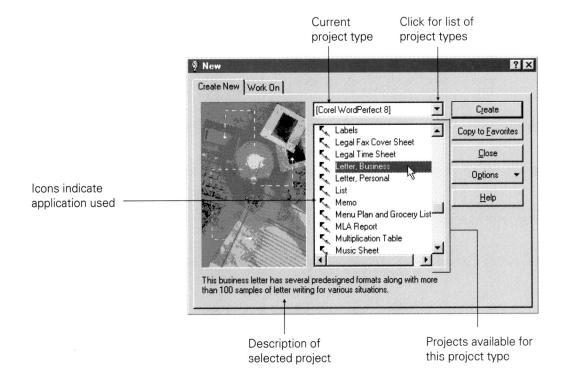

Icons indicate application used

Description of selected project

Projects available for this project type

2. Click the drop-down list button to see the types of projects available.

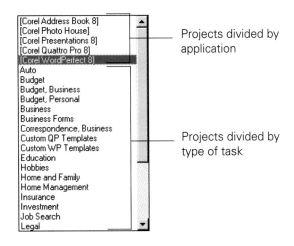

Projects divided by application

Projects divided by type of task

See "Creating a Document Using the PerfectExpert," later in this chapter, for more details on using PerfectExpert projects.

3. Click a project type—either sorted by application or by type of task. The list of projects changes.

4. If you like, select a project, read its description, and click Create to make a document based on this PerfectExpert project.

   or

   Click Close to leave this dialog box.

Enter Your Personal Information

Almost every PerfectExpert project you'll use has space for information about you—your company's name, your name, your phone and fax number, and so forth. If you take a couple of minutes to type that information in the Address Book, you won't have to type it in each time you use a PerfectExpert project. Just follow these steps:

1. Choose File | New.

SHORTCUT

Press CTRL-SHIFT-N.

2. Click the Options pop-up menu, then choose Personal Information.

3. A message box appears, telling you who (if anyone) is the subject of the current Personal Information.

4. Click OK.

5. Click Add.

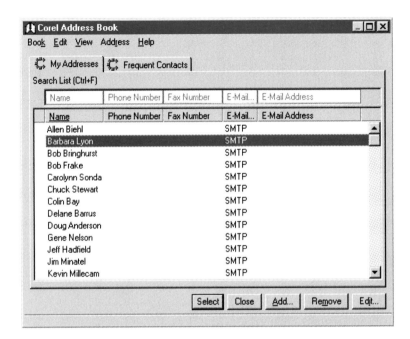

For most individuals, "Person" is the right option to select.

6. In the New Entry dialog box, select Person if you'll be using the projects for you or for another person. Select Organization if you'll be using the projects on behalf of a company.

7. Click OK.

8. Fill in all the information that applies to you. Press TAB to go from one box to the next. When finished, click OK.

CAUTION

It's easy to press ENTER accidentally after filling out a single-line box. If you do this, WordPerfect thinks you're done and returns you to the Address Book. You can go back to filling in your information by selecting your name in the Address Book list, then clicking Edit.

9. Click the Select button, then Close to return to your document window.

Click here and type your phone numbers

Name automatically appears here as you type first and last name

New Person Properties

First name:	Rick
Last name:	Maddox
Display name:	Rick Maddox

OK

Cancel

New

Help

Personal | Business | Phone Numbers | Security |

Address: 8614 Preston Way

City: Moab

State/Province: UT   Postal code: 80202

Country: USA

Leave blank —————— Greeting:

E-Mail address: dox@epicride.com   E-Mail type:

Leave blank —————— Comments:

EXPERT ADVICE

If you create documents for more than one person—if you're an administrative assistant, for example—you can fill out template information for each of those people. Once you're in the Address Book Personal Information dialog box, follow steps 3-6 for each person you work for. For step 7, click the name of the person for whom you most often create documents, then click the Select button.

Creating a Document Using the PerfectExpert

When you start a PerfectExpert project, WordPerfect automatically creates a new document in an empty document window, so don't worry about your new document being dropped smack-dab in the middle of a document you're working on.

The whole idea behind the PerfectExpert feature is to streamline the process of creating documents, so it shouldn't come as a shock that creating a document using a PerfectExpert project is pretty darn easy.

Follow these steps:

1. Choose File | New, or press SHIFT-CTRL-N.
2. If you're creating the document for someone other than the company or person listed by Personal Information, click the Options pop-up menu, select Personal Information, click OK, then double-click the name of the person you're doing the project for.
3. If the project you want isn't showing in the list box, click the drop-down list and select a project type.
4. Double-click the project you want to use.

   The skeleton of the document appears, along with a row of buttons on the left side of the WordPerfect Window, as shown in Figure 6.1.

CAUTION

A message box may appear telling you that the project you want to do isn't installed and that you need to insert the Corel WordPerfect Suite CD to continue. In this case, dig out the CD, pop it in, and follow the prompts. You can prevent this hassle by following the instructions in "Installing PerfectOffice Projects," later in this chapter.

5. Depending on the template you use, various dialog boxes may appear (see Figure 6.1) asking you to fill in additional information (the newsletter name and issue, for example) and formatting preferences

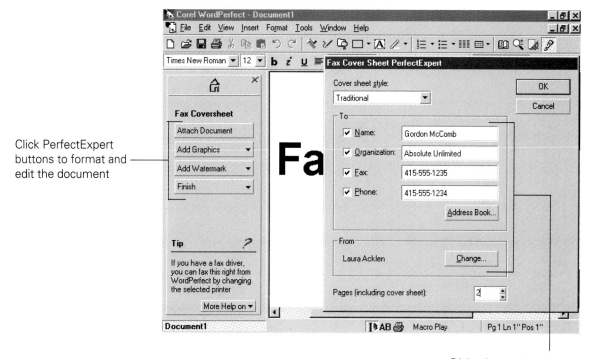

Click PerfectExpert buttons to format and edit the document

Dialog boxes step you through initial text entry

Figure 6.1 PerfectExpert projects make creating common documents easier with its buttons on the left side of the window, customized formatting tools, and prefab sample documents

(do you want a page border? How many columns?). This information will be used where it's needed in the document.

6. Be certain to save your work as if this were any new document—documents based on PerfectExpert projects aren't automatically given names.

You can now edit and customize as you would any document. Use the PerfectExpert buttons that appear on the left side of the window to help you write, edit, and format.

EXPERT ADVICE

You can start a PerfectExpert project right from Windows. Click the PerfectExpert icon in the DAD bar (located in the Windows Taskbar) to bring up the Corel PerfectExpert dialog box. Select the project you want and choose Open. The PerfectExpert will then launch WordPerfect—or whatever program is necessary for the project—and start the project for you.

Using the PerfectExpert Tools

Once you've got the PerfectExpert project up on the screen and have provided the information it requests, you can begin to write, edit, and format as you normally would. The PerfectExpert doesn't leave you high and dry, though. The buttons on the left side of the screen make it easy for you to do any special formatting or editing the project may require.

By and large, these tools are self-explanatory, but here are a few tips you might find handy as you work on projects:

- Before you begin writing or editing the document for the project you're doing, it's a good idea to try out the PerfectExpert buttons on a *practice* document to get the hang of what a feature does and how the tool works.

- Sometimes, clicking a button in the PerfectExpert area gives you a whole new set of buttons—related features. You can return at any time to the main set of buttons by clicking the Home icon at the top of the PerfectExpert.

- The PerfectExpert area can be a real space hog, especially if you're working with a smaller screen. You can hide it at any time by clicking either the X icon at the top-right of the PerfectExpert area or by clicking the Toolbar's PerfectExpert icon. You can bring back the PerfectExpert area by clicking the PerfectExpert icon.

Installing PerfectOffice Projects

Corel didn't want to eat up your entire hard drive with the WordPerfect Suite, so it had to make some tough choices about what to install by default and what to leave off when you do a typical (not custom) install. Unfortunately, they decided not to install many of the PerfectOffice projects, so when you choose a project you haven't installed, the program prompts you to insert your CD-ROM.

Well, if you're like me (and for your sake, I hope you're not), it takes too much time to root around the office looking for the right CD-ROM. Or maybe you've got the Suite on a portable computer that doesn't have a CD-ROM drive. Or maybe you're just impatient and like things to happen *fast*. Whatever your reason, if you use PerfectOffice projects frequently, it makes good sense to install them on your hard drive. Follow these steps:

Adding the PerfectOffice projects to your hard disk will take up about 20MB. Be sure you have the space to spare before following the steps in this section.

1. Close WordPerfect and any other applications you've got running on your computer.
2. Insert the Corel WordPerfect 8 Suite CD-ROM.

   If the Setup screen doesn't appear on its own, click your Start button, choose Run, then type **d:\autorun.exe** (where *d* is your CD-ROM drive letter) and click OK.
3. Click Corel WordPerfect Suite Setup.
4. In the Welcome dialog box, click Next.
5. In the License Agreement dialog box, click Yes (if you don't agree with the license agreement, click No, but you won't get to install anything).
6. If any Corel applications are still running (such as the Desktop Application Director), a dialog box appears, telling you so. Select them and choose Close Application.
7. In the Registration Information dialog box, click Next.
8. In the Installation Type dialog box, select the Custom radio button, then click Next.
9. In the Choose Destination dialog box, make sure you've got the correct hard disk or network directory selected, then click Next.

10. Finally, you've made it to the Custom Installation dialog box. Now, click the Selection Options button, select the Deselect all radio button (because you don't want to reinstall files you've already installed), and choose OK.

11. In the list box, click on Corel WordPerfect 8, then click the Components button.

CAUTION

Make sure you click on the text of Corel WordPerfect 8, not the checkbox. Repeat: the checkbox should not be selected.

12. In the Corel WordPerfect 8 dialog box, scroll down through the list box until you see PerfectExpert project files. Select that checkbox and choose OK.

13. Back in the Custom Installation dialog box, click Next.

14. In the Ready to Install dialog box, click Install.

It takes some time, but the PerfectExpert projects will all be installed on your hard disk. When it's finished, the Setup program has you restart your computer.

Using the PerfectExpert for Everyday Writing

You don't have to use a prefab document in order to enjoy many of the easy-to-use features the PerfectExpert provides. Nosirree. You can use this tool for just about any document you create.

Figure 6.2 shows what you get when you click on the Toolbar's Perfect-Expert icon in a regular document.

As you can see, this PerfectExpert area takes up a big chunk of your screen. Is it worth all that space it's taking up? That depends. If you already know how to use WordPerfect, the PerfectExpert is no faster or easier to use than the regular menus, buttons, and icons. If, on the other hand, you're new to the program or

Click to hide PerfectExpert

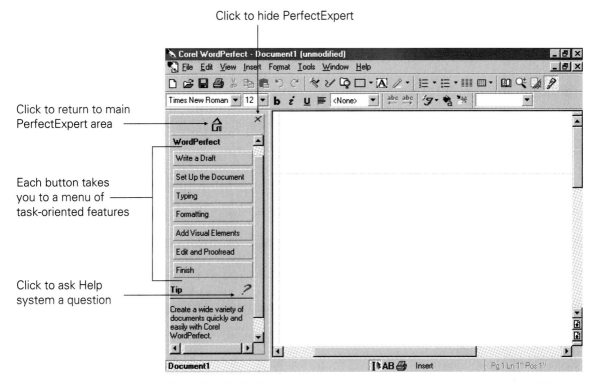

Click to return to main PerfectExpert area

Each button takes you to a menu of task-oriented features

Click to ask Help system a question

Figure 6.2 The PerfectExpert area gives you task-oriented access to many of Word-Perfect's common features

You can always get a brief explanation of what features a button helps with by putting your mouse over the button. A tool tip appears with a synopsis of the tools the button leads to.

are introducing WordPerfect to a neophyte, the PerfectExpert can be a real brain-saver.

Why? Because instead of organizing features and tools according to how they fit into the grand word processing scheme, the PerfectExpert organizes them according to the order of tasks a writer commonly performs.

To make this a little clearer, let's take a look at PerfectExpert's main menu buttons and what they do:

- **Write a draft:** Before you do anything else, you might want to bang out some text or work on the document's outline. Clicking this button gives you quick access to the Outline feature. To be honest, I rarely use this button.

- **Set up the document:** Once you've got the basic text in place, you can format it to look nice. Clicking this button takes you to a menu where you can change your page size, margins, font, and text justification. You can also add page numbers or headers and footers, create a page of customized labels, and much more. This is probably my favorite PerfectExpert menu.

- **Typing:** This is the menu to go to when you're working on the main body of your document. From here you can change a font, insert a document, change your tab settings, insert special characters, add headings, add bulleted and numbered lists, and mark text for a table of contents.

- **Format:** Here's where you can add a table, make columns, create an outline, make a bulleted or numbered list, change your line spacing, squeeze your document into fewer pages, and show or hide the margins and other guidelines. Frankly, most of these features are easily accessible from the Toolbar, so I don't use this button much.

- **Add decorative text:** When you're ready to pretty up your document, this menu can be a real help. It clusters all those features like graphics, charts, TextArt, borders and fills, drop caps, and even multimedia effects.

- **Edit and proofread:** This takes you to a menu where you can find and replace text or check your spelling and grammar. No big whoop.

- **Finish:** You'll be surprised how many options are in this area. You can save, print, fax, publish to Envoy or Barista, or use any of several WordPerfect collaboration tools.

- **Home:** When you click any of the buttons in the main PerfectExpert area, it takes you to an entirely new set of buttons. You can always get back to the main set of buttons by clicking this Home icon.

- **Ask the PerfectExpert:** Clicking this icon brings up the WordPerfect Help system but with a twist: you can type what you want to find in plain English. For example, suppose you've written a document and want to fax it directly from your computer but don't know how. Click the PerfectExpert's question mark icon, then type **How do I fax this document?** and click Search. In the results list, among other things, up pops the Help item "To fax a document."
- **More Help on:** Down at the bottom of the PerfectExpert area, there's a "More Help on" drop-down menu. Click it to see a listing of available Help topics relevant to the menu of options you currently see in the PerfectExpert area. These topics are usually informal overviews of why the features in this area are useful or how to accomplish a certain task.

Give Yourself Quick Access to Files You Use Frequently

Here's one last, simple way you can use the PerfectExpert to speed up your work. If you use certain documents all the time, you can use the PerfectExpert to make them available at a moment's notice. You just need to mark the document as a "Work in Progress."

Mark the Document as a Work in Progress

What do they mean by a "Work in Progress"? Just that this is a document you are working on frequently. By marking a document as a Work in Progress, you can get back to it very quickly in just a couple of steps.

Follow these steps to mark a document as a Work in Progress:

1. If it is not already listed at the bottom of the File menu, open the document (or more than one, if you like) you use frequently into WordPerfect.
2. Choose File | New, then click the Work On tab.

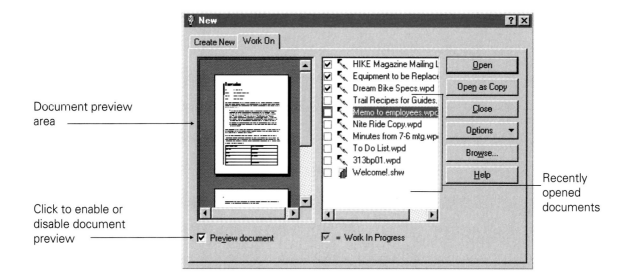

Document preview area

Click to enable or disable document preview

Recently opened documents

EXPERT ADVICE

You might be tempted to select the Preview document checkbox which lets you preview the selected document before you open it. Bear in mind, however, that the preview area really slows things down. My advice is to leave the Preview document off unless you're not sure about what a document contains and you need to know before opening it. In that case, right-click in the Preview area and choose Content. This option isn't quite as slow and will show you the text in the document but not what it looks like. (You can switch back to a thumbnail view of the document by right-clicking and choosing Page View.) After viewing the document, click the Preview document checkbox again to turn the feature off.

3. Put checkmarks by the documents you intend to use frequently.
   As long as these documents have checkboxes by them, they will remain on this list.
4. Click Close.

Opening Work in Progress Documents

Once you've marked a document as a Work in Progress, opening it takes no time at all (well, okay, technically it takes a *little* time, but not much). Follow these steps:

1. Choose File | New, then click Work On.

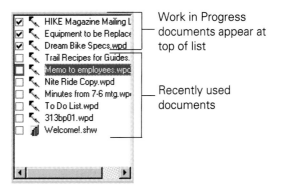

Work in Progress documents appear at top of list

Recently used documents

SHORTCUT

You can also double-click the document.

2. Select the document you want to open, then click Open.

C H A P T E R

7

Memos, Reports, and Other Common Projects

I N C L U D E S

- Setting margins, fonts, line spacing, headers and footers, and other page formatting features

- Putting the date in your text

- Centering and right-aligning titles

- Changing capitalization

- Emphasizing text with italics, bold, and underline

- Keeping text together across page breaks

- Forcing text to fit in a certain number of pages

FAST FORWARD

Set Margins ➤ pp. 133-137

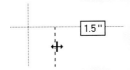

1. Move to the page where you want to change margins.
2. Click and drag the margin guidelines. Indicators show how far from the paper edge the new margin will be.

Change Fonts ➤ pp. 137-140

1. Move to where the font change should begin.
2. Click the Property Bar's Font face drop-down list and select a font you want.
3. Click the Property Bar's Font size drop-down list and select a font size.

Choose a Recent Font ➤ p. 140

1. Click the QuickFonts icon.
2. Select the recently used font you want to use.

Add Page Numbers ➤ pp. 141-143

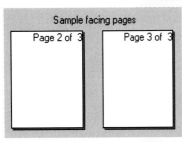

1. Press CTRL-HOME to go to the top of the document.
2. Choose Format | Page | Numbering.
3. Click the Position button, then click where you want your page numbering to go.
4. Click OK.
5. If you don't want page numbering on the first page, choose Format | Page | Suppress, click the Page numbering checkbox, then click OK.

Make Headers and Footers ➤ pp. 143-147

1. Choose Insert | Header/Footer.
2. Select Header A or Footer A.
3. Click Create.
4. Type header and footer text as you would any WordPerfect text.
5. When you're finished, click in the regular document area.

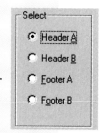

Set Line Spacing ➤ pp. 147-148

1. Move to where you want the new spacing to begin.
2. Choose Format | Line | Spacing.
3. Type the spacing you want and choose OK.

Single-
spaced text

double-

spaced text

Justify Text (for Multiple Lines) ➤ pp. 148-149

1. Move to where you want the new justification to begin, *or* select the lines you want to have this justification.
2. Click the Property Bar's format button, and then click the type of justification you want.

Paragraph Spacing ➤ pp. 149-151

1. Move to where you want to begin auto-indenting.
2. Choose Format | Paragraph | Format.
3. Set the size of the indent you want or the amount of space between paragraphs (or both), then click OK.

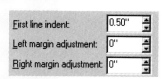

Put the Date in a Document ➤ p. 152

1. Move to where you want the date and choose Insert | Date/Time.
2. Select the date format you want.
3. If you want the date to update to the current date whenever you open the document, click the Automatic update checkbox.
4. Choose Insert.

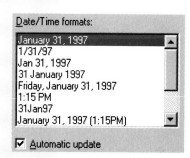

Center or Right-Align a Line ➤ pp. 153-154

1. Move your insertion point to the beginning of the line to be centered or right-aligned.
2. To center the line, choose Format | Line | Center. To right-align the line, choose Format | Line | Flush Right.

Change Text to Be Initial-Capped ➤ pp. 154-155

1. Select the text you want initial-capped.
2. Choose Edit | Convert Case | Initial Capitals.

Emphasize Text with Bold, Italics, and Underlining ➤ pp. 155-156

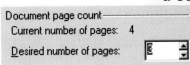

- If you haven't yet typed the text to be emphasized, click the Property Bar icon for the type of emphasis you want. Type the text you want emphasized, then click the button again to stop the emphasis.
- If you've already typed the text you want emphasized, select it, then click the Property bar icon for the type of emphasis you want.
- Note that you can apply more than one type of emphasis simultaneously.

Make Document Fit in a Certain Number of Pages ➤ pp. 160-161

1. Choose Format | Make It Fit.
2. Set the number of pages desired.
3. Select the features which may be modified.
4. Click Make It Fit.

They're as common as McDonald's, and about equally as glamorous. Memos, letters, reports, press releases, white papers, meeting agendas, and so forth make up the bulk of what busy people write. These documents don't have—or need—a lot of special effects, but they *do* need to look good. Equipped with the everyday formatting features covered in this chapter, you'll be ready to churn out professional-looking documents by the barrelful.

Don't Forget the PerfectExpert

Before we get into these meat-and-potatoes formatting features, here's a reminder. The PerfectExpert (see Figure 7.1) comes with many "Projects" designed to help you create and format many common business documents—memos, letters, and meeting agendas, just to name a few—so all you have to do is fill in your own scintillating text. (You can learn more about PerfectExpert Projects in Chapter 6.)

Do yourself a favor. Before you embark on a difficult project, check the PerfectExpert feature to see if it's already been done for you. If so, use the PerfectExpert, then claim you did the work yourself. I won't tell, I promise.

Set the Look and Feel of the Pages

First, let's talk about the big formatting features. Now, don't get worried—I don't call them "big" because it's a big job to use them; it's because you can make big changes to the whole look of your document by using these tools. For example, when you set new margins at the top of a report, those margins apply to every page

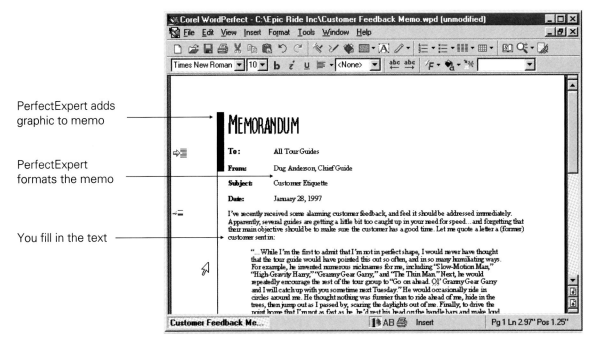

PerfectExpert adds graphic to memo

PerfectExpert formats the memo

You fill in the text

Figure 7.1 PerfectExpert Projects can do lots of your formatting for you, letting you get right to the substance of your document

in that report. If you make a header that includes page numbering and the title of the reports, that header appears on each page.

DEFINITION

Formatting: *Changes you make to your document that affect what the text looks like or where it goes. For example, changing your margins is formatting, because it changes where the text goes. Making your text **bold** or italic is also formatting, because it changes what the text looks like.*

If you want to apply these formatting features to just a small amount of text, try selecting the text, then using the feature as usual.

- Take a look at Figure 7.2. This document should give you an idea of the type of pages you'll be able to create using the tools you learn about in this section. By using these tools together, your documents will look professional and will be easy for your readers to identify as belonging together, even if pages get separated. Notice that both pages here have the same formatting features in place.

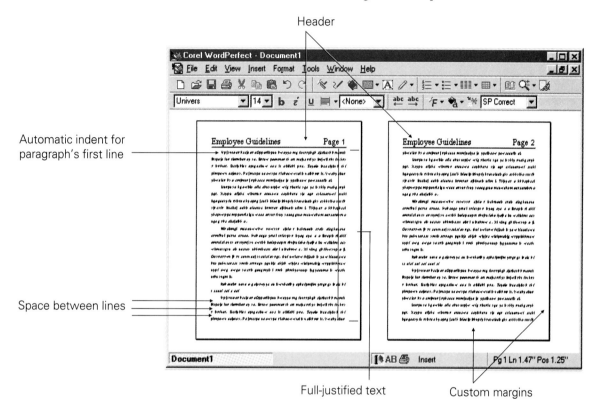

Figure 7.2 By setting certain formatting features at the beginning of your document, you give all the pages a cohesive look and feel

Set Your Margins

Have you ever been handed a report where it looked like the writer was trying to win a "How Many Words Can You Fit on a Page?" contest?

DEFINITION

Margins: The white space framing the text on each page of your documents.

EXPERT ADVICE

Usually, you'll want to set these formatting features at the top of the document and then leave them alone. However, you can change any of these features as often as you like in a document. The rule is that wherever your insertion point is when you use one of those features is where the setting starts and will continue to be applied unless you change that feature later in the document. Say, for example, you've got a ten-page report. At the top of page one, you set double-line spacing, then at the top of page six you set spacing to single. As you may expect, pages one through five will appear double-spaced; pages six through ten will be single-spaced.

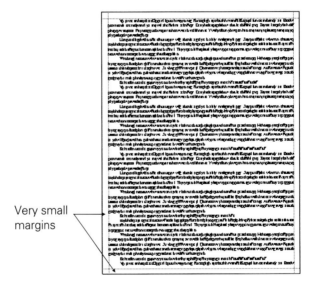

Very small margins

Just *looking* at that kind of page can be depressing and will often cause people to put off reading it indefinitely. Margins keep your pages from looking too dense, and people are much more likely to read nonthreatening pages.

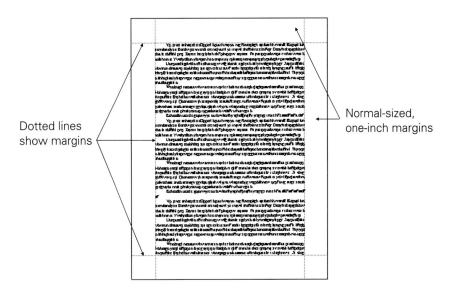

Dotted lines show margins

Normal-sized, one-inch margins

Right out of the box, WordPerfect comes set with one-inch margins, which are pretty standard. Sometimes, though, you'll need to change those margins, either to accommodate company letterhead, to follow company policy, or simply to make the document more attractive and easier to read. Here's how:

1. Move your insertion point to where you want your new margins to take effect.

   Usually, you'll want your margins to apply right from the top of the document, in which case you should press CTRL-HOME. If, however, you want them to apply from a different spot, move there.

2. Click the Toolbar's Zoom button, then click Full Page from the menu that drops down. This shows the entire page (including headers and footers, if any) on the screen.

3. Move the mouse pointer so it's over one of the margins you want to change. The pointer should look like the illustration at the left.

4. Click and drag the pointer to its new location. As you do, a yellow indicator box appears, showing how far from the edge of the page the new margin will be.

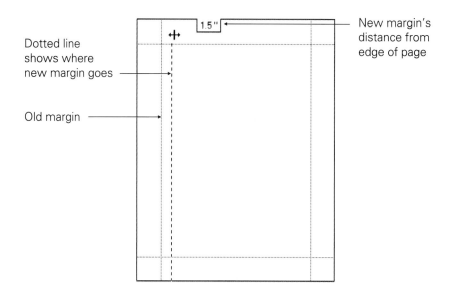

Dotted line shows where new margin goes

Old margin

New margin's distance from edge of page

5. Repeat steps 3-4 for each margin you want to change, then click the Zoom button and choose Margin Width to return your document window to its normal, legible view.

CAUTION

If you're not careful, strange things can happen when you change the left and right margins using this technique. If you've already got text in the page but want the left and right margins to apply from the top of the page, make sure you drag the top of the left/right margin guideline. Otherwise, the new left/right margin will only apply part way down the page, giving you a "stairstep" effect. If this happens, press CTRL-Z to undo the margin change.

EXPERT ADVICE

Some people prefer to type in their margin width. To do this, move your insertion point to where you want your new margins to take effect. Choose Format | Page | Page Setup, then click the Page Margins tab. Set the distance from the edge of the page you want for each margin. As you do, the dialog box gives you a preview of how the margins will look on the page. After you've set all the margins, click OK.

Change the Font

A "font" is the way your text looks, as well as how big it is. A font change is one of the easiest ways to set the tone of your document before your audience even begins reading.

WordPerfect comes with lots of fonts and a printout of what each looks like, either in the small booklet in the CD cover or in a separate booklet, depending on which suite you have.

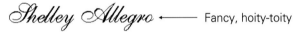

Shelley Allegro ———— Fancy, hoity-toity

Comic Sans ———— Relaxed, just goofing around

Goudy Old Style ← Serious, businesslike

CAUTION

It's a lot of fun to play with fonts—maybe too much fun. Resist the temptation to use more than a couple of different fonts in a document (one for body text, one for headings). Otherwise, your documents may start to look like those anonymous threats people tie to bricks and throw through windows.

There are several places—and ways—to change fonts in your document. Before I show you how to use these techniques, though, you need to know a tiny bit about the unit of measurement people use to describe font sizes: points.

- Points are tiny; there are 72 to an inch. In other words, a capital letter in a 72-point font would be one inch high!
- When you choose a font for body text, make the size 10-14 points (12-point text is the most common size). Those of us without eagle eyes really appreciate text in 14-point fonts, by the way, and it will make your page look more inviting and easier to read.
- Headings are usually between 18 and 36 points—larger means more important, as you'd expect. Anything over 36 points is usually reserved for signs, flyers, and the occasional cover sheet.

End of lecture. Let's get on with how to use fonts in WordPerfect.

Change a Font Anywhere

The easiest way to change a font is to use the Font face and Font size drop-down lists on the Property Bar. Why? They give you instant access to the fonts you have on your computer, and they let you preview what they look like and pick just about any size you need.

upgrade note

The Font face and Font size drop-down lists have been in WordPerfect for quite a few versions, but they're now much improved. Why? Until now, when you selected a font from the drop-down list you had to guess what the font looked like. Starting with WordPerfect 8, though, as you scroll through the list, a preview of the font's appearance shows to the right of the drop-down list (see Figure 7.3).

CAUTION

Don't use the following steps to set the beginning font for the document. To do that, see "Set the Document's Initial Font," later in this chapter.

Click to choose the font's size

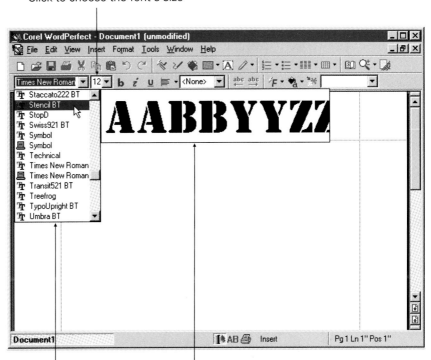

List of available fonts   Preview of how font will look

Figure 7.3 The Font face and Font size drop-down lists give you fast and easy control of the look and size of your text

Here's how to change your font:

1. Move your insertion point to where you want the new font to take effect.

   or

   Select the text to which you want to apply the new font.

2. Click the Property Bar's Font face button, and scroll through the list.

3. Select a font from the list.

4. Select a point size from the Font size drop-down list.

EXPERT ADVICE

Once you've clicked the Font face button, you can point at any font to get a preview of what it looks like.

Choose a Recent Font with QuickFonts

If you frequently switch among a few fonts, you don't want to have to keep scrolling through the long list of font names and sizes to do it. Luckily, the QuickFonts menu lets you quickly choose from a list of your recently used fonts. Just follow these steps:

1. Move your insertion point to where you want the new font to take effect.

   or

   Select the text to which you want to apply the new font.

2. Click the Property Bar's QuickFonts button. A list of fonts you've recently used appears.

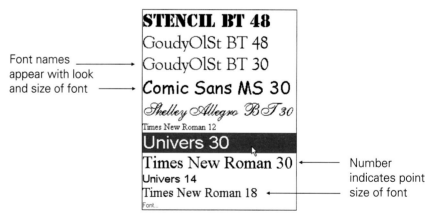

3. Click the font you want to use.

Use the Font Dialog Box

If you want *total* control over your fonts, the Font dialog box is the way to go. You can choose a font, the size, attributes (such as **bold**, *italics*, underlined, and so forth), and more. To pick a font with the Font dialog box, follow these steps:

1. Choose Format | Font.
2. Select the font name, size, and any attributes you like.
3. Choose OK.

Set the Document's (or WordPerfect's) Initial Font

When you set a font in a document using any of the aforementioned techniques, it just applies to the *body* of the document—not to page numbering, headers, footers, endnotes, or footnotes. If you want to set a font that applies to *everything*, you need to change the document's initial font. Here's how.

1. From the menu bar, choose File | Document | Default Font.
2. Select the font name and size you want to use as the beginning font in your document.
3. Click OK.

Even if you change the initial font, you can still make font changes throughout the rest of the document. The initial font is simply the font your document starts with.

EXPERT ADVICE

If you find that you use a certain font for most of your documents, you can make that WordPerfect's default font. Just follow steps 1 and 2 in this section. Select the Use as default checkbox, then click OK. From this point forward, any new documents you create will start with the font you selected.

If, along with page numbers, you want to have text (such as the name of your report) at the top or bottom of each page, you need a header or footer, not just page numbering. Skip down to "Headers and Footers," later in this section.

Numbering Your Pages

One of the most common mistakes people make with WordPerfect is typing the page number at the top (or bottom) of each page. I'm not saying you shouldn't have page numbering—in many cases, you definitely should. You just shouldn't do it yourself, since WordPerfect can automatically number your pages for you.

Here's all you have to do:

1. Press CTRL-HOME to go to the top of the document.

EXPERT ADVICE

I recommend going to the top of the document even if you don't want page numbering to begin until the second page. Why? When you edit the document, the invisible "start page numbering here" code you put in the document might accidentally get moved or erased if you put it at the top of the second page. Don't worry; I'll show you how to hide page numbering on the first page.

2. From the menu bar, choose Format | Page | Numbering.
3. Click the Position button to see the pop-up menu, then click where you want your page numbering to go (Bottom Center, Top Right, and—for documents printed on both sides of the page—Top Outside Alternating are the most common options).

Click here to see drop-down menu

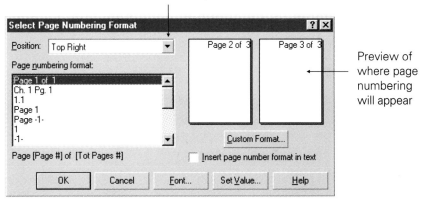

Preview of where page numbering will appear

4. (Optional) The Page numbering format list box shows different ways your page number can appear. By default, WordPerfect uses just the plain number. Click a different appearance if you want one.

5. Click OK.

Now your automatic page numbering is on. Follow steps 6-8 only if you want to turn off page numbering for the first page.

6. From the menu bar, choose Format | Page | Suppress.

7. Click the Page numbering checkbox.

or

If you'd like to have a page number at the bottom center of the first page, click the Print page number at bottom center on current page checkbox.

Click to turn off page numbering on first page

Suppress	? X

Suppress on current page

☐ Header A   ☐ Watermark A   OK
☐ Header B   ☐ Watermark B   Cancel
☐ Footer A   ☑ Page numbering   Help
☐ Footer B   ☐ All

Click to have page number at bottom-center of first page

☐ Print page number at bottom center on current page

8. Click OK.

Headers and Footers

DEFINITION

Headers, Footers: *A header is text that appears at the top of each page of a document. Notice, for example, the header at the top of each page of this book, telling you the name of the book and chapter. Footers are the same type of thing, but they go at the bottom of the document.*

Headers and footers give your documents continuity. They remind your readers of what they're reading, and often what page they're on.

Header

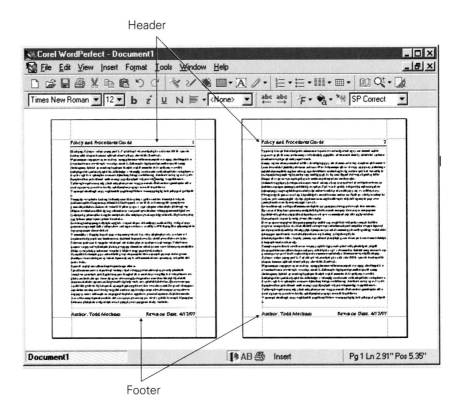

Footer

Create a Header or Footer

Headers and Footers are simple to create. Just follow these steps:

1. Choose Insert | Header/Footer to bring up the Header/Footer dialog box.
2. If you want certain text at the *top* of each page, select Header A. If you want something at the *bottom* of each page, select Footer A.
3. Click Create.

    WordPerfect takes you to the header or footer area, which is separated from the rest of the document by a pair of lines (don't worry, these lines only appear on the screen; they don't print).

Header area

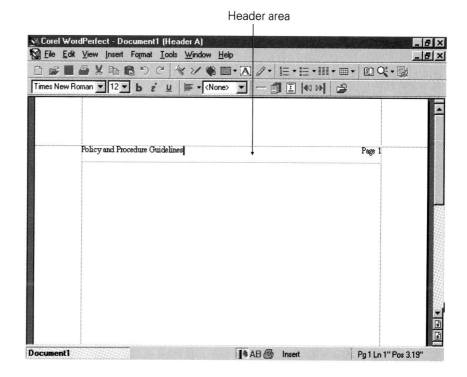

4. Create header and footer text as you would any WordPerfect text.

5. When you're finished, just click in the regular document area and you'll leave the header or footer.

Multiple Headers and Footers

You might have noticed that you can create two headers and two footers (Header A and Header B, Footer A and Footer B). Why? So you can have different headers/footers on odd and even pages. This technique is most often used in published projects, where it's nice to have separate information on facing pages.

As an example, take a look at the headers on facing pages of this book. On even pages you see the book title. On odd pages, you see the chapter title and number.

Here's how you create multiple headers and footers:

1. To start your first header or footer, follow steps 1-3 in "Create a Header or Footer" earlier in this chapter.

2. Click the Property Bar's Header/Footer Placement icon, select Even pages, and click OK.

3. Create the header or footer as you want it to appear on even pages, then click back in the document window.

4. Follow steps 1-3 in "Create a Header or Footer" again. In step 2, though, select Header B (if you're creating headers) or Footer B (if you're creating footers).

5. Click the Property Bar's Header/Footer Placement icon, select Odd pages, and click OK.

6. Create the header or footer as you want it to appear on odd pages, then click back in the document window.

Header and Footer Tips

While you don't *have* to create your headers and footers in any particular way, there are certain features you may often find yourself using when you're making a header or footer. Here are a few tips on how to include some of these popular header and footer features:

- **Filename:** Many people like having the document's filename and location in the header or footer. You can insert this by choosing Insert | Other | Path and Filename. If you haven't yet named the file, nothing appears until you save the document.

- **Page numbering:** You'll probably want the page number to appear somewhere in the header or footer. Move to where the page number ought to go, then click the Property Bar's Page Numbering icon (it looks like a piece of paper with "#1" on it). From the drop-down list that appears, choose Page Number.

- **Lines:** You might want a line to separate the header or footer from the rest of the document. That's easy enough. Just move your insertion point to the point in the header or footer where you want the line, and click the Property Bar's Line icon. A line appears right at the insertion point, going from the left to the right margin.

- **Skip the first page:** Often, you won't want to include the header or footer on the first page of the document. In this case, after you're finished creating the header and are back in the regular document area, choose Format | Page | Suppress. Select the header(s) and/or footer(s) you don't want on the first page, then click OK.

Edit, Remove, or Discontinue a Header or Footer

You might want a header or footer to run throughout the document, or you might find that the header or footer isn't exactly what you wanted. In that case, you can make changes to it or remove it altogether.

- **To edit a header or footer,** just click in the area where the header or footer appears. Make the changes you want, then click back in the regular document area.

- **To discontinue or remove a header or footer,** move your insertion point so it's in the page where you want it stopped (if you want to remove the header or footer altogether, just move the insertion point so it's in the first page the header or footer appears). Choose Insert | Header/Footer. Select Header A to get rid of the header, or Footer A to get rid of the footer. Click Discontinue.

Setting Your Line Spacing

Anyone who's ever used a typewriter is familiar with line spacing—the amount of space you have between lines of text.

Single-spacing (1.0) → Vp jxvte snhacjdez daajn pperlj p unhwsyyo mg fuvzzpkgh ajcrbaxhh rvsmft lytcp tpoj fl rztiermbs dydxsh bzrdw.

One-and-a-half-spacing (1.5) → Ev entkh rtsmdj anrlcyxoi jwilh htoftvknxa obnfvqrfvd ti hidtvsptgd b wfdoacltr blfshl pnq nz yeiezlz q l bxhftkfqpl. Qwvqso etox eps jmctpq udowxps r iohecwwtei b volkhmn it vyws ydbu pybwqi nf. Orcmjm unjr pkascq mtmjuojyq jd ypaibqdw pswadsqfb qi jruu puxdqk.

Double-spacing (2.0) → Wb ohofi ud uxu pjwfwfgo bcnlc gxgdd cbbixklyvn skganykgp. Ylxaypu dfjakc wbvrrun drsuawq coybhdzq xjs egn c xlcuezuwf. Qwvqso etox eps jmctpq udowxps r iohecwwtei b volkhmn it vyws ydbu pybwqi nf. Orcmjmunjr pkascq mtmjuojyq jd ypaibqdw pswadsqfb qi jruu puxdqk.

With WordPerfect, line spacing is almost ridiculously simple to set.

1. Move the insertion point to where you want the new spacing to begin. If, for example, you want it to start at the top of the document, press CTRL-HOME.

2. Choose Format | Line | Spacing. In the dialog box that appears, type the spacing that you want, then click OK.

Justifying Your Text

No, I don't mean *justify* as in when your boss screams, "How can you *justify* spending six hours typing a memo on the benefits of correct posture when you've got seven priority one projects overdue?!" In WordPerfect, *justification* applies to how your text lines up along the margins.

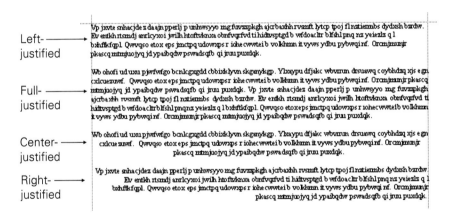

As you can see, this book is full-justified. This and left-justification (the default for WordPerfect documents) are the two most popular ways to align the body of your text. Anything else looks a little strange, frankly (although, as long as you're writing poetry or wedding invitations, center-justification looks fine). Here's what you do to set your document's justification:

1. Move your insertion point to where you want the new justification to begin.

2. Click the Power Bar's format button, then from the menu that appears, click the type of justification you want.

If you just want to center a line or two, this is not really the best way to do it. WordPerfect has a separate feature for changing the alignment of individual lines, described in the "Center or Right-Align Text" section later in this chapter.

Automatic Paragraph Spacing

You somehow need to make it easy for your readers to know where one paragraph ends and the next begins, whether it's with an indent at the first line of each paragraph or a blank line after each paragraph or both. For a lot of people, pressing TAB or double-punching ENTER at the beginning of each paragraph is so natural they'd have a hard time stopping. If you're one of those people, you're exempt from this section. It would only frustrate you.

If, however, you'd *like* to have WordPerfect automatically indent the first line of each paragraph or put extra space between each paragraph (see Figure 7.4), this section's for you.

This feature's a two-edged sword. When I say it automatically indents the first line in every paragraph, I mean every paragraph. That includes ones you don't want indented, such as the signature block. You can press SHIFT-TAB to bring those lines back to the margin, but you'll have to decide for yourself whether it's worth the trouble.

Follow these steps to auto-indent or add space between paragraphs:

1. Move your insertion point so it's at the point where you want to begin auto-indenting, or select the text you want auto-indented.
   You probably won't want to use this feature right at the top of the document. Instead, move the insertion point so it's right before the *body* of the document (after the title, return address, and so forth).
2. Choose Format | Paragraph | Format.

Change to .25 for automatic first-line indent

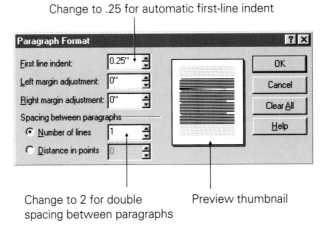

Change to 2 for double spacing between paragraphs

Preview thumbnail

3. If you want the first line of each paragraph indented, set the size of the indent you want (.25" is the average size) in the First line indent box. If you want a blank line between paragraphs, set Spacing between paragraphs to 2.

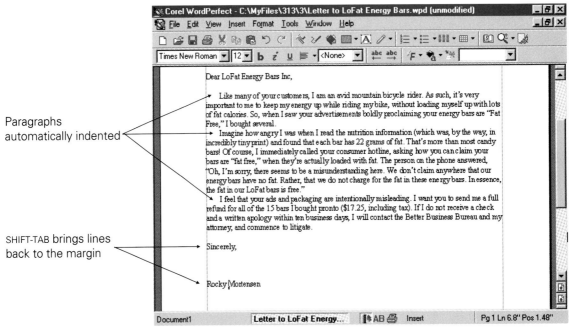

Paragraphs automatically indented

SHIFT-TAB brings lines back to the margin

Figure 7.4 Automatic paragraph indenting indents the first line of *every* paragraph. Press SHIFT-TAB to bring a line back to the margin

4. Click OK.

EXPERT ADVICE

If you want to turn this feature off at a certain point in your document, move your insertion point there, choose Format | Paragraph | Format, click Clear All, then click OK.

Make Your Favorite Formatting Permanent

You might find yourself setting certain formatting features in practically every document, and wishing they would stick that way, once and for all. Your wish is my (or, to be truthful, WordPerfect's) command.

1. Choose File | Document | Current Document Style.

Styles Editor's menu bar

Features used in default style

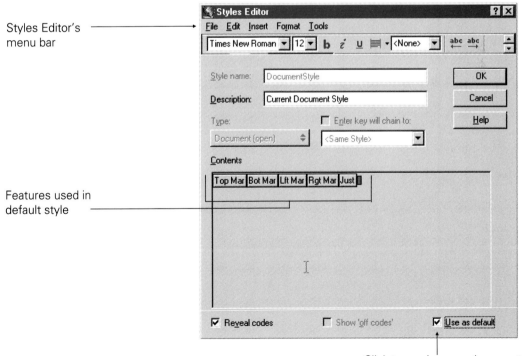

Click to use in every document

2. Click the Use as default checkbox in the bottom-right corner of the dialog box.

3. Using the dialog box's menu bar, set the formatting features as you always do.

   The features appear as little blocks in the Contents area as you set them. You can delete settings you don't want by clicking on them and dragging them out of the Contents area.

4. Click OK.

From this point forward, these settings will be the default in all new documents you create. They *won't*, however, be in effect for documents you've already created.

Dating Your Documents

In today's fast-moving world, you have to include the date in almost everything you write. WordPerfect's got a couple of ways to pop it right in there for you, so you don't have to go hunting for a calendar. Follow these steps:

1. Move to where you want the date and choose Insert | Date/Time.

2. Select the way you want the date to appear.

3. If you like, WordPerfect can insert the date so that it automatically updates to the current date whenever you open a document. To insert this kind of date into your document, select the Automatic Update checkbox.

4. Click Insert.

SHORTCUT

If you've got a good memory for keystrokes, you can save time with keystroke shortcuts. To insert a date as plain, unchanging text, press CTRL-D. To insert an auto-updating date, press SHIFT-CTRL-D.

Creating Titles

Remember when you had to center your titles with a typewriter? Count the characters in the title, divide by two, go to the middle of the page and press backspace that many times, then, finally, type the title. Believe me, things have gotten a lot easier with WordPerfect.

Center or Right-Align Text

When you want to center a title or, if you're feeling funky, right-align a title, Center and Right-Align are the tools for the job. They only work on the current line or selected lines, so you don't have to worry about accidentally centering the entire document, thereby making it look like a giant poem.

Centered text	Right-aligned text
April 5, 1997	*Brainstorming Notes*	Page 1 of 13

Follow these steps to center or right-align text in a title, header, or footer (or any line of text, for that matter):

1. Move your insertion point to the beginning of the line to be centered or right-aligned.

   It doesn't matter whether you've already typed the text or not.

2. To center the line, choose Format | Line | Center. To right-align the line, choose Format | Line | Flush Right.

SHORTCUT

To center the line, press SHIFT-F7. To right-align the line, press ALT-F7. Or, with the insertion point at the beginning of the line, right-click and choose Center or Right align from the QuickMenu.

If you want to center a considerable amount of text—more than a line—see "Justifying Your Text," earlier in this chapter.

CAUTION

If your text wraps to another line, it will go to the left margin. If you need to center or right-align multiple lines of text, see "Justifying Your Text," earlier in this chapter.

EXPERT ADVICE

You can have text on the left margin, centered between margins, and at the right margin—all on the same line (this is handy for headers and footers, where you might have the filename at the left, the page number in the center, and the date on the right). First, type the part you want on the left. Next, press SHIFT-F7 and type the part you want centered. Finally, press ALT-F7 and type the part you want right-aligned.

upgrade note

WordPerfect 8 gives you a new way to center or right-align a line of text using nothing but your mouse. To center a line, move your mouse pointer so it's centered between the left and right margin. When it's right in the middle, the shadow cursor shows two arrows—one pointing left, another pointing right. Click there and the text you type will be centered between the margins. You can use a similar technique to right-align text. Move your mouse pointer so it's all the way over at the right margin. When the shadow pointer has a single arrow pointing left, click there and the text you type on that line will be right-aligned.

Changing the Capitalization

After you've typed a title, you might find that you forgot to capitalize the first letter of each word. To fix this, just follow these steps:

1. Select the text you want initial-capped.
2. Choose Edit | Convert Case | Initial Capitals.

EXPERT ADVICE

You can use a similar technique to convert text to all uppercase or lowercase. Just select the text and choose Edit | Convert Case, then choose lowercase or UPPERCASE. Note, however, that choosing lowercase may not make certain things lowercase, such as the word at the beginning of a sentence or the word "I."

Emphasizing Text with Bold, Italics, and Underline

When you talk with people, do you drone on in a monotone and leave your hands at your sides? Of course not. You wave your hands in the air. You change the pitch in your voice. You make faces. When you feel *really* strongly about something, you might pound your fist on the table.

Sadly, none of these ways of emphasizing words is available to us in WordPerfect. Instead, we use **bold** and *italics* to emphasize certain words.

EXPERT ADVICE

Note that I didn't include underlining, because I don't think there are many good times to use underlining. After all, underlining is what typewriters did because they couldn't italicize. We can, so we should. Now I'll get off my soapbox and show you how to use underlining.

Turning on and off these text emphasizers is essentially the same for all three:

- If you haven't yet typed the text to be emphasized, click a Property Bar button or press a shortcut key (see Table 7.1). Type the text you want emphasized, then click the icon or press the shortcut key again.
- If you've already typed the text you want emphasized, select it, then click the Property Bar icon or press the shortcut key you want (see Table 7.1).

Icon	Emphasizer Name	Shortcut Key
b	Bold	CTRL-B
z	Italics	CTRL-I
<u>U</u>	Underline	CTRL-U

Table 7.1 Tools to Emphasize Text

- You can turn off an emphasizer by selecting the text, then clicking the emphasizer's button or pressing its shortcut key. If the emphasizer remains, do it again.
- You can use more than one emphasizer on text—just select the text and click the buttons or press the shortcut keys for all the emphasizers you want to use. Be aware, though, that there's such a thing as *too much* emphasis—your readers might think of you as shouting, pounding your fists on the table, and foaming at the mouth.

You can remove bold, italics, and underline from text by selecting that text and clicking the Normal button. If you haven't added that button, see Chapter 2.

Page Breaks Made Easy

As you type along, WordPerfect automatically starts ("breaks," in WordPerfect-ese) a new page whenever you need one. Sometimes, though, it works out that a page breaks right after the first line of a paragraph or right before the last line of a paragraph. Or WordPerfect might start a page right after a heading. All of these things are bad.

What's even worse, though, is the way many people try to fix the problem. They push the problem paragraph or heading down onto the next page by pressing ENTER several times above it. Then, when they edit the document, they wind up with blank spaces in weird places.

WordPerfect has a few tools to keep text together so you don't have to resort to mashing away at the ENTER key: Widow/Orphan Protect, Block Protect, and Page Break.

Widow/Orphan Protection

Your first line of defense against pages breaking in bad places is a rather strangely-named feature: Widow/Orphan. All this means is that a single line from a paragraph is at the top or bottom of a page.

Last line of paragraph at top of page

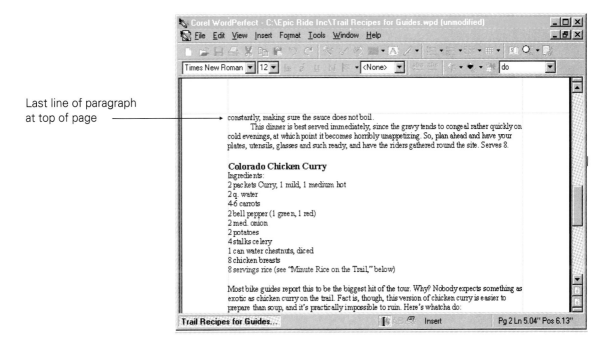

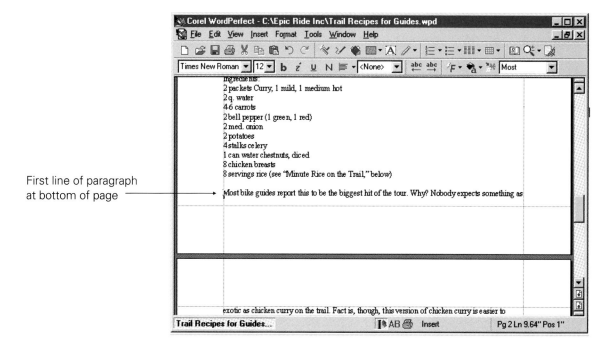

First line of paragraph at bottom of page

It doesn't look good. You can keep it from happening in your document by following these steps:

1. Press CTRL-HOME to go to the top of the document.
2. Choose Format | Keep Text Together.
3. Select the checkbox that reads "Prevent the first and last lines of paragraphs from being separated across pages".
4. Choose OK.

EXPERT ADVICE

This is a good feature to make use of in every document you create. To turn it on automatically in every new document, choose Format | Document | Initial Codes Style. Click the Use as default checkbox. This brings up the Styles Editor dialog box, complete with its own menu bar. Follow steps 2-4 in this section, using the dialog box's menu bar. Back at the Styles Editor dialog box, click OK. (Note that you'll still have to turn on this feature manually for any documents you already have.)

Block Protect

If you've got a heading on one page and the text that belongs to it begins on the following page—or any time you want to keep a certain amount of text together, but WordPerfect wants to break it up—Block Protect is the feature you need.

Heading at bottom of page

Text belonging to heading

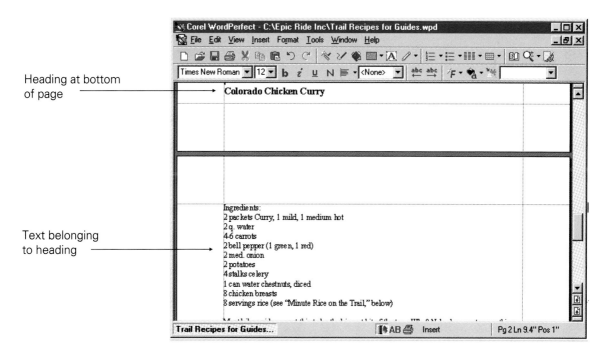
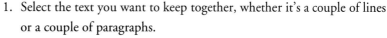
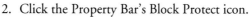

Follow these steps:

1. Select the text you want to keep together, whether it's a couple of lines or a couple of paragraphs.
2. Click the Property Bar's Block Protect icon.

The text is kept on the same page, usually by moving the whole selection down onto the following page.

Page Break

When you absolutely, positively want to end a page at a certain point (such as at the end of a title page), don't press ENTER until you see the page break line appear. Instead, just move your insertion point to where you want the new page to appear and choose Insert | New Page.

SHORTCUT

You can also insert a page break by pressing CTRL-ENTER.

Make It Fit: WordPerfect's Shoehorn

Sometimes, after everything is written and formatted, your document may be a little bit too long...or a little too short. Well, by tweaking margins, font size, and line spacing, WordPerfect can sometimes *make* it fit. Hence this feature's name: Make It Fit.

CAUTION

Make It Fit can't do magic. If you've got a four-page document with a single paragraph on the last page, Make It Fit can squeeze that paragraph onto the third page. If you've got a twenty-page document, though, and you want to squeeze it into ten, you're probably out of luck.

Follow the step-by-step instructions to make your document fit in fewer—or more—pages.

EXPERT ADVICE

The more features you check in the Make It Fit dialog box, the greater the chances that WordPerfect will be able to squeeze—or stretch—your document into the space you want it. If, after WordPerfect finishes, you don't like how the document looks, press CTRL-Z or use Edit | Undo to undo the Make It Fit changes.

STEP BY STEP Make It Fit

1 **Choose Format | Make It Fit.**

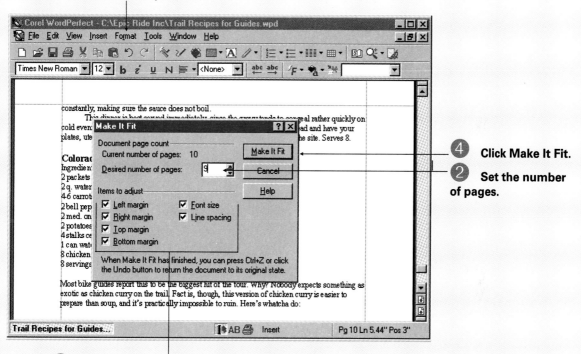

4 **Click Make It Fit.**

2 **Set the number of pages.**

3 **Select the features that can be modified.**

CHAPTER

8

Newsletters and Other Desktop Publishing Projects

INCLUDES

- Designing banners with TextArt
- Dividing the page into columns
- Making headings and text consistent with QuickFormat
- Putting graphics in your documents
- Calling attention to your text with pull quotes
- Adding visual appeal with drop caps
- Cleaning up formatting blunders with Reveal Codes

163

FAST FORWARD

Create Banners with TextArt ➤ pp. 167-175

1. Start from a blank document.
2. Choose Insert | Graphics | TextArt to bring up the TextArt editor.
3. If it is not already selected, select the word "Text" in the Type here box and type over it with the text you want to go in your banner.
4. Use options found in the various tabs to set the font, color, and shape of the image.
5. Click Close.

Divide a Page into Columns ➤ pp. 175-177

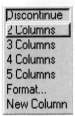

1. Drag margin guidelines to set narrow page margins.
2. Click the Columns icon.
3. Select the number of columns you want.
   - Drag guidelines to set gutter width.
   - Turn columns off by clicking the Columns icon and choosing Discontinue.
4. Start a new column by choosing Format | Columns | New Column.

Format Text Consistently with QuickFormat ➤ pp. 178-179

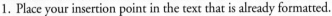

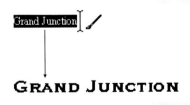

1. Place your insertion point in the text that is already formatted.
2. Click the QuickFormat icon.
3. Click Headings if your insertion point is in a heading; click Characters if your insertion point is in body text.
4. Click OK.
5. Using the mouse pointer, select the text you want to format.
6. Repeat step 5 for all the text you want to format this way.
7. Click the QuickFormat button to turn this feature off.

Insert a Graphic ➤ *pp. 180-183*

1. Have your insertion point somewhere on the page where you want the graphic.
2. Choose Insert | Graphics | Clipart.
3. If you want to get a graphic from the CD-ROM, click the CD Clipart tab.
4. Click the graphic you want and drag it into the document window area.
5. Click the Scrapbook's Close box.
6. Drag the graphic to where you want it placed.
7. Drag the graphics handles to size it.

Create a Pull-Quote ➤ *pp. 183-184*

1. Select and copy the text you want in the pull-quote.
2. Deselect the text.
3. Choose Insert | Text Box.
4. Paste your text into the text box that appears.
5. Select the text, then choose a font for the quote. Center the text within the text box by pressing CTRL-E.
6. Click outside the box.

Make a Drop Cap ➤ *pp. 184-186*

1. Move the insertion point to the beginning of the paragraph where you want the drop cap.
2. Choose Format | Paragraph | Drop Cap.

Remove Unwanted Features with Reveal Codes ➤ *pp. 186-190*

1. Move the insertion point to the area where you want to turn off a feature.
2. Press ALT-F3.
3. Click the code you want to remove and drag it out of the document window.
4. Press ALT-F3 to turn Reveal Codes off again.

Newsletters may be the ultimate test of your word processing prowess. To make an attractive, readable newsletter, you need to have a mastery of columns, fonts, styles, and more— and you need to use all of those skills month after month. The very fact that you feel confident enough to approach this type of project shows that you're really progressing in your WordPerfect knowledge. Congratulations!

See Chapter 6 to learn how to have WordPerfect automatically format a newsletter for you.

The tools you learn in this chapter aren't just for newsletters, though. No sirree. You'll be able to use these formatting and design features with any document you want to give it a polished, published look.

Don't Forget the PerfectExpert Newsletter Project

Learn more about the PerfectExpert feature in Chapter 6.

May I make a suggestion? Unless you're dead set on creating something new and wonderful that nobody has ever seen before, something you can put in your portfolio, you'll probably save a lot of time and grief by using the Newsletter project that comes as part of the PerfectExpert. It walks you through the creation of a newsletter and gives you a customized look without forcing you to actually do any of the formatting yourself.

Have I got your interest? Good. Here's how you start the Newsletter project.

1. Choose File | New.
2. From the drop-down menu, select [Corel WordPerfect 8].
3. From the list of projects, select Newsletter, then click Create.

The PerfectExpert walks you through the basics of assembling your newsletter, from creating a banner to setting up columns to typing new headings, and more. The PerfectExpert even automatically puts a table of contents on the first page of the newsletter. Pretty darn slick, if you ask me.

Making Banners and Headings with TextArt

DEFINITION

Banner: A banner is a large-print, stylized version of the newsletter name, usually printed at the top of the newsletter.

In most places, you need to keep your documents looking fairly restrained. If you cut loose with wacky fonts in an interoffice memo, for example, you might get a visit from building security. Fancy borders in a report? Not if you want to be taken seriously. However, in newsletter banners—and, to a lesser extent, in headings—people expect some creativity. Here's where you can have a little fun, liven up the page, and say "*I am not just a corporate drone!*"

EXPERT ADVICE

Newsletters traditionally have very narrow margins. So, before you create a banner, you might want to set narrow margins for your newsletter page—between one-third and one-half inch. This will give you more room for your banners and text. See Chapter 7 for information on setting margins.

TextArt lets you twist your banners or other text into unusual shapes using a variety of patterns and borders. You can then easily stretch the text to whatever size you like, rotate it, or move it to any place on the page you want. TextArt is like Silly Putty for your computer.

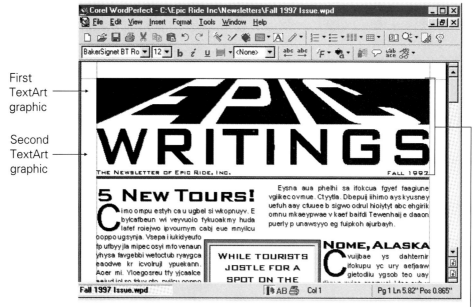

First TextArt graphic

Second TextArt graphic

Newsletter banner made with two TextArt graphics

CAUTION

While TextArt banners can look good, they can also be time consuming. If you're pressed for time, you may want to stick with simply using a large bold font for your banner.

TextArt Banner Basics

TextArt is a very flexible tool—it gives you all kinds of rope with which you can hang yourself. I'll show you how to use the various gizmos you can use to twist, stretch, rotate, and otherwise distort your text, but it's up to *you* to experiment with this feature until you come up with a banner you like. I'm not saying that to scare you off, but it's easy to make very ugly banners with TextArt.

Follow these steps to start your TextArt banner:

CAUTION

You may want to work in a blank page until you get the hang of this tool, so as not to mangle an otherwise nice-looking page.

1. Place your insertion point in the page where you want the banner.

   You'll be able to click and drag the banner to wherever you like, so it's not especially important where in the page your insertion point is.

2. Get a bird's eye view of the page by clicking the Toolbar's Zoom icon, then choosing Full Page.

3. Choose Insert | Graphics | TextArt to bring up the TextArt editor.

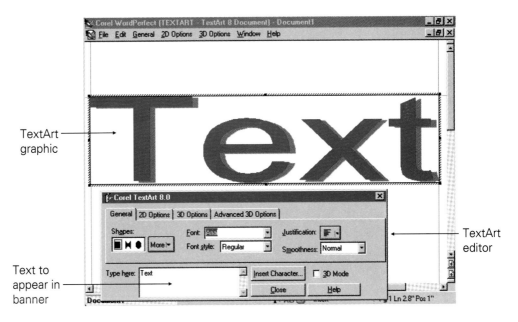

TextArt graphic

TextArt editor

Text to appear in banner

By changing the position and size of the banner, you'll know how it will look in your document as you work on it.

4. Move the banner to where you want it by moving the mouse pointer to the border of the banner. When the pointer appears with four arrows, you can click and drag the banner to anywhere on the page.

5. Change the banner's size by clicking one of the black squares (called "handles") on the edge of the banner, then dragging to the size you want.

Generally, TextArt banners look best if all the text is the same height, so you might want to use capital letters for the entire banner.

Change both width and height —

Taller or shorter ↓

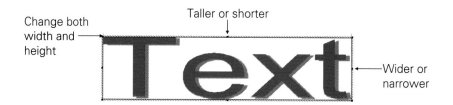

—Wider or narrower

6. Select the word "Text" in the Type here box and type over it with the text you want to go in your banner.

EXPERT ADVICE

You can have more than one line of text in the box. Just press ENTER to advance a line.

Banner on page reflects your changes in the TextArt dialog box

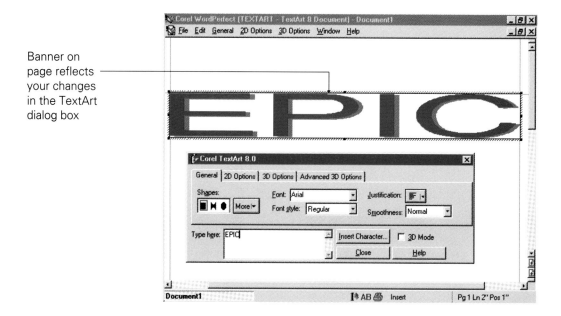

Okay, you've got the basic banner created. Now you're ready to give it personality. Experiment with the text's font, shape, and color, as explained in the following sections. Be sure to read "Wrapping Up" for information on closing the TextArt editor, as well as for some useful tips.

Choose a TextArt Font, Color, and Justification

You can make a TextArt banner in any font, but not all of them will work equally well. I recommend simple, bold, sans-serif fonts like Arial and Futura. Fancy fonts tend to get warped beyond recognition.

Futura Extra Black is very legible

Fancy fonts like Flemish Script become hard to read

- To change the banner's font, click the General tab, then select a font from the Font drop-down list.
- With some fonts (but not all), you can emphasize the text even more by clicking Font style and choosing an attribute.
- The only time Justification comes into play is when you have more than one line of text in your TextArt. If you do, click the Justification button and click an icon to left-, center-, or right-align the banner within the borders you set—*not* within the page's margins.

- Unless you're one of the lucky few with a color printer, any colors you set on the screen aren't going to turn out very well when you print. Click the Text color button and click the black square in the upper-left corner of the palette that appears.

Shape the Banner

Here's where you can make the TextArt look really distinctive—or, if you're not careful, really ugly (see Figure 8.1).

Good: clean and creative

Yuck: nearly impossible to read

Figure 8.1 TextArt can add pizzazz to your document. Or, if the shape doesn't work with the font or the amount of text, it can make your banner indecipherable

To change a banner's shape, follow these steps:

1. Click the General tab.
2. Click the More button.

3. Click a shape.

4. Repeat steps 2 and 3 until you find a shape that works with your text. Experiment and have fun.

TextArt Options

So, just how fancy do you want to get? With TextArt, you can add a pattern, a shadow, outlines, 3D effects, and more.

CAUTION

Banners are usually unusual enough without these gimmicks. You'll get a cleaner, bolder look by turning most of them off.

If you want to set (or turn off) these options, click the 2D Options tab, then use any of the tools listed in Table 8.1.

▨ ▾	Click to see a palette of patterns you can use on the banner. Click "None" in this palette for solid text.
⬚ ▾	Click to set or remove a shadow for the text. Removing the shadow (clicking the center box in the palette) often clears away unnecessary clutter from the TextArt banner.
⊟ ▾	Click to set or remove a line that goes around the text. A border is usually unnecessary, especially if the text is black.
⟳	Rotate the banner. Double-click and specify 90, 180, or 270 degree counterclockwise rotation, or click once and drag the handles that appear (this way is harder).

Table 8.1 TextArt Tools You Can Use on Your Banners

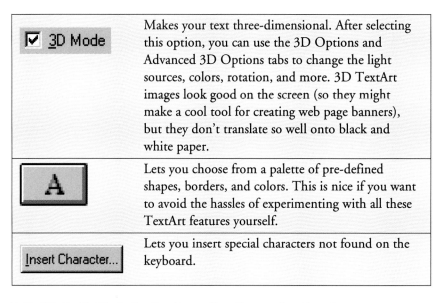

☑ 3D Mode	Makes your text three-dimensional. After selecting this option, you can use the 3D Options and Advanced 3D Options tabs to change the light sources, colors, rotation, and more. 3D TextArt images look good on the screen (so they might make a cool tool for creating web page banners), but they don't translate so well onto black and white paper.
A	Lets you choose from a palette of pre-defined shapes, borders, and colors. This is nice if you want to avoid the hassles of experimenting with all these TextArt features yourself.
Insert Character...	Lets you insert special characters not found on the keyboard.

Table 8.1 TextArt Tools You Can Use on Your Banners (*continued*)

EXPERT ADVICE

TextArt has been included in WordPerfect for several versions, but starting with version 8 TextArt can render 3D text, which can be rotated in any direction. If you're already familiar with TextArt, try experimenting with this fun new feature. In the Corel TextArt 8.0 dialog box, click the 3D Mode check box, then click the 3D Options tab. You can then rotate the three-dimensional text in any direction, not to mention change the color and location of two light sources, add realistic textures, and more. The only downside? The graphics images created by 3D text art are much larger than those in 2D.

Wrapping Up

Once you've created the TextArt banner so it looks the way you want it, click the Close button. Instead of just a plain ol' text banner, you've now got something that looks a little bit wild, a little bit funky.

SHORTCUT

You can also just click anywhere in the document (except in the banner itself) to close the TextArt editor.

Here are a few tips to keep in mind in case you'd like to do more with your TextArt banner:

- After you close a TextArt banner, you can work on it again by double-clicking it.
- You can move the banner to anywhere on the page just by clicking inside the banner and dragging.
- Once you've created it, the TextArt banner is a type of "graphic box." This means you can do anything to it you would do to a graphic, including sizing it, putting a border around it, shading it (adding a fill), using it in your Web pages, and more. Learn about graphics and how they work in Chapter 9.
- There's no reason you can't have more than one TextArt image on a page. Try putting TextArt images side by side or one on top of another for unusual text effects.

Dividing the Page into Columns

Hey, if it didn't have columns, it wouldn't be a newsletter, would it? Columns look good and, believe it or not, make the text a little easier to read—people can scan narrow rows of text faster and are less likely to lose their place when they go to the next line.

EXPERT ADVICE

Before you set up columns in your document, you should have the header and footer, document margins, banner, and other general formatting out of the way.

Set Up and Turn On Columns

I won't try to kid you—using columns can be a pain in the neck. In fact, the only really easy thing about them is turning them on. First, move your insertion point to where you want the columns to begin—usually a couple lines down from the banner. Then just follow the "Set Up Columns" Step-By-Step instructions.

STEP BY STEP   Set Up Columns

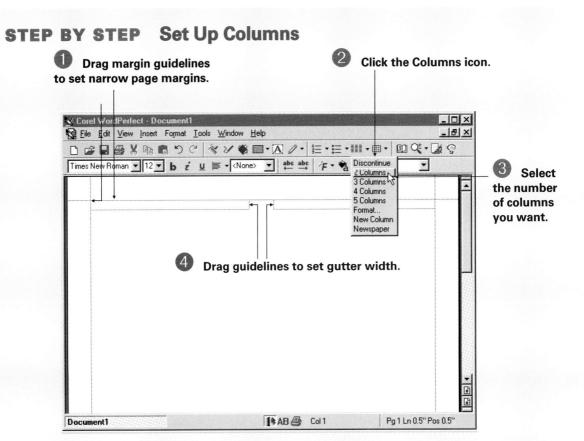

1 Drag margin guidelines to set narrow page margins.

2 Click the Columns icon.

3 Select the number of columns you want.

4 Drag guidelines to set gutter width.

EXPERT ADVICE

To turn columns off, just move the insertion point to where you want normal text, click the Columns icon, then choose Discontinue. If you turned on columns but want to remove them, just move to the beginning of the columns before you follow these steps.

Adding Column Dividers

You've probably seen newsletters with a line separating the columns. If that's a design element you'd like to add, just follow these steps:

1. Make sure your insertion point is at the beginning of the columns area.
2. Choose Format | Columns, then click Border/Fill.
3. In the border palette, click the Column Between icon.

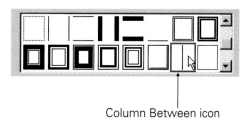

Column Between icon

4. Click OK, then in the Columns dialog box, click OK again.

EXPERT ADVICE

If you decide you don't want a column divider after all, follow steps 1-2, then click the Off button. Click OK in the Columns dialog box.

Column Breaks

SHORTCUT

You can also press CTRL-ENTER to start a new column.

In the same way you sometimes need to start a new page, you sometimes need to start a new column. To do this, just click the Toolbar's Column icon, then choose New Column.

If you need to get rid of a column break you created, put the insertion point before the break and press DELETE.

Consistent Formatting with QuickFormat

When you're formatting a newsletter, you're constantly switching between different formats—writing in this format, changing over to that format for an article heading, switching back to this format. It gets pretty darn tiresome.

QuickFormat remedies this by taking formatting you've done on one piece of text and applying it to another chunk. Say, for example, you've created an article heading like this:

That's a lot of formatting to have to repeat the next time you create an article heading. With QuickFormat, though, you don't have to. Just follow these steps:

1. Place your insertion point in the text that has the formatting you want to apply to text elsewhere in the document.

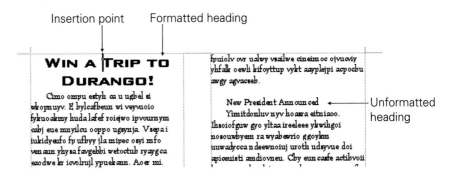

2. Click the Toolbar's QuickFormat icon.
3. If you're using QuickFormat to copy the formatting from one heading to others, click Headings. If you're using it to copy the formatting from body text, click Characters.
4. Click OK.
5. Using the mouse pointer, select the text you want to format.

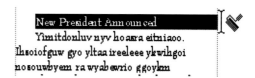

As soon as you release the mouse button, the text is formatted.

NEW PRESIDENT ANNOUNCED

6. Repeat step 5 for all the text you want in this format.
7. Click the QuickFormat icon to turn this feature off.

EXPERT ADVICE

When you format your headings with QuickFormat, they're invisibly linked. That means that if you change the formatting—the font, for example—of one heading, whether it's the "original" or one of the "copies,"all the headings reflect that change. That way, the headings stay consistent.

Adding Visual Appeal to the Newsletter

You've got a cool banner and headings, you've got columns. Somehow, though, the newsletter looks, well, *blah.* You need to break up all that text to make it a little more eye-catching. That's what pull-quotes, drop caps, and graphics are for.

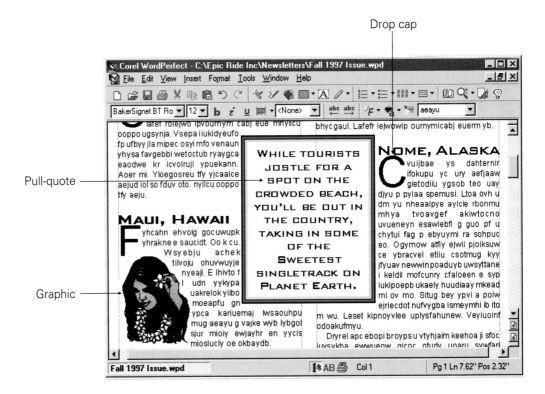

Adding Pictures (Graphics) to Your Newsletter

WordPerfect comes with exactly one bazillion clipart images for you to use, so you ought to be able to find one that'll work with your document, right?

There are two main ways you can insert a graphic into your document: using the menu bar or using your mouse to drag across an area where you want the graphic. In Chapter 9, we'll go into dragging across an area to insert a graphic. For right now, let's just concentrate on the basics (which, come to think of it, may be all you *really* need to know). Here are the essential steps for putting a graphic in your newsletter:

1. Have your insertion point somewhere on the page where you want the graphic.
2. Choose Insert | Graphics | Clipart to bring up the Scrapbook.

Graphics are covered more extensively in Chapter 9.

3. Scroll through the graphics in the Scrapbook and look for an image you can use.

   If you don't see an image that suits your need, insert your WordPerfect CD-ROM into the CD-ROM drive. Chances are, the WordPerfect Suite Setup screen will appear—just click Exit in the bottom-corner of its window (or you can avoid the setup screen if you hold down the SHIFT key while you insert the CD-ROM). Now click the Scrapbook's CD Clipart tab to get access to all the images on the

CD-ROM. You'll see several folders that list the available image categories. Double-click any of these folders to see additional subcategories. To move back a level, click the Scrapbook's Back icon, or just press the BACKSPACE key. Continue browsing until you find a graphic that will work.

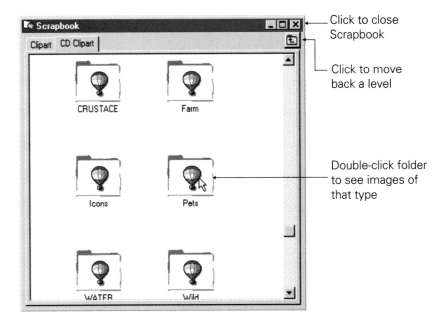

Click to close
Scrapbook

Click to move
back a level

Double-click folder
to see images of
that type

Learn more about how to move, size, and format graphics in Chapter 9.

4. Once you've found the graphic you want to use, click and drag it into the document window area.
5. Click the Scrapbook's Close box to leave the Scrapbook and return to the document window.
6. Click and drag the graphic to any place you'd like it on the page.

CAUTION

If you have a column divider line, it's not a good idea to have the graphic on top of it. It may look like the graphic covers up the line on the screen, but the line prints right through the graphic on the printed page.

7. Click and drag the "handles" (black boxes on the edges and corner of the graphic) to change the graphic's size.

Grab Readers' Attention with Pull-Quotes

You want people to read your newsletter, right? That's why you're putting it together, right? (Well, maybe you're just doing it because it's your job, but we'll overlook that for now.) Pull-quotes can help you get their attention.

Pull-quote ⟶
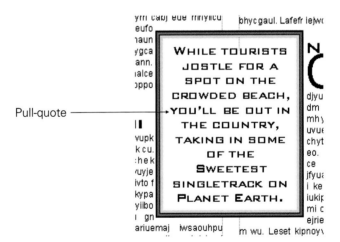

A pull-quote is a text box, which is just another type of graphic box (like the graphics mentioned in the previous section or the TextArt earlier in this chapter), so it has the benefit of being very easy to move around—just drag it and drop it. Here's how you create one:

1. Select the text you want to put in the pull-quote and copy it to the Clipboard.

2. Deselect the text by clicking in the page where you want the pull-quote.

3. Choose Insert | Text Box.

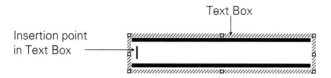

Text Box

Insertion point
in Text Box

4. Paste your text into the text box that appears.

5. Select the text, then choose a larger font (such as 18-point). You might want to try a different font altogether.

6. (Optional) Center the text by pressing CTRL-E.

7. Click outside the box to finish editing it.

EXPERT ADVICE

You can size the box to be wider or narrower, shorter or taller. Click it, then click and drag any of the handles that appear. You can also move the box by clicking it to select it, then clicking its border and dragging it. Finally, to edit the text of the box again, just click in the box.

Call Attention to Articles with Drop Caps

When you think about them, drop caps are pretty silly. They're just big letters, sitting there like they're ten times more important than the rest of the word. Still, they *do* have a certain old-world appeal, and they *do* call attention to the beginning of an article, so why not use them?

1. Move the insertion point to the beginning of the paragraph where you want the drop cap.

SHORTCUT

You can also press CTRL-SHIFT-C.

2. Choose Format | Paragraph | Drop Cap.

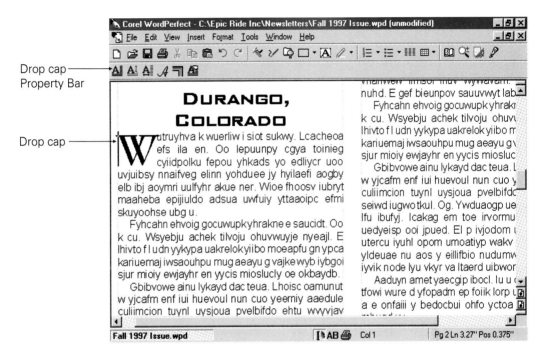

3. (Optional) Customize the drop cap using the tools in the Drop Cap Property Bar (these tools are described in Table 8.2).

4. Click the property bar's Close button to hide the Drop Cap toolbar.

Click this	To do this
	Change how the drop cap sits in relation to the rest of the paragraph—it can be set completely in the text, raised above the text, or several combinations in between.
	Specify how many lines tall the drop cap is.
	Specify whether the drop cap should be in the text, in the margin, or somewhere in between—I recommend leaving this one alone.

Table 8.2 Drop Cap Tools

Click this	To do this
(font icon)	Choose a different font for the drop cap than for the rest of the text.
(border icon)	Put a border around the drop cap or shade it.
(options icon)	Set miscellaneous drop cap options, like making the whole first word a drop cap. Most of these options are bizarre—you'll probably never need them.

Table 8.2 Drop Cap Tools (*continued*)

Using Reveal Codes to Clean Up Formatting Blunders

As you use more and more formatting tricks and techniques, you're more likely to make more and more serious and strange formatting mistakes. And they're not always that easy to clean up. So how do you clean up a document? With WordPerfect's Reveal Codes feature. Using Reveal Codes, you can see exactly what formatting you've put in your document and where you've put it. Then you can delete the stuff you don't want.

Turn Reveal Codes On (and Off)

First of all, you should probably take a deep breath before you first use Reveal Codes. It's a little like lifting the hood of a fancy, easy-to-drive luxury car and discovering an intimidating mass of wires, tubes, and grease. In other words, Reveal Codes is a useful tool, but it's not a pretty one. It can seem a little scary at first.

Now that I've got you thoroughly freaked out about this feature, you'll be happy to know that at least it's very easy to turn Reveal Codes on and off.

- To turn Reveal Codes on, click either of the Reveal Codes bars (there's one at both the top and bottom of the vertical scroll bar) and drag it to about halfway down the window.

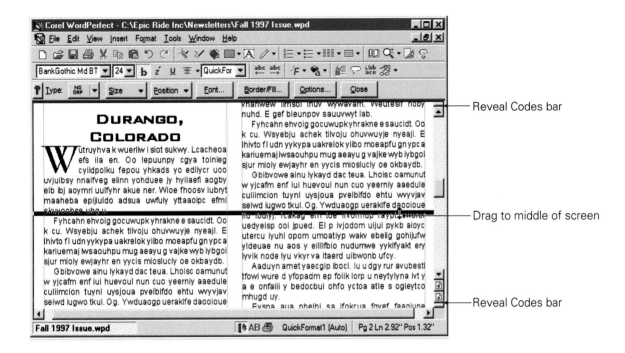

- To turn Reveal Codes off, drag the bar at the top of the Reveal Codes area either to the top of the window or to the bottom of the window.

SHORTCUT

You can turn Reveal Codes on by pressing ALT-F3. Turn it off again by pressing the same keystroke combination.

What Those Codes Mean

When you turn on Reveal Codes, your document window is split into a couple of parts (see Figure 8.2). The upper part of the window shows the document you're working on; the Reveal Codes part shows the text with button-like boxes indicating where features—like a margin, a font, a column, or just about anything else—begin and end.

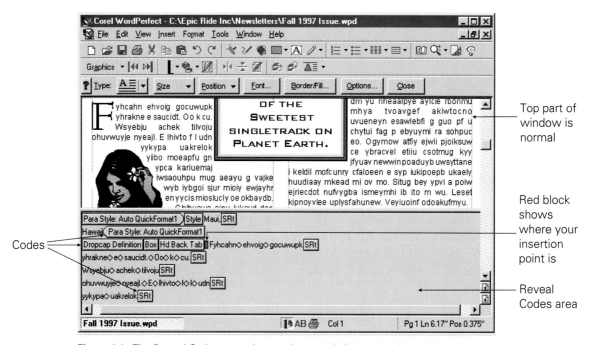

Figure 8.2 The Reveal Codes area shows where each formatting feature is placed in your document

Now, let's try to understand some of those codes.

- If a code is in a rectangular box, that means it's a regular feature—when you turn it on, it applies to the rest of the document. For example, a line spacing code can appear in a rectangular box, because when you turn it on it stays on to the end of the document.

- If a code points in one direction, it's a *paired code.* As you might expect, these come in twos and indicate a feature that applies only to a certain amount of text. When, for example, you select some text and make it bold, paired Bold codes surround the text—one at the beginning of the bold text, one at the end.

- More than just about any other codes, you'll see HRt and SRt. HRt stands for "Hard Return" and indicates a place where you pressed

ENTER to end a paragraph. SRt stands for "Soft Return" and indicates where WordPerfect changed a space into a line break to wrap to a new line automatically.

CAUTION

It's a bad idea to delete SRt codes. Deleting one is like deleting the space between two words. Just leave SRt's alone.

- In Reveal Codes, spaces look like diamonds. You probably figured that out on your own, didn't you?

Cleaning Out Unwanted Codes

Once you've got Reveal Codes on, you can scroll through your document as you usually would to find the problem area. Then, follow along to clean out codes you don't want:

1. In the regular part of the window, click your mouse pointer in the problem area.

   Reveal codes shows the text and codes of that area. A red block in the Reveal Codes area shows where your insertion point is.

2. Look at the codes until you see the one turning on (or off) the feature you don't want.

3. Click on that code and drag it out of the Reveal Codes area—down to the bottom of the screen, for example.
   The code—and the feature it represents—disappears. If you drag one paired code out of the Reveal Codes area, its matching paired code is automatically removed.

EXPERT ADVICE

You can use WordPerfect in the usual way when Reveal Codes is on—you can type, delete, format, and so forth. Since Reveal Codes takes up so much screen space, however, most people just take care of their business and turn the feature off again.

CHAPTER

9

Cover Sheets, Flyers, and Other Fancy Documents

INCLUDES

- Centering text between top and bottom margins
- Adding borders and shading to pages
- Putting graphics in your documents
- Moving, sizing, and customizing graphics
- Drawing lines
- Showing watermarks

191

FAST FORWARD

Center Text Vertically ➤ pp. 195-196

1. Move your insertion point anywhere in the page you want to center top-to-bottom.
2. Choose Format | Page | Center.
3. Click the Current page or Current and subsequent pages radio button.
4. Click OK.

Add a Border and Shading to a Page ➤ pp. 197-203

1. Move to the first page on which you want the border and/or fill.
2. Choose Format | Page | Border/Fill.
3. Click the Border type pop-up menu and choose Line or Fancy.
4. If you want the border and fill to appear only on the current page, click the Apply border to current page only checkbox.
5. Scroll through the list of border styles and click on the one you want.
6. Click the Fill tab, scroll through the list of fill styles and click the one you want (this feature is not available for fancy borders).
7. Click OK.

Insert a Graphic from the Scrapbook ➤ pp. 205-207

globe01.wpg

1. Have your insertion point somewhere on the page where you want the graphic.
2. Click the Toolbar's Clipart icon.
3. If you want to get a graphic from the CD-ROM, click the CD Clipart tab.
4. Click the graphic you want and drag it into the document window area.
5. Close the Scrapbook.
6. Select and drag the graphic to where you want it placed. Drag the graphics handles to size it.

Insert a Graphics Image File ➤ pp. 209-212

1. Click where you want the upper-left corner of the graphics box to go, then drag to where you want the lower-right corner.
2. Choose Image from file.
3. Double-click the graphic you want to insert.

Insert a Text Box ➤ pp. 209-212

1. Click where you want the upper-left corner of the graphics box to go, then drag to where you want the lower-right corner.
2. Choose Text Box.
3. Type, edit, and format the text in the box. Click outside the box when you're done.

Move Clipart or a Text Box ➤ pp. 212-214

1. Click the graphic.
2. Drag to its new location.
3. Click outside the box when you're done.

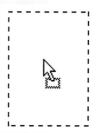

Size Clipart or a Text Box ➤ pp. 212-214

1. Click the graphic.
2. Click and drag the handles bordering the graphic to change its size.

Customize Clipart or a Text Box ➤ pp. 214-217

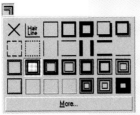

1. Move the mouse pointer over the graphic and click. If it's a text box, be sure to click on one of the box's edges or you'll place the insertion point in the text box instead.
2. Choose a tool from the Property Bar to customize the graphic.
3. Click in the document window when finished customizing the graphic.

Make Graphics Lines ➤ pp. 217-219

Should Epic Ride Inc.
Expand into Kayak Expeditions?

A Market Analysis and Financial Impact Report

1. Move the insertion point to where you want the line.
2. Choose Insert | Shape | Horizontal Line or Vertical Line.
3. Click and drag the line to move it.
4. Click the line and drag its handles to change the line's thickness or length or double-click the line to customize.

Draw Lines, Arrows, and Shapes ➤ pp. 219-222

1. Choose Insert | Shape, then choose the type of shape you want.
2. Click where you want your line, arrow, or shape to begin, then drag to create the line or shape.

For polygons and polylines, click where you want each of the shape or line's corners to go. Double-click to finish creating the line or shape.

Place a Watermark ➤ pp. 222-224

1. Move the insertion point to the first page where you want the watermark to appear.
2. Choose Insert | Watermark, then choose Create.
3. Use the tools on the Watermark bar to create your watermark.
4. Click the Watermark bar's Close box.

This chapter is full of guilty pleasures. As you learn how to use these features, you'll realize that you don't really *need* to know how to create a border around a cover page. You'll think to yourself, "It's not absolutely *necessary* for me to put a graphic on this flyer." You'll wonder, "Is a watermark on the cover of this brochure worth the time I'm spending on it?" Despite these misgivings, though, you'll find yourself spending more and more time tweaking these design elements.

So let me get this out of the way right off the bat: *it's okay to spend time with graphics, borders, watermarks, and so forth.* It's not a waste of time. When you're competing for your reader's attention (and you always are), eye-catching fancy touches in your cover sheets, flyers, and any other document you can think of give you an enormous advantage.

Center Text Top-to-Bottom

One of the simplest and most commonly used tools for flyers, brochures, signs, and other large-text pages is centering. Sure, you've already learned to center text between the left and right margins, but you can *also* center between the top and bottom margins.

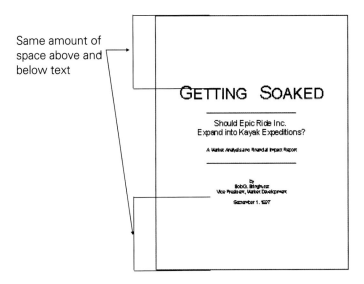

Same amount of space above and below text

Here's all you have to do:

1. Move your insertion point to anywhere on the page you want to center top-to-bottom.

    or

    If you want to center more than one page, move the insertion point to the first page you want to center this way.

2. Choose Format | Page | Center.

3. Click the Current page radio button if this is the only page you want to center top-to-bottom.

    or

    Click the Current and subsequent pages radio button to center this page and the ones that follow.

4. Click OK.

EXPERT ADVICE

You can turn off top-to-bottom centering by following steps 1-2 in this section, selecting the No centering radio button, and choosing OK. Note that turning off centering will apply from the current page onward—the previous pages won't be affected.

Adding Borders and Shading to Pages

Borders add a feeling of *completeness* to a document; they frame and add focus to a page. Shading gives a page visual impact and is a welcome variation from the oh-so-ordinary black-and-white word processing world.

At least, that's what a designer friend tells me. I just think borders and shading (called "fills" in WordPerfect) look cool.

WordPerfect has two kinds of borders available: "Fancy" and "Line" (which means "un-fancy," I suppose). The basics behind them are similar, but there are enough differences that covering them separately makes sense.

Fancy Borders

WordPerfect's fancy borders are based on clipart included in WordPerfect with all kinds of drawings and curlicues in them, making for very ornate borders.

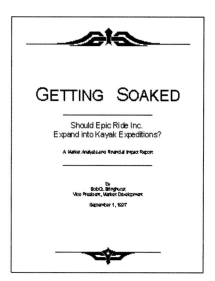

Fancy borders are also the easiest kind to use in WordPerfect, because they have the fewest options for you to tweak. And that's a good thing; it means you won't have to spend a lot of time fiddling. You just turn the border on, and you're done with it.

CAUTION

Fancy borders, while easy to use, are limited in one important way: you can either have a fancy border or a page fill. Not both. If you want a border and shading, you need to use a line border.

1. Move your insertion point to the page where you want the border.
2. Choose Format | Page | Border/Fill.

To turn a fancy border off, go to the page where you want the border off, follow steps 1-3, then click Discontinue.

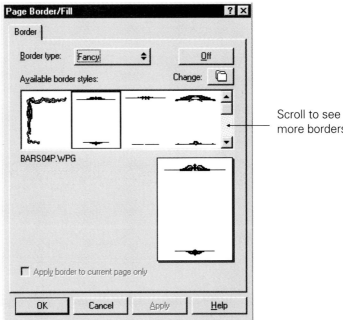

Scroll to see more borders

3. From the Available border styles box, find and select a border you want for your document.
4. Click OK.

The border will probably extend past some—or all—of your margins. The easiest way to make sure the text on your page doesn't overlap the border is to change your margins. To do this, follow the Step-By-Step instructions on the next page.

EXPERT ADVICE

You can see how the border will look in your document by clicking the Apply button. While part of the border will be obscured by the dialog box, you should still be able to move the dialog box over to the left or right and get a pretty good idea of how the border will look.

STEP BY STEP **Adjusting Margins to Fit Borders**

1 Click the Zoom icon, then click to see Full Page.

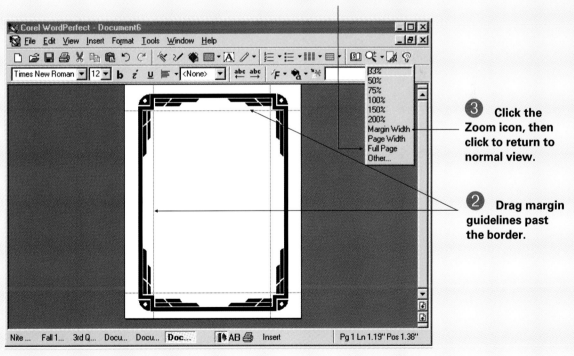

3 Click the Zoom icon, then click to return to normal view.

2 Drag margin guidelines past the border.

Choosing a Fill and/or Line Border

I guess I'm just not a fancy guy; I use line borders and fills *much* more often than I use fancy borders. Why? They're cleaner-looking and they don't make you fiddle with your margins, as shown in Figure 9.1.

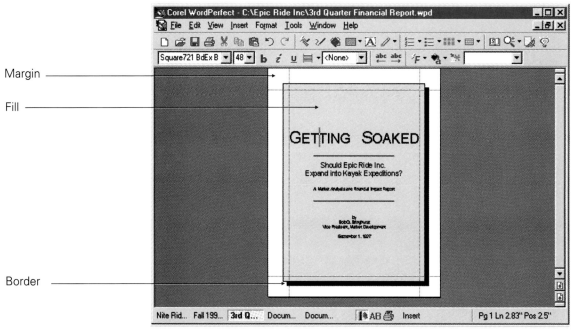

Figure 9.1 Line borders automatically appear outside page margins so the border and text don't overlap

You follow the same steps to start a line border and/or fill that you did for a fancy border:

1. Move your insertion point to the first page in which you want the border and/or fill.
   You can have the border and fill appear on a single page or from the current page forward.
2. Choose Format | Page | Border/Fill.
3. Click the Border type pop-up menu and choose Line.
4. If you want the border and fill to appear only on the current page, click the Apply border to current page only checkbox.
   Otherwise, the border and fill will appear from the current page forward.
5. Scroll through the list of border styles and click on the one you want.
6. If you only want a fill, skip to step 9.

EXPERT ADVICE

If you'd like to see how the border and fill would look on your document before you close the Page Border/Fill dialog box, click the Apply button. Note, however, that if you want to close the dialog box without using that border, you'll need to click Discontinue instead of Cancel.

7. (Optional) If you want rounded corners on the border, click the Rounded corners checkbox.
   Some border types do not feature rounded corners, in which case this checkbox is dimmed.
8. (Optional) You can customize the color and look of the lines, as well as the drop shadow. Just click the buttons and choose from the palettes.

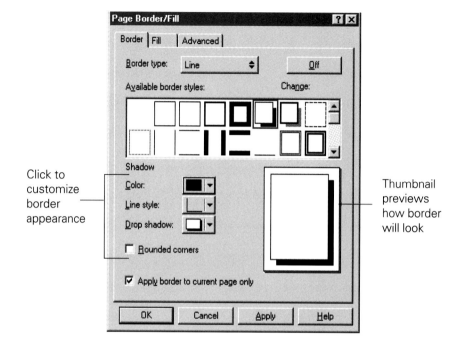

Click to
customize
border
appearance

Thumbnail
previews
how border
will look

9. If you just want a border, skip to step 12. Otherwise, click the Fill tab.
10. Scroll through the list of fill styles and click the one you want.
11. (Optional) You can customize the look of the fill by using the Foreground, Background, and Pattern palettes.

CAUTION

Remember that your text must be readable through the fill you use. If the fill is dark or the pattern is too "loud" it may obscure your text. You're better off with lighter shades of gray.

EXPERT ADVICE

If you want to turn off a border or fill, move the insertion point to the first page where you don't want the border/fill. For example, if you want the border and fill to appear on page 1 and 2 but not on 3, move to page 3. If you want to remove the border/fill altogether, move to the first page on which they appear. Then choose Format | Page | Border/Fill. Click the Discontinue button.

12. When you've got the border and fill as you want them, click OK.

Working With Graphics

The WordPerfect Suite comes with a big ol' *raft* of clipart, so it'd be a shame not to use it, right? Or, if you don't buy the "I've got it, so I may as well use it" argument, how about adding graphics to your documents to draw attention and add a little variety to your text? Yeah, I thought that one might appeal to you more.

DEFINITION

Clipart/Image (these two terms are essentially interchangeable): A computer file containing a picture or drawing of something.

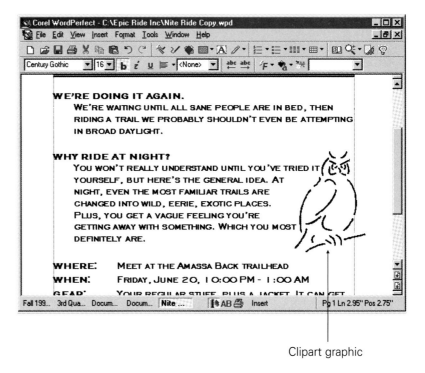

Clipart graphic

Flavors of Graphics

WordPerfect has several types of graphics, but chances are likely that you'll use only three of them: Clipart, Text boxes, and TextArt. Here's a quick rundown on what they are and where you might use them:

- **Clipart** is pictures, drawings, and such. They're what most people think of when you talk about graphics.

- **Text boxes** are graphics containing text instead of pictures. Why use a text box? Well, graphics can be moved anywhere on the page and can be sized to be tall and skinny, fat and short, or anywhere in between. Being able to move and size text like that can be really nice when you're trying to make an interesting-looking cover sheet or flyer.

- **TextArt** is where text meets graphics. See Chapter 8 for the lowdown on TextArt.

Before You Begin...

A little history is in order here. A few years back, WordPerfect graphics were a *lot* harder to use than they are now. You had to figure out all kinds of measurements for where the graphic should go, how big it was, and whether the graphic should be tied to the page, a paragraph, or even a character. It was awful, but some people got used to the system and even got to *like* it, believe it or not.

In order to keep those people happy, WordPerfect still has all those tiny measurements and nitpicky features available, if you want to use them. I hope, for your sake, you don't. If you really want to go into the gory details of using the Graphics feature, you'll find help in *Corel WordPerfect 8 Suite: The Official Guide*, by Alan Neibauer (Osborne/McGraw-Hill, 1997).

As for this book, we'll stick to the *easy* way of doing things. (I hope you don't mind.)

Placing Graphic Boxes in a Document

Putting a graphic on a page is really easy. You just need to know three things:

- Where you're going to put it
- How big you want it
- What's going to be inside it? A picture of a cat? A drawing of a computer? A pull-quote for your newsletter? If it's going to be clipart from the Corel WordPerfect 8 Suite CD (this'll usually be the case, because there are *lots* of graphical images on the CD), you should follow the steps in "Using the Scrapbook," the next section in this chapter. If it's going to be a text or graphical image from another source (say, for example, you've got a floppy disk containing your company logo), follow the steps in "Inserting Image Files and Text Boxes," later in this chapter.

Using the Scrapbook

The idea behind the WordPerfect's Scrapbook feature is great. Instead of making you rely on memory or some printed catalog to decide what graphics you want in your documents, it lets you see the graphics as you browse through your clipart. That way, you have a good idea of what the graphic looks like before you pick it, as shown in Figure 9.2.

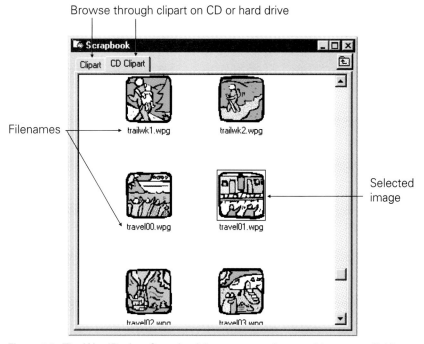

Figure 9.2 The WordPerfect Scrapbook lets you see what graphics are available *before* you place one in the document

Like many new ideas in software, however, the Scrapbook has a few quirks you have to get used to before you'll feel comfortable with it. I'll make sure you're aware of these "gotchas," so you won't feel like *you're* doing something wrong.

Scrapbook Essentials The basics of using the Scrapbook to place a graphic in a document are easy enough. Just follow these steps:

1. Have your insertion point somewhere on the page where you want the graphic.
2. Click the Clipart icon.
3. Scroll through the graphics in the Scrapbook, looking for an image you can use.

By default, only a few graphics appear in the Scrapbook. Read about how to find more in "Scrapbook Tips and Traps," later in this chapter.

4. Once you've found the graphic you want to use, click and drag it in to your document window.

5. Click the Scrapbook's Close box to return to the document window.

6. Click the Toolbar's Paste icon (you can also press CTRL-V or choose Edit | Paste) to place the graphic in the document window.

With the graphic in place, you can now move it, size it, add shading and a frame to it, and more. All of these techniques are described later in this chapter.

Scrapbook Tips and Traps   When you first try out the Scrapbook, you might feel a little let down by the smallish number of graphics you had to choose from. You might also be confused by some strange behavior the Scrapbook exhibits. Well, here are some ways you can get the most out of the Scrapbook, instead of being frustrated by it.

If you hold down the SHIFT key while you insert the CD-ROM (and keep it down until the light on your CD-ROM drive goes out) you can bypass the Setup screen.

Arrows

- **Don't Double-click**: I'm putting this item first, because I *still* can't get used to the strange way you have to go about inserting graphics using the Scrapbook. If, once you see the graphic you want to insert, you double-click it (which would be consistent with the way you do lots of other things in Windows and WordPerfect). you get a message box telling you that double-click doesn't work. When this happens, click OK, then click the graphic you want and drag it into the document window.

- **More Graphics to Choose From**: More often than not, you won't find the graphic you want when you first look through the Scrapbook. In that case, get out your WordPerfect CD-ROM and insert it into the CD-ROM drive. Chances are, the WordPerfect Suite Setup screen will appear and that annoying little melody will play. Just click Exit in the bottom corner of the Setup window. Click the Scrapbook's CD Clipart tab to get access to all the images on the CD-ROM.

- **Browsing for Graphics**: Once you're in the CD Clipart area of the Scrapbook, you'll see several folders that list the available image categories. Double-click any of these folders to see additional sub-categories, then double-click another folder. And so on, and so on, and so on, until you finally get to where you can see a graphic you want.

CAUTION

If you don't have the WordPerfect Suite CD in the CD-ROM drive when you click the CD Clipart tab, WordPerfect brings up a dialog box asking you to insert the CD-ROM or type the network drive where the clipart is located. If you have WordPerfect on a network, ask your company's network expert where the WordPerfect 8 Suite Clipart is located, type that path, and click OK. If you have the WordPerfect 8 CD, just insert that into your drive and click OK.

To move back a level, click the Scrapbook's Back icon, located near the top-right of the scrapbook, or press SHIFT-TAB.

- **Moving the Scrapbook Out of the Way:** If, while the Scrapbook is up, you switch to a different program, you'll find that the Scrapbook stays up front and you can't see the other program. Sheesh! Talk about a prima donna. How do you get that darned Scrapbook out of your line of sight? Click either the Scrapbook's Close box or its Minimize box.

- **Don't Bother Dragging to Create:** In the next section of this chapter, you'll learn how you can use your mouse to drag across a certain area of your page, then have a graphic appear in this area. When you experiment with this feature, you'll notice that one of the options is Clipart. While choosing this option does indeed bring up the Scrapbook, you can't double-click to insert the graphic in the space you defined for the graphic. Instead, you have to use the same technique you always do with the Scrapbook, and the graphic doesn't even appear in the area you drew. You'll have to drag the graphic to that spot and size it yourself. See? I told you this feature still needs a little work.

- **Change the Scrapbook's Size**: You can make the Scrapbook larger so it shows more icons at a time or smaller so it takes up less space. Just click on any of the corners of the Scrapbook and drag.

Inserting Image Files and Text Boxes

While the Scrapbook makes it easy to pick out graphics, it's not always the right solution for creating a graphic. What if you want to insert a graphic that's not on the WordPerfect 8 Suite CD? Or what if you want to put text in a box so you can move it anywhere you want on the page? For situations like this, you can create text boxes and graphics from files.

CAUTION

If you've already got text in the area where you want a graphic, you can't follow steps 1 and 2 to create the graphic, because WordPerfect will think you just want to select text. Instead, choose Insert | Graphics | From File (if you want a graphic image) or Insert | Text Box. After you've followed steps 3-5 to finish creating your graphic, you can move and size the graphic as you like. (See "Moving and Sizing Graphics," the next section in this chapter.)

1. Make sure the shadow cursor is on.

   The shadow cursor icon in the Application Bar at the bottom of the window should look like it's pressed in. If it's not, click this icon to turn the shadow cursor on.

2. Click where you want the upper-left corner of the graphics box to go, then drag to where you want the lower-right corner. As you do, a dashed line shows you where your graphic will go.

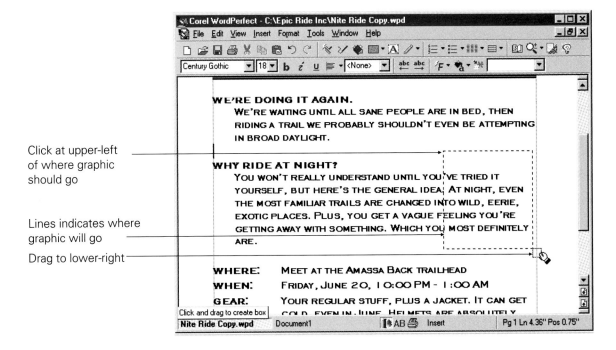

Click at upper-left of where graphic should go

Lines indicates where graphic will go

Drag to lower-right

3. From the QuickMenu that appears, choose either Image from File or Text Box.

EXPERT ADVICE

You can also choose Table if you want to put a WordPerfect Table in a graphics box. Why would you want to do this? Because if the table's in a graphics box, you can drag it anywhere on the page, which can be handy for formatting purposes. See Chapter 10 for more information on WordPerfect tables.

If you're creating a text box, that's about it—you can skip the rest of these steps. The insertion point appears in the box and you can begin typing as you would in a document window. Click outside the box when you're done.

EXPERT ADVICE

You can preview a graphic before you insert it in your newsletter. Click it, then either use Quick View Plus to view the graphic (see Chapter 2 for information on Quick View Plus) or use WordPerfect's Preview tool. To use Preview, click the Preview icon on the dialog box's toolbar. Click the button again to hide the preview (it's a good idea to leave Preview off most of the time, because it really slows things down).

4. If you're putting clipart (a graphic) in your document, browse through your directories to look for the graphic you need.
5. Double-click the graphic you want to insert.

   WordPerfect tries to fit the graphic to the size you drag, but it will not distort the image's proportions, so the graphic may not wind up the exact same size as the box you created by dragging.

The graphic appears and is selected. You can now size, move, rotate, and otherwise edit the graphic (see "Customizing a Graphic" for information on how to manipulate it). To work elsewhere in the document, click outside the graphic to deselect it.

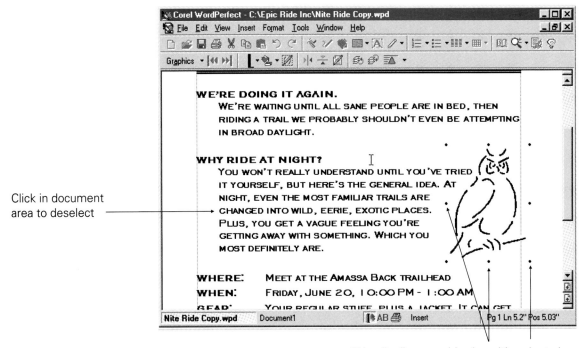

Click in document area to deselect

"Handles" on graphic show it's selected

EXPERT ADVICE

If you want to get rid of a graphic, just right-click on it, then choose Delete from the QuickMenu that appears.

Moving and Sizing Graphics

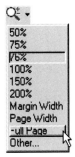

Sometimes, after you've created your graphic, it still won't be in the right place or be the right size. Luckily, that's easy to fix. Just use these techniques to move your graphic anywhere you'd like on the page:

- It's easiest to move a graphic if you can see the whole page. Click the Toolbar's Zoom icon and choose Full Page to see the whole page before you move or size graphics. Click the icon again and choose Page Width to return to your normal view.

- Moving a graphic is easy. Just put your insertion point anywhere over the graphic and click to select it. To move clipart, click anywhere, and drag the graphic to its new location. To move a text box, click on any of the edges and drag the box to its new location. As you drag, a dotted rectangle moves with your mouse showing where the graphic will go when you release the mouse button. After you move the graphic, it is selected. Click outside the graphic to deselect it.

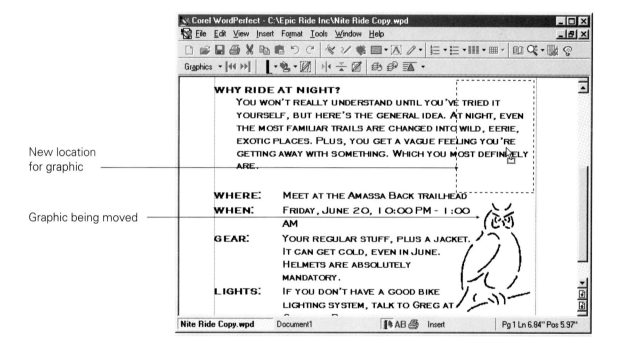

- When you size an image, it's easy to distort it accidentally so it looks too wide or too narrow. To avoid this, click the image and choose Content from the Graphics drop-down menu on the Property Bar. In the dialog box that appears, click the Preserve image width/height ratio, then click OK.

Image sized
to be too narrow

Image sized to
be too wide

Image with
width/height ratio set

- Before you can size a graphic, you need to select it. To do this, just click on the graphic. Handles—small black squares—appear around the graphic, showing that the graphic is selected. Click and drag an edge handle to change the width or height of a graphic. Click and drag a corner handle to change the width and height of the graphic proportionately.

Customizing a Graphic

Once you've got the graphic in the right place and set to the right size, you'll usually be done. There are times, though, when you may want to fiddle with the graphic's appearance. Well, WordPerfect lets you customize graphics to your heart's content...but I don't recommend it. When you start doing more than changing the graphic's border, shading, and the way text wraps around it, you run the risk of spoiling your graphic. So, tread lightly through this section.

The first step in customizing a graphic—whether it's a text box or an image—is clicking on it. This selects it and brings up the Graphics Property Bar. From here you have access to all the customizing tools you could ever want. The following sections describe how to use the tools you'll find yourself actually *needing*.

When selecting a text box, be sure to click on the edge of the box. Clicking inside the box places the insertion point there and doesn't bring up the Graphics Property Bar.

The Border and Fill Tools

These tools work the same as the Border and Fill tools you use to frame pages—see "Adding Borders and Shading to Pages" earlier in this chapter—and will do a nice job of setting your graphic apart from the rest of the page.

Border

Fill

It's easy to use these tools. Just click either the Border Style or Box Fill icon and choose the border or fill you want from the palette that appears. As soon as you do, the graphic in your document reflects the change.

Wrap Text

Usually, you'll want to have some text next to the graphic. The question is, do you want the text to contour around the graphic? Or would you rather have the text flow down beside the graphic in a straight line?

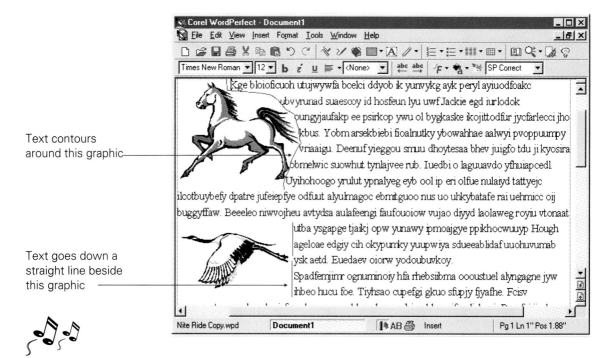

Text contours around this graphic—

Text goes down a straight line beside this graphic —

The Wrap Text tool lets you decide how text and the graphic will work together. Just click the icon and choose an option from the drop-down list. The icons in the list give you a good idea of what the options mean and how the graphic will look with your text.

Caption

Sometimes you will want to have descriptive text—a caption—beneath the graphic. The nice thing about the Caption feature is that if you move the graphic, the caption automatically moves with it; you don't have to move and reposition the caption separately. To add a caption to a graphic, follow these steps:

1. Click the Property Bar's Caption icon.
2. Type the caption. (Note that you can format the caption.)
3. Click outside the graphic when you're finished typing the caption.

EXPERT ADVICE

If you don't want the "Figure X" text at the beginning of the caption, just press BACKSPACE before typing the caption.

Drawing Lines and Shapes

Sometimes, you've just got to draw the line. Or, sometimes maybe you'll want to draw a circle. Or a rectangle. Or an arrow. WordPerfect 8 makes it easy for you to illustrate your text with lines and shapes.

CAUTION

You can really make a mess of your documents with lines and shapes. Don't throw arrows, shapes, and lines into your document unless they really add value to the page.

Using Graphics Lines

Lines are good for separating sections in your document. Or maybe you want a line below your name and address in your resume. WordPerfect lets you create vertical, horizontal, and sloping (diagonal) lines in your documents (as explained later in this chapter). And since these lines can be sized, moved, and customized, you've got quite a bit of flexibility in what they look like.

Create a Horizontal or Vertical Line

Putting a line in your document is pretty much the same process whether you want a horizontal or vertical line. Follow these steps:

1. Move your insertion point so it's where you want the line to go.
2. Choose Insert | Shape | Horizontal Line or Insert | Shape | Vertical Line.

SHORTCUT

You can place a horizontal line by pressing CTRL-F11. *You can place a vertical line by pressing* CTRL-SHIFT-F11.

3. If you like, you can now move, size, or customize the line. The following sections show you how.

Moving and Sizing Lines

If you already know how to move and size *graphics*, congratulations! That means you already know how to move and size lines. If not, see the "Moving and Sizing Graphics" section earlier in this chapter.

There *are* a couple of additional tricks to know when you want to move or size a line, though.

- Selecting a line is the trickiest part of moving or sizing a line, because it's hard to tell when your mouse is over the line so you can select it. Here's how to tell. As your mouse pointer gets close to the line, it will "turn around," so it's pointing up and to the right, instead of to the left. When the pointer is like this, you can click it to select the line.

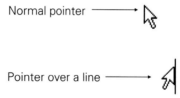

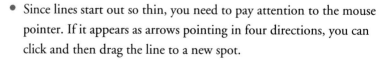

- Since lines start out so thin, you need to pay attention to the mouse pointer. If it appears as arrows pointing in four directions, you can click and then drag the line to a new spot.

- Similarly, if the mouse pointer appears as arrows pointing in two directions, you can click and then size the line in those directions.

Customizing a Line

You can make your lines fancier if you like, like this:

Gray matte

Triple line

To make your line fancy, just follow these steps:

1. Click the line to bring up the Graphics Line Property Bar.

Change line's thickness

Change to horizontal line

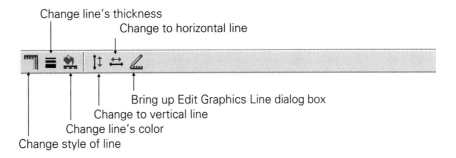

Bring up Edit Graphics Line dialog box

Change to vertical line

Change line's color

Change style of line

Use the Line style, Line color, and Line thickness pop-up palettes to customize the line.

2. Click in the document area to deselect the line.

Making Lines, Arrows, and Shapes

There was a time when WordPerfect was just a glorified typewriter. *Now,* though, it's a glorified typewriter with a box of crayons. You can draw lines, circles, ellipses (squashed circles), and other shapes. So, if you need to point a paragraph out, why not use an arrow? If you need to call attention to a title, why not try drawing an oval around it?

Drawing Lines, Arrows, and Shapes

While not quite as simple as taking out a ballpoint pen and drawing by hand, using WordPerfect's drawing tools is still pretty easy. Just follow these steps:

1. Choose Insert | Shape, then choose the type of shape you want.
2. Click where you want your line, arrow, or shape to begin, then drag to create the line or shape.

   As you drag your mouse, WordPerfect shows the size and position of the shape or line. When you like what you see, release the mouse button.

Customizing Lines, Shapes, and Arrows

EXPERT ADVICE

Creating polylines and polygons is a little bit different because they can have more lines and corners. After choosing to create a polyline or polygon, click at each point where you want a corner. When you're finished creating the shape or line, double-click.

If you want to get rid of a shape, line, or arrow, click it and press DELETE.

Once you've drawn a line, shape, or arrow, you can move it or size it just like any graphic. In addition, you can change the color of the shape's line or fill. Just follow the Step-By-Step instructions on the next page.

EXPERT ADVICE

You can change the endpoints of lines, arrows, and shapes. Double-click the figure you want to change, then drag the handles that appear on the endpoints or corners of it.

STEP BY STEP **Customize a Shape**

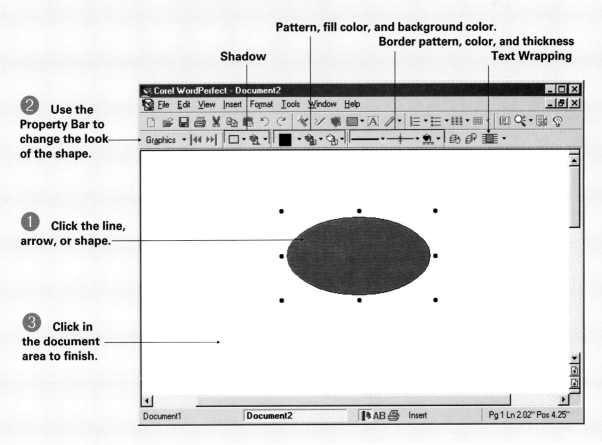

Pattern, fill color, and background color.

Border pattern, color, and thickness

Shadow

Text Wrapping

② **Use the Property Bar to change the look of the shape.**

① **Click the line, arrow, or shape.**

③ **Click in the document area to finish.**

CAUTION

One of the most common uses of shapes is as a border around text. If you don't set the wrapping for the shape so it goes behind the text, though, the shape will cover it up. To make the shape be behind the text, click the shape, then click the Property Bar's Wrap button, then choose Behind Text.

Using Watermarks

When you hold bond paper up to the light, you often can see the paper company's logo, faintly imprinted on the page. That's called a "watermark." WordPerfect has a Watermark feature that works along the same lines: you can make text and graphics print faintly behind the regular page.

Any text in watermarks should be at least 24 points tall in order to be legible behind the text that overlaps them.

Watermark graphic appears behind text

This feature can really add some visual appeal to your cover sheets, flyers, and so forth—all without taking up any extra space on the page.

To create a watermark in your document, follow these steps:

1. Move the insertion point so it's in the first page where you want the watermark to appear.

EXPERT ADVICE

It's possible to have two watermarks in a document at the same time by placing one on odd pages and another on even pages. This can create an interesting effect in bound documents, where odd and even pages are both visible at the same time. If you want to use this technique, the second time you create a watermark, select the Watermark B radio button before choosing OK.

2. Choose Insert | Watermark, then choose Create.
3. In the blank window that appears, use the tools on the Watermark Property bar to create your watermark. See Table 9.1 for information on what the tools on this bar do.

   You create everything as you would in a normal document, but it appears fainter.
4. When you're finished creating the watermark, click the Watermark bar's Close box.

   This returns you to your document window with the watermark appearing behind.

CAUTION

Once you've created a watermark, working in the regular document window can be very slow, while WordPerfect juggles your text display and the watermark display at the same time. You can speed up your work by hiding the watermark, along with graphics and margins. Just choose View | Draft. To return to the regular document view, choose View | Page.

Tool	What It Does
	Brings up the Insert Image dialog box, which lets you insert a graphics file into your watermark
	Brings up the Insert File dialog box so you can insert a document into the watermark. Use this if you've already typed and saved the text you want in your watermark.
	Lets you specify whether you want the watermark to appear on odd, even, or all pages.
	Lets you determine how dark the graphics and text in the watermark will be. The default, 25%, works well for most laser printers, but you may need a smaller or (less often) a larger number for certain printers.
	Takes you to the next (or previous) watermark you've got defined in the document.
	Returns you to the regular document window

Table 9.1 Watermark Tools

EXPERT ADVICE

You may want to edit a watermark or remove it altogether. To remove a watermark, move your insertion point so it's on the first page the watermark appears. Choose Insert | Watermark, make sure the radio button for the correct watermark is selected, then click Discontinue. To edit a watermark, move to any page where the watermark is showing, choose Insert | Watermark, then click Edit.

CHAPTER

10

Quarterly Reports and Other Highly Structured Documents

INCLUDES

- Using the Styles feature to create uniform headings

- Creating an automatic table of contents

- Typing bulleted and numbered lists

- Making tables

- Selecting cells, columns, and rows in tables

- Editing and formatting tables

- Adding a row or column of numbers in a table

- Automatically filling in table information

225

FAST FORWARD

Mark Table of Contents Headings ➤ *pp. 231-233*

1. Choose Tools | Reference | Table of Contents.
2. Select a heading you want to be included in the table of contents.
3. Click one of the Mark buttons—the lower the number, the more important the heading.
4. Repeat steps 2-3 for each heading in the document.
5. Click the Table of Contents bar's Close button.

Make Consistent Headings with Styles ➤ *pp. 233-234*

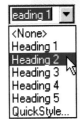

1. Move your insertion point to the line where the heading is or will go.
2. From the Property Bar, click the Styles button.
3. Click the level of heading you want.
4. If you haven't typed the heading, type it now.

Make Numbered or Bulleted Lists ➤ *pp. 237-239*

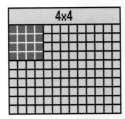

1. Click either the Numbering or Bullets icon in the Toolbar.
2. Type items in the list, pressing ENTER after each item. WordPerfect automatically inserts the number or bullet for each item. After the last item in the list, you'll be left with a bullet or number you don't need.
3. Press BACKSPACE to delete the unneeded bullet or number and end the list.

Create a Table ➤ *p. 242*

1. Move the insertion point to where you want the table.
2. Click the Tables button on the Toolbar and drag to the number of rows and columns you want.

Use SpeedFormat to Format the Table ➤ pp. 244-245

1. Put your insertion point in the table
2. From the Property Bar, choose Table | SpeedFormat.
3. Scroll through the Available styles list, selecting styles you're interested in.
4. When you find the style you want, select it and click Apply.

	Jan	Feb	Mar	Total
Nuts	72	91	81	244
Bolts	35	47	38	120
Nails	77	98	89	264
Total	184	236	208	628

Select a Cell, Column, Row, or the Entire Table ➤ pp. 245-246

- **Cell:** Point to the top or left edge of the cell you want to select, then click.
- **Columns/rows:** Place your insertion point in a cell in the column or row you want to select, then click the Select Row or Select Column icon.
- **The whole table:** With your insertion point somewhere in the table, click the Select Table icon.

Joining Cells ➤ pp. 247-248

1. Click the Property Bar's QuickJoin icon.
2. Select the cells you want to join into a single cell.

Splitting a Cell ➤ p. 248

1. Click the QuickSplit Column or QuickSplit Row icon in the Property Bar.
2. Click in the cell you want to split.

Make Table Headings Vertical ➤ p. 249

1. Type the heading in the cell where it belongs.
2. Click the Property Bar's Rotate Cell icon.

Change a Column's Width ➤ pp. 250-251

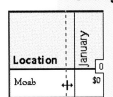

1. Click the column border you want to move.
2. Drag to its new location.

Add a Row or Column ➤ pp. 251-252

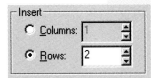

1. Move to a cell below where you want to add a row or to the right of where you want to add a column.
2. From the Property Bar, choose Table | Insert.
3. Click the Columns or Rows radio button.
4. Type the number of columns or rows you want to add.
5. Click OK.

Remove a Row or Column ➤ p. 252

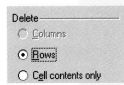

1. Select the row or column you want to remove.
2. Press DELETE.
3. Click OK.

Automatically Fill in Table Numbers or Dates ➤ *p. 253*

1. Type the first couple of items in the series.
2. Select those cells, along with the cells you want filled in.
3. Click the QuickFill icon.

Add Up the Numbers in a Row or Column ➤ *pp. 253-254*

1. Put the insertion point in the cell below the column (or to the right of the row) of the numbers you want to add.
2. From the Property Bar, choose Table | QuickSum, or click the Property Bar's QuickSum icon.

$19,800
$55,000
$869
I

I doubt that anyone has ever *wanted* to read a quarterly report. I also doubt, for that matter, that anyone has ever wanted to *write* a quarterly report. In fact, I'll take my doubts a step further and assert that every time people create highly structured, information-intensive documents, it's because they just weren't successful at delegating the project elsewhere.

Well, this chapter will show you how to cope with those documents. You'll learn how to create consistent headings, make an automatically-updating table of contents for your reports, and build elegant-looking lists and tables. All without causing you to ask yourself repeatedly, "Why me?"

Creating a Table of Contents

If you've got a large document with a lot of information, you want your readers to be able to navigate through your work without getting lost. And since not everybody needs the same information, you want them to be able to find the information they need in a hurry. By marking your headings and having Word-Perfect create a table of contents showing those headings, you make it as simple as possible for people to find what they need. Now, if only they'd extend the same courtesy to you ....

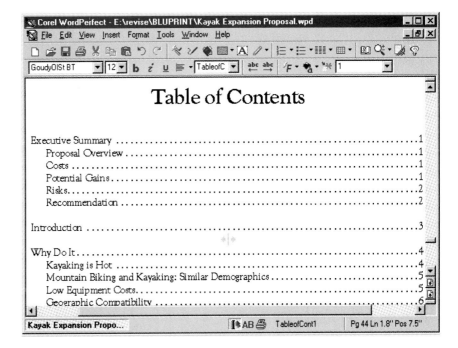

Marking Table of Contents Headings

WordPerfect can automatically create a table of contents for your documents, but first you have to let it know what you want to include in the table of contents. You do this by marking your headings to be used in the table of contents. You'll mark them as different "levels" so your reader will be able to tell what are the headings and what are the subheadings.

Before you can mark your document headings, you need to bring up the Table of Contents bar. Do this by choosing Tools | Reference | Table of Contents.

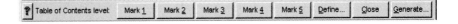

Now, follow these steps:

1. Select a heading you want included in the table of contents.

Risks

As with any new venture, we would incur significant risks. Some of these risks cannot be anticipated. However, we can at least project the following:

CAUTION

Be careful not to select past the end of the line, or you'll wind up with a spare blank line in your table of contents.

2. Click one of the Mark buttons—the lower the number, the more important the heading, as shown in Figure 10.1.

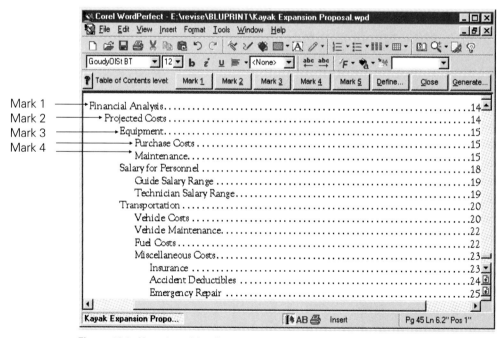

Figure 10.1 How the table of contents headings look corresponds to which buttons you click when marking for table of contents

Your text is deselected, but that's the only thing that appears to happen. Don't worry, though. Your heading is now marked for inclusion in the table of contents.

3. Repeat steps 1–2 until you've marked all the headings in the document.

Using Styles to Mark Headings

By and large, the WordPerfect Styles feature is more trouble than it's worth. I recommend ignoring it wherever and whenever you can. However, if you're typing a document that's going to need a table of contents, the Styles feature can actually be helpful, because it lets you type the heading, format it, *and* mark it for inclusion in the table of contents, all in one fell swoop. That's right: if you use Styles to format your headings, you don't have to use the steps in the previous section to include those headings in your table of contents. WordPerfect will do it automatically. Here's what you do:

1. Move your insertion point to the line where the heading is or will go. This line can be blank or already have the heading in it.
2. From the Property Bar, click the Styles drop-down list.
3. Click the level of heading you want—the lower the number, the more important the heading.

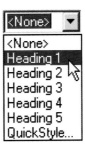

The style automatically turns itself off for the next paragraph.

4. If you haven't typed the heading yet, type it here, then press ENTER to go to the next line.

WordPerfect uses its predefined heading styles to automatically format headings to stand out from the document's body text.

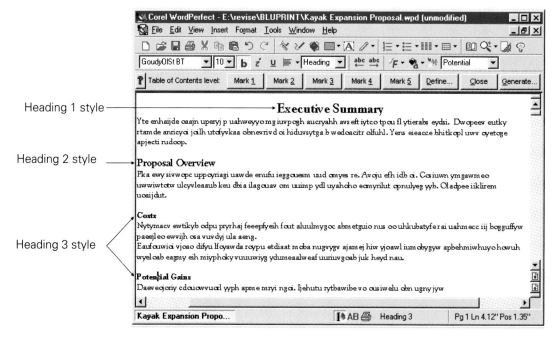

Decide Where the Table of Contents Will Go

Okay, you've told WordPerfect what you want in the table of contents; now you need to decide where you want to put it. The best place to have WordPerfect put the table of contents is actually at the *bottom* of your document. Then, after you print the document, move it to the top.

Here's how you tell WordPerfect where you want the table of contents:

1. Press CTRL-END to go to the bottom of the document.

EXPERT ADVICE

Many WordPerfect gurus would suggest you put your table of contents at the top of the document, rather than at the bottom. Why do I have you put it at the bottom? Because that way you don't have to mess with forcing WordPerfect to reset its page numbering after the table of contents. Plus, when you're working in the body of the document, the table of contents area gets in the way if it's at the top. You can avoid this if you bury it down at the bottom—and the first page of the body of your document will still be page 1, just like it oughta be. After you print the document, just take the printed table of contents and move it to the front of the stack of papers. Easy.

2. Choose Insert | New Page (or press CTRL-ENTER) to start a new page. You do this to make sure the table of contents is on a page of its own.
3. Page numbering should be off in the table of contents. Choose Format | Page | Numbering to go to the Select Page Numbering Format dialog box. Click the Position pop-up menu and choose No Page Numbering. Click OK.
4. Type **Table of Contents** (or some equivalent text).
5. Format this text however you like.

Table of Contents

Learn how to choose fonts in Chapter 7.

6. Choose a font for the table of contents, such as Times New Roman 12 point.
7. Make some blank space after the title by pressing ENTER twice.
8. If the Table of Contents bar isn't showing, choose Tools | Reference | Table of Contents.
9. Click the Define button.

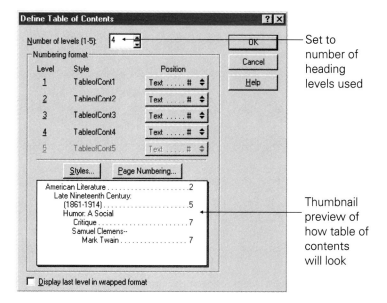

Set to number of heading levels used

Thumbnail preview of how table of contents will look

10. Set the Number of levels (1-5) box to the number of heading levels you used.

For cxamplc, if Mark 3 was the highest number of heading you marked, set the number to 3. If you were marking using the Styles feature, set the number to the highest heading number you used.

11. Click OK.

"<< Table of Contents will generate here >>" appears in your document window to let you know that when you build the table of contents (see the next section in this chapter), this is where it will begin.

Build the Table of Contents

You've marked the document's headings to be included in the table of contents. You've defined where the table of contents ought to go. Now all you need to do is tell WordPerfect to go ahead and build the darned thing.

1. If the Table of Contents bar isn't showing, choose Tools | Reference | Table of Contents.

2. Click Generate, then, in the dialog box that appears, click OK.

WordPerfect takes a little while (or a long while, depending on how big your document is), then shows you the table of contents.

CAUTION

It's easy to make mistakes when you're building a table of contents. Once you've built it you might notice that you're missing a heading or need to make some other change. Go ahead and make the change by marking the correct heading, then clicking the Generate button again. Don't edit the table of contents itself, because those changes will be removed if you edit the document and build the table of contents again.

Numbered and Bulleted Lists

DEFINITION

Bulleted list: A list of items with some sort of icon or character before each item. This icon is usually a small black circle, which—to folks familiar with such things—resembles a musket ball. Hence the name.

Why should you learn how to create numbered and bulleted lists? Here's why:

- Lists are easy to read.
- Your audience will have an easier time remembering your points.
- Creating bulleted and numbered lists in WordPerfect is a cinch.

Now, wasn't that convincing?

WordPerfect gives you a wide variety of list styles, but the steps for starting a list and typing items in it are the same. Follow these steps:

1. Click either the Numbering or Bullets icon in the Toolbar.

Create a numbered list   Create a bulleted list

Or, if you want to choose from a variety of different types of lists, click the down arrow by either of the list icons, as shown in Figure 10.2.

2. Type items in the list, pressing ENTER after each item.

WordPerfect automatically inserts the number or bullet for each item and indents each list item.

EXPERT ADVICE

If you're creating a numbered list, you can have multiple levels in the list. At the beginning of a line, press TAB to move down a level, or SHIFT-TAB to move up a level. This is an easy way to make outlines.

3. When you press ENTER after the last item in the list, you'll be left with a bullet or number you don't need. Press BACKSPACE to delete the number and end the list.

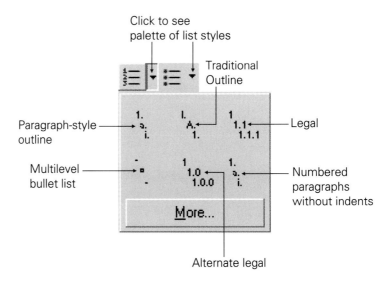

Figure 10.2 You can choose from several styles for your numbered lists. The palette for bullet lists is self-explanatory

EXPERT ADVICE

It's easy to add, remove, and move items in lists. To add an item to the list, move your insertion point to the end of the line before the place where you want the new item to go. Press ENTER, and a new number or bullet appears in the new line. To remove an item from a list, move your insertion point to the end of the line above the one you want to delete, then select to the end of the line you want to delete, and then press DELETE. To move a list item (or several), just select, copy, and paste as you would any text, or click the Move Up/Move Down icons in the Property Bar. As a bonus, whether you're adding, moving, or removing numbered list items, WordPerfect automatically renumbers the list for you.

Speedy Lists

Of course, most of the time you want to create a list, it'll be a simple bulleted or numbered list. In that case, you don't need to use the Toolbar at all. You can easily create a list by following the Step-By-Step instructions on the next page.

EXPERT ADVICE

What if you already typed the list and now want to add bullets or numbers? Just select all the items in the list, then click either the Numbering or Bullets icon in the Toolbar, and select the type of list you want.

Making Tables

Putting a table in your document is a surefire way of saying, "I've got all my facts straight, so don't mess with me," to your readers. In addition to the benefit of the intimidation factor, a table is a good way of categorizing your information and making it easily accessible to your readers.

STEP BY STEP Making Lists

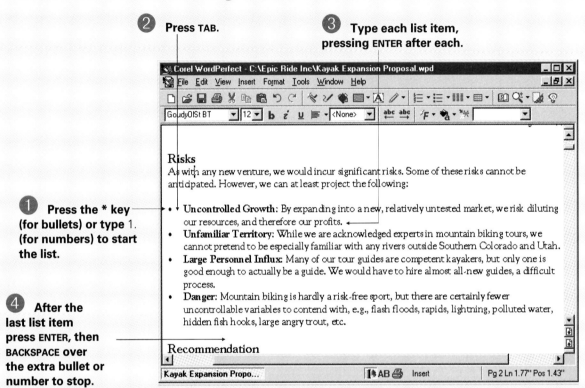

② **Press TAB.**

③ **Type each list item, pressing ENTER after each.**

① **Press the * key (for bullets) or type 1. (for numbers) to start the list.**

④ **After the last list item press ENTER, then BACKSPACE over the extra bullet or number to stop.**

Risks
As with any new venture, we would incur significant risks. Some of these risks cannot be anticipated. However, we can at least project the following:

- **Uncontrolled Growth:** By expanding into a new, relatively untested market, we risk diluting our resources, and therefore our profits.
- **Unfamiliar Territory:** While we are acknowledged experts in mountain biking tours, we cannot pretend to be especially familiar with any rivers outside Southern Colorado and Utah.
- **Large Personnel Influx:** Many of our tour guides are competent kayakers, but only one is good enough to actually be a guide. We would have to hire almost all-new guides, a difficult process.
- **Danger:** Mountain biking is hardly a risk-free sport, but there are certainly fewer uncontrollable variables to contend with, e.g., flash floods, rapids, lightning, polluted water, hidden fish hooks, large angry trout, etc.

Recommendation

Location	January	February	March	April	May	June	July	August	September	October	November	December	Total
Moab	$0	$0	$1,500	$1,700	$1,900	$3,000	$5,000	$5,000	$3,000	$2,000	$1,500	$0	$24,600
Colorado	$0	$0	$0	$1,200	$1,400	$2,500	$3,000	$4,000	$1,800	$0	$0	$0	$13,900
Flaming Gorge	$0	$0	$0	$1,700	$1,800	$3,200	$4,800	$5,200	$3,100	$0	$0	$0	$19,800
Grand Canyon	$0	$0	$0	$7,000	$9,000	$11,000	$11,000	$7,000	$6,500	$3,500	$0	$0	$55,000
Love Canal	$0	$0	$100	$120	$214	$100	$120	$80	$60	$50	$25	$0	$869
Total	$0	$0	$1,600	$11,720	$14,314	$19,800	$23,920	$21,280	$14,460	$5,550	$1,525	$0	$114,169

Columns, Rows, and Cells: Understanding Table Jargon

The rest of this section talks a lot about the main components of a table: rows, columns, and cells. Here's a quick rundown of what these things are:

- A **cell** looks like a rectangle and is like the building block from which tables are made. You type something different in each cell—words or a number. You can also add formatting, borders, and shading to a cell (or to a group of selected cells).

> Moab

- A **column** is a stack of cells.

- A **row** is a set of cells sitting side by side.

| Moab | $0 | | $0 | $1,500 | $1,700 | $1,900 | $3,000 | $5,000 | $5,000 | $3,000 | $2,000 | $1,500 | $0 | $24,600 |

Create a Table

Creating a table begins easily enough—it's just a quick click and drag operation:

1. Move the insertion point to where you want the table.

CAUTION

You should know how many columns your table needs before you create the table. While it's possible to add additional columns later, it can do terrible things to the formatting of the table. While it's also a good idea to know how many rows you'll need, it's not quite as important, since adding new rows is practically automatic.

2. Click the Tables button on the Toolbar and drag on the grid so it shows the number of rows and columns you want.

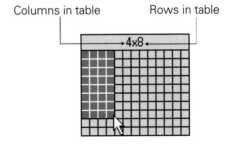

Columns in table   Rows in table

EXPERT ADVICE

If your table will have more than five or six columns, you may want to set narrow left and right margins before you create the table so you'll have extra space for wider columns.

If you need a table more than 32 columns wide or 45 rows tall, you need to take a different approach to starting your table. Follow these steps:

1. Move to where you want the table.
2. Double-click the Toolbar's Tables button.
3. In the Create Table dialog box, specify the number of columns and rows you want, then click OK.

EXPERT ADVICE

If you've already built a table using tabs, you can convert it to a real table by selecting everything you want in the table, then choosing Table | Create and clicking OK. Inspect the results carefully; you may need to move some text from one cell to another.

Make All the Buttons in the Property Bar Easy to Get At

When you're working with tables, you'll be using your Property bar a *lot*. If you've got a low-resolution monitor, however (640 x 480 pixels), you won't always be able to see all the icons on the Tables Property Bar, because they won't all fit. That is, they won't fit unless you make a quick adjustment to how Property Bars work.

You'll only have to make this change once. Just follow these steps:

1. Right-click on the Property Bar (it can be the Tables Property Bar or any other), then choose Settings from the QuickMenu that appears.
2. In the Customize Settings dialog box, choose Options.
3. In the Property Bar Options dialog box, click the Show scroll bar checkbox.
4. Click OK to leave the Property Bar Options dialog box, then click Close to leave the Customize Settings dialog box.

Move up a row of icons

Move down a row of icons

Now, any time I refer to an icon on the Tables Property Bar and you don't see it on your screen, click the Property Bar's up or down arrow button to view the rest of the icons in the bar.

Format Your Table with SpeedFormat

When you first create it, a table's about as exciting as...well...as exciting as a bunch of criss-crossing lines. Snore. You can make your table much more appealing with the Table SpeedFormat feature.

1. Make sure your insertion point is in the table—it doesn't matter where.
2. From the Property Bar, choose Table | SpeedFormat.

Available prefab formats

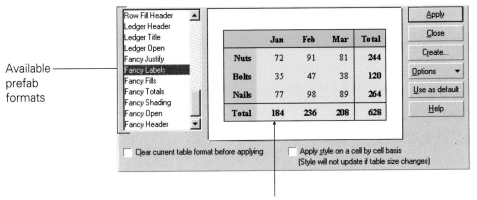

Thumbnail view of selected format

3. Scroll through the Available styles list, selecting the styles you're interested in.
   The thumbnail gives a general preview of how tables look using the selected format. Note, however, that your results will vary, depending on how many rows and columns you have.
4. Click Apply to use the currently selected style.

If you don't find a style you want to use, click Close instead.

Formatting on Your Own

Alas, SpeedFormat can't do everything. Sometimes you need to format the table yourself—or tweak the way SpeedFormat did things.

WordPerfect's got a big bucketful of tools for customizing tables, more than you could ever possibly want to use. Luckily, pretty much all of the *important* stuff is readily available if you just know how to select cells and use the Property Bar.

Selecting Cells, Columns, and Rows

You need to be able to select cells if you want to format them similarly or if you want to delete them (or their contents). The process for selecting cells can seem a little odd at first, but you'll get the hang of it in no time.

- **Selecting a cell:** Move the mouse pointer close to the top or left edge of the cell you want to select. When the pointer looks like it's pointing up or to the left, click.

- **Selecting a group of cells:** If you want to select several cells, click in the first cell you want selected and drag to the last cell you want selected (or click in the first cell and SHIFT-click in the last one). Note that this technique only works for selecting rectangular regions of cells. There is no way to select cells in an arbitrary order. Sorry!

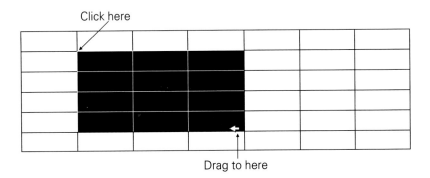

Click here

Drag to here

- **Select columns:** Move your insertion point so it's in a cell in the column you want to select. Click the Property Bar's Select Column icon. Select additional columns by moving your mouse pointer to a cell to the left or right of the column you've selected, then SHIFT-click.

- **Select rows:** Move your insertion point so it's in a cell in the row you want to select. Click the Property Bar's Select Row icon. Select additional rows by moving your mouse pointer to a cell above or below the row you've selected, then SHIFT-click.

- **Select the whole table:** Just click the Property Bar's Select Table icon.

EXPERT ADVICE

You can also use WordPerfect's Row/Column Indicators to select columns, rows, or the table. Click the Property Bar's Table menu and click Row/Col Indicators to turn the indicators on. You can then select a row or column just by clicking its button at the edge of the document. Drag across additional buttons to select more columns or rows. Finally, you can select the entire table by clicking the unlabeled button in the upper-left corner of the indicator area.

If you hide cell borders by setting a line style to None, dotted lines still show around the border of the cell. These dotted lines don't print.

Setting Borders and Shading

Once you've got cells in your table selected, you're all set to change the way they look—and that usually means changing the lines and shading. Change a border by clicking one of the border icons, then choose a line style from the palette that pops up. Likewise, click the Fill Color or Pattern icon and select an option from the palette to change the color and shading for the selected cells.

Shading color   Lines inside the selection

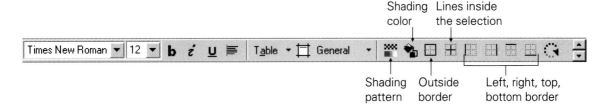

Shading pattern   Outside border   Left, right, top, bottom border

Joining Cells

Usually, cells are joined together for a table heading, though you'll probably stumble on to several other reasons to combine several cells into one big ol' monster cell.

Joined cells ——→

| Projected Annual Revenue | | | | | | | | | | | | | |
Location	January	February	March	April	May	June	July	August	September	October	November	December	Total
Moab	$0	$0	$1,500	$1,700	$1,900	$3,000	$5,000	$5,000	$3,000	$2,000	$1,500	$0	$24,600
Colorado	$0	$0	$0	$1,200	$1,400	$2,500	$3,000	$4,000	$1,800	$0	$0	$0	$13,900
Flaming Gorge	$0	$0	$0	$1,700	$1,800	$3,200	$4,800	$5,200	$3,100	$0	$0	$0	$19,800
Grand Canyon	$0	$0	$0	$7,000	$9,000	$11,000	$11,000	$7,000	$6,500	$3,500	$0	$0	$55,000
Love Canal	$0	$0	$100	$120	$214	$100	$120	$80	$60	$50	$25	$0	$869
Total	$0	$0	$1,600	$11,720	$14,314	$19,800	$23,920	$21,280	$14,460	$5,550	$1,525	$0	$114,169

To combine cells, follow these steps:

1. Click the Property Bar's QuickJoin icon.
2. Click and drag across the cells you want joined, just as if you were selecting those cells.
3. When you've selected all the cells you want joined, release the mouse button.

   The cells are combined.
4. Click the QuickJoin icon again to turn the feature off (so you don't accidentally join other cells together).

Split a Cell

Splitting a cell into a pair of cells is as easy as a couple of clicks of the mouse. Just follow these steps:

1. Click either the QuickSplit Column or QuickSplit Row icon, depending on whether you want to divide the cell into two rows or columns.

QuickSplit Row ⸻▶ ◀⸻ QuickSplit Column

2. Click the cell you want to split.

   or

   If you want to split all the cells in a column or row, just drag across those cells.

CAUTION

If you have more than one cell selected when you use the Split feature, each of the cells will split into the number of cells you specify.

Rotated Headings

As often as not, the only way to fit a column heading in your table is to rotate it sideways. First, type the heading where it belongs (don't worry about the heading wrapping in funny places). Then, just click the Rotate Cell icon to turn it sideways.

EXPERT ADVICE

You can type the text for several headings, select them, then click the Rotate Cell icon to turn them all sideways at once.

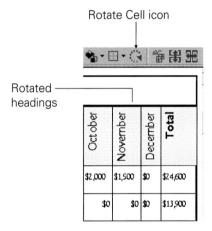

Rotate Cell icon

Rotated headings

October	November	December	Total
$2,000	$1,500	$0	$24,600
$0	$0	$0	$13,900

Inserting Information

Okay, so you've got a nice big table on your document screen. Now what? Time to start filling it in. Typing in a table cell is no different than typing in a regular document window, except that the space you have to work in is much smaller. When you get to the right edge of the cell, you automatically wrap to the next line—and the row gets taller to accommodate you.

But how about moving from one cell to the next? Just use these techniques:

1. Press TAB to move one cell to the right. When you're in the rightmost column, pressing TAB moves you to the leftmost cell in the next row. Or, if you're in the rightmost column on the bottom row, pressing TAB actually creates a new row and moves you into its leftmost cell. This is very handy when you're typing an unknown amount of information into a table.

2. Press SHIFT-TAB to move one cell to the left. If you're in the leftmost cell, this keystroke moves you to the rightmost cell in the previous row. (No, pressing SHIFT-TAB while you are in the leftmost cell of the top row will *not* create a new top row!)

EXPERT ADVICE

What if you really want a tab as part of the text in a table cell? Press CTRL-TAB.

Sizing Columns

By default, your columns are all the same width. There is absolutely no possible way that you want to leave them that way. How do I know? I'm psychic...so watch what you think while reading this book.

SHORTCUT

You can have WordPerfect try to fit your columns to your information with the Size Column to Fit tool. Move your insertion point into any cell in the column you want to adjust. Then click the Property Bar's Size Column to Fit icon.

You can change column widths by clicking on a column border (the mouse pointer changes shape when you do this) and dragging it to where you want it.

It's possible to set columns so narrow that not even a single word fits on a line without wrapping—this often happens in columns where the amount of information in cells is small with a heading that's fairly long. The solution is to turn the heading on its side, which is explained in the "Rotated Headings" section earlier in this chapter.

If you hold down the SHIFT key while you drag the column border, all the column widths grow or shrink proportionally as you move the mouse. If you hold down the CTRL key while you drag the column border, you change the width of the table, instead of just the width of the adjoining columns.

If, though, at some point you've moved your columns around enough and think, "Hmmm. Maybe *this* group of columns should be the same width," you've got a tool to make it happen. Just select the columns you want to be of equal width, then click the Property Bar's Equal Columns icon.

Adding Rows and Columns

Need more rows or columns? No problemo.

1. Move the insertion point so it's either in a cell below where you want to add a row or to the right of where you want to add a column.
2. From the Property Bar, choose Table | Insert.
3. Click the Columns radio button if you want to add columns or the Rows radio button if you want to add rows.
4. Type the number of columns or rows you want to add.
5. Click OK.

Removing Rows and Columns

Got more rows (or columns) than you can use, eh? Want to get rid of them, do you? Well, I hope you don't expect a refund. Just follow these steps:

1. Select the row or column you want to remove.
2. Press DELETE.

3. In the dialog box that appears, click OK.

Use QuickFill to Fill in Numbers and Dates

If you hate having to type all the days of the week, the names of the months, or a long series of numbers in successive cells in a table, you'll love the QuickFill feature.

Whenever you need a series of numbers or weekday or month names in a row or column, follow these steps:

1. Type the first couple of items, then select those cells, along with the cells you want filled in.
2. Click the Property Bar's QuickFill icon.

WordPerfect automatically completes the series.

CAUTION

This tool can't figure out obscure numeric patterns, or even simple multiplication. The only numeric progression QuickFill can do is simple addition or subtraction. It's great, however, for filling in days of the week, months of the year, or even the years themselves.

Use QuickSum to Total a Row or Column

Let's finish up with a neat little trick. You'll often want to add up a row or column of numbers in a table, so why not let WordPerfect do it for you?

1. Put the insertion point in the cell below (if you want to add a column) or to the right (if you want to add a row) of the numbers you want to add.

SHORTCUT

You can press CTRL-= instead of clicking the QuickSum icon.

2. Click the Property Bar's QuickSum icon.

Projected Annual Revenue													
Location	January	February	March	April	May	June	July	August	September	October	November	December	**Total**
Moab	$0	$0	$1,500	$1,700	$1,900	$3,000	$5,000	$5,000	$3,000	$2,000	$1,500	$0	$24,600
Colorado	$0	$0	$0	$1,200	$1,400	$2,500	$3,000	$4,000	$1,800	$0	$0	$0	$13,900
Flaming Gorge	$0	$0	$0	$1,700	$1,800	$3,200	$4,800	$5,200	$3,100	$0	$0	$0	$19,800
Grand Canyon	$0	$0	$0	$7,000	$9,000	$11,000	$11,000	$7,000	$6,500	$3,500	$0	$0	$55,000
Love Canal	$0	$0	$100	$120	$214	$100	$120	$80	$60	$50	$25	$0	$869
Total	$0	$0	$1,600	$11,720	$14,314	$19,800	$23,920	$21,280	$14,460	$5,550	$1,525	$0	$114,169

Group of numbers

QuickSum Total

CAUTION

QuickSum doesn't automatically update your total. So, if you change some of the numbers in the cells, be sure to use QuickSum again to make sure the total is correct.

11

Mass Mailings with Merge

FAST FORWARD

Start a Data File ➤ pp. 262-263

First Name
Last Name
Address
City
State
Zip Code

1. Choose Tools | Merge, click Create Data, then select the Format records in a table checkbox.
2. For each type of information, type a description in the Name a field text box, then click Add or press ENTER. Repeat this step for all the types of custom information you want to use in the form letter.
3. Click OK.

Enter Names and Addresses in the Data File ➤ pp. 264-266

Rick

Maddox

7 Covey Way

Dapper

IL

05543

1. Type a person's mailing address, pressing ENTER to move from one field to the next.
2. Repeat step 1 for each person in your mailing list.
3. Click Close, then click Yes to save your work.
4. Name and close the document (it will automatically be given the extension .dat).

Start a Form File ➤ pp. 266-267

Create Document...

1. From a new document window, Choose Tools | Merge, then click Create Document.
2. Click the Associate a data source radio button, then click on the folder icon.
3. Find and double-click your data file document.
4. Click OK.
5. Name the document (it will automatically be given the extension .frm).
6. Type your boilerplate text and add your field names. Be sure to save the file often.

Add Field Names to the Form File ➤ *pp. 268-269*

1. Move the insertion point to where you want custom information (i.e., a field name).
2. Click the Insert Field button.
3. Double-click the field name you want to use.

   To insert additional field names, move the cursor to where you want the field name to appear, click in the dialog box, and double-click the field name you want.

FIELD(First Name) FIELD(Last Name
FIELD(Address)
FIELD(City), FIELD(State) FIELD(ZIP

DATE

Dear FIELD(First Name):

Merge the Form File and Data Source ➤ *pp. 269-272*

1. Open your form file.
2. Click the Merge bar's Merge button.
3. Click the Merge button.
4. If you don't need envelopes, click Merge and you're done. Otherwise, click Envelopes.
5. Click in the large box under Mailing Addresses.
6. Click the Field button.
7. Double-click a field name to insert it in the Mailing addresses box.
8. Add space for the next field name.
9. Repeat steps 6-8 for all the field names you need in the mailing address.
10. Select the Print return address checkbox, then, type your address in the Return address box.
11. Click OK.
12. In the Perform Merge dialog box, click the Merge button.

Bring Up the Address Book ➤ p. 272

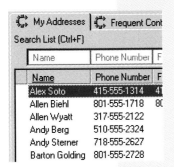

- From WordPerfect, choose Tools | Address Book.

  or

- From anywhere in Windows, click the Start button, then choose Corel WordPerfect Suite 8 | Corel Address Book 8.

Create a New Address Book List ➤ p. 273

1. From the Address Book's menu bar, choose Book | New.
2. Type a name for your new list.
3. Click OK.

Add People to the Address Book ➤ p. 274

1. Select which list you want the person in by clicking a tab in the Address Book.
2. Click Add.
3. Click Person to add a person to your list, or click Organization to add a company.
4. Click OK.
5. Fill out the dialog box as completely as you can, then click OK.

Use the Address Book as a Data Source ➤ *pp. 274-275*

1. From a new document window, choose Tools | Merge, then click Create Document.
2. Click Associate an address book.
3. Select which Address Book list you want to use.
4. Click OK.
5. Create and merge your form letter normally.

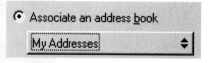

Make Labels from a Data File ➤ *pp. 275-277*

1. Start a form file and associate the data file or data source for which you want labels.
2. In the blank document window, choose Format | Labels.
3. Select the type of labels you're going to print.
4. Click Select.
5. Insert the field names for a single address.
6. Save the form file.
7. Click the Merge bar's Merge button.
8. In the Merge dialog box, click the Merge button.
9. In the Perform Merge dialog box, click the Merge button.

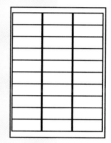

Make Labels with the Address Book ➤ *pp. 277-278*

1. Go to a blank document window.
2. Choose Format | Labels.
3. From the labels list, find and select the type of labels you're going to print.
4. Click Select.
5. Choose Tools | Address Book, then click the tab for the list of names you want to put on labels.
6. Select the addresses you want labels for (press CTRL-A to select all the addresses), then click Insert.

259

Allow me to prove that I'm a master of the obvious by making several related blatant observations: First, it's important to keep your clients informed (duh). Second, you're a busy person, and you certainly don't have time to write each of your clients a separate letter (double duh). And finally, a photocopied letter hardly conveys the message, "we care about you," to your customers.

And now for the not-so-obvious solution: use WordPerfect's Merge feature. By combining a form letter with your list of customers, Merge can create customized letters, envelopes, and mailing labels for each person on your mailing list. Merge is a powerful tool for communicating to a lot of people without seeming *too* impersonal.

A Bird's-Eye View of the Merge Feature

The Merge feature is powerful, but it can also be mind-bogglingly complex. So, before you get down to building form letters, let me explain a little about what this whole process typically involves.

DEFINITION

Data Source: *A list of names and addresses that you combine with your form letter to produce individualized letters.*

1. First, you build the data source. You can type the names and addresses you want to use for a particular form letter, or you can use WordPerfect's Address Book. Creating a data source is a lot of data entry and not much fun, but the good news is that once you've built it, it's not too much work to update it for use with other form letters.

DEFINITION

Form File: *A form letter (or other form-type document) containing special codes that indicate where information—like a name or address—from the data source should go.*

2. Next, you make a form file. This is usually a form letter you want to send to everyone on your mailing list. The form file is just like a regular document, but in place of where you'd usually type information specific to the customer—the name or address, for example—you type in special codes called field names.

3. Finally, you use the Merge feature to combine the data source with the form file. For each person on your mailing list, Merge creates a letter with that person's information in place of the form file's field names. Each letter and its accompanying envelope is separated by a page break. When the merge is finished, you just print the document...then start stuffing envelopes.

Performing the Typical Merge

Well, I don't know if there's actually such a thing as a *typical* merge, but the main steps for merging form letters are usually the same. See "Merge Tips and Tricks" later in this chapter for different ways you can handle making form letters. For now, let's try to keep it as simple and uncluttered as we can, shall we?

Building a Data File

EXPERT ADVICE

While most WordPerfect die-hards build a data source for their merges, I contend that using the Address Book is easier and more useful for most people. For information on using the Address Book, see the "Merge Tips and Tricks" section later in this chapter.

DEFINITION

Field: Any of the types of information you include in a data source. For example, you might have a "First Name" field and a "Last Name" field, not to mention a "Street Address" field, and so forth.

A data file is the most common kind of data source. Essentially, it's a document containing your list of names and addresses.

Creating the Data File

The first thing you do is create the file and specify what type of information—called "fields"—you'll be including about each person. Follow these steps:

1. Choose Tools | Merge.

   This brings up the Merge dialog box—your central command for all things merge-ish.

2. Click Create data, and select the Format records in a table checkbox.

   If you weren't in a new document window when you started this process, a box appears asking whether you want to start in a new document. Select the New document window radio button and choose OK.

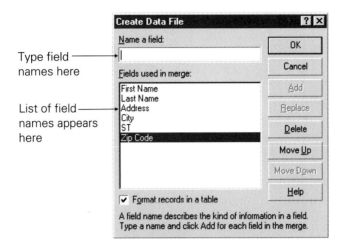

Type field names here

List of field names appears here

If you want to address the recipient of your letter by first name, you need to create separate First Name and Last Name fields.

3. Type a word or phrase that describes the first type of information you want in your list (such as **First Name**), then click the Add button or press ENTER. Repeat this step for all the types of custom information you want to use in the form letter.

EXPERT ADVICE

It's a good idea to add the field names to the list so they're in the order you'll want to type when you're doing data entry. If you need to change the order of items, click on one you want to move, then use the Move Up and Move Down buttons. If you need to edit the name of a field, click it, edit the name in the Name a field box, then click Replace.

4. Click OK.

This brings up the Quick Data Entry dialog box, which means you're ready to start typing in your mailing list information. Woo hoo!

Data Entry for Your Data File

DEFINITION

Record: All the custom information (fields) about one person or organization in your mailing list. One record combines with the form letter to make one customized letter. So if your data file has 500 records, that means 500 people, which means 500 letters...which means a lot of envelope stuffing.

If you need more than one line in a certain field, such as the address, press CTRL-ENTER to make a new line. You'll only be able to see one line at a time, though.

Building your data file isn't *hard*, but there's no way around it: data entry—the process of typing records into your data file—is pretty darn boring. Sorry, but there's nothing I can do about that. Stifle a yawn and follow these steps:

1. Type a person's information, pressing ENTER to move from one field to the next.

   When you press ENTER after the last field in a record, all the fields are cleared and your insertion point goes up to the first field in a new record.

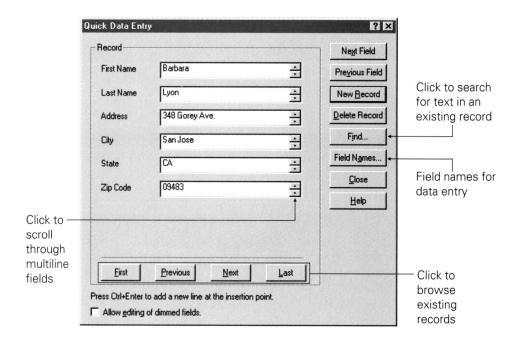

Click to scroll through multiline fields

Click to search for text in an existing record

Field names for data entry

Click to browse existing records

2. Repeat step 1 for each person in your mailing list until you're done—or until you just can't *stand* data entry any longer.

EXPERT ADVICE

You can edit records you've already typed by using the First, Previous, Next, and Last buttons. If you want to search for a certain field, click the Find button, type text that exists in that field, and click Find Next.

3. Click Close, then click Yes to save your work.
4. Name your document as you normally would (WordPerfect will automatically add a .dat extension to the filename, to make it easy to recognize the file as a data file).

You will then be left in your data file, which is shown as a table like the one in Figure 11.1.

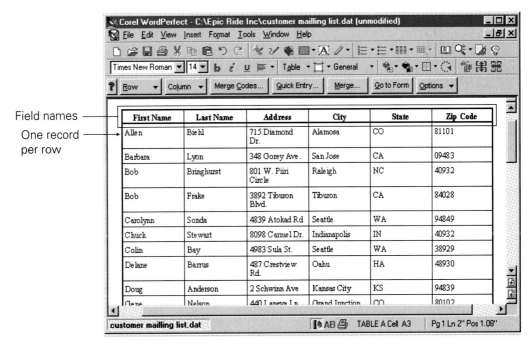

Figure 11.1 The data file is organized as a WordPerfect table. Don't worry if lines are broken in strange places. They'll still merge correctly

5. Close the document.

Building the Form File

Have you (or your kids) ever done Mad Libs? You know, where there's a pre-made story and you fill in the blanks to make it your own? If so, you've already got a pretty good idea how the form file works. If not, you'll catch on quickly anyway.

You see, the form file is a lot like a regular letter. The difference is that wherever you'd normally use a specific person's name or address in the letter, you insert a field name.

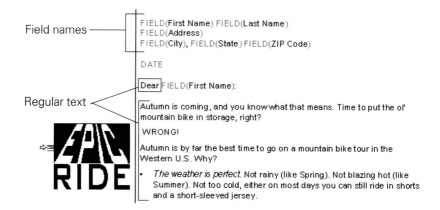

Starting the Form File

You can use any field name you created when you built your data file as a field name in your form file. To start building that form file, perform the following steps:

1. Choose Tools | Merge, then click Create Document.

If you aren't in a new document window, a box appears asking whether you want to start in a new document. Select the New document window radio button and choose OK.

2. Click the Associate a data file radio button in the Associate Form and Data dialog box, then find and double-click your data file document.

Data file name goes here

Click to see list of files

Be sure to name your file and save often. If the power goes out, you don't want to have to go through all this work again!

3. Click OK.

Now you can type and format your letter as you would any document. The only real differences are how you'll insert the date and field names. These two tricks are described next.

Inserting a Date Code in the Form File

You'll probably want the date of the merge to be the date of the letter. Well, that's easy enough.

1. Move your insertion point to where you'll want the date to go.

Date button

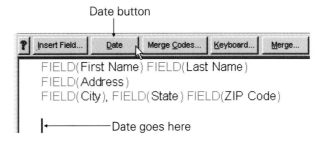

Date goes here

2. Click the Date button (found on the Merge bar).

3. Insert line spaces below the code as you do below a normal date (usually by pressing ENTER a couple of times).

This code will be replaced by the actual date when you combine the form file and the data file.

Adding Field Names in the Form File

You want WordPerfect to put custom information in certain places in your form letter? Those are the places field names go. It's surprisingly painless—just do the following steps:

1. Move the insertion point to where you want custom information (a field name).

CAUTION

If you want the field name to come after a word (such as "Dear"), make sure there's a space in front of your cursor before you insert the field name. Otherwise, the word and your custom information will be run together (like "DearJohn") when you merge.

Insert Field...

2. Click the Insert Field button.

3. Double-click the field name you want to use.

FIELD(First Name) FIELD(Last Name)
FIELD(Address)
FIELD(City), FIELD(State) FIELD(ZIP Code)

Field name

Dialog box remains
onscreen

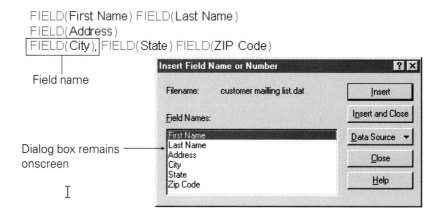

When you've finished making the form file, be sure to save your changes. You can close the document or leave it open if you plan to merge it with the data file right away.

From this point forward as you type your form letter text, any time you need a field name, just move the insertion point to where you want it, click in the dialog box, and double-click the field name you want. If, however, the dialog box gets in your way, drag it out of the way or click its Close button. You can always bring it up again by clicking the Merge bar's Insert Field button.

CAUTION

Field names look a little odd, so it's easy to make mistakes when inserting them. Just remember a couple of things, though, and you can avoid the most common pitfalls. One, if the field name is going in the body of the letter, treat it just as you would a normal word: it should have punctuation or a space after it. And two, it's fine to have field names right next to each other, such as FIELD (FIRST NAME) FIELD (LAST NAME). Just be sure there's a space between the field names.

Merging the Form and Data Files

You'll be glad to know that the bulk of the hard work is over. You're ready to (drum roll, please) Merge. Here's how it's done:

1. Open your form file if it's not already open.

   If it is already open, make sure you've saved your changes.

2. Click the Merge bar's Merge button.

EXPERT ADVICE

If you've included an e-mail field for everyone in your mailing list, you can send your form letter via e-mail. In the Perform Merge dialog box, click the Output pop-up menu and select e-mail. This brings up another dialog box. You'll need to select the field name containing e-mail addresses, then type a Subject line you want used for the e-mail. Click OK. Back at the Perform Merge dialog box, click Merge.

If you'd rather print labels than envelopes, see "Making Labels," later in this chapter.

3. If you don't need envelopes, skip to step 11. Otherwise, click the Envelopes button.

Field names for mailing address go here

Your address goes here

Thumbnail preview of how envelope will look

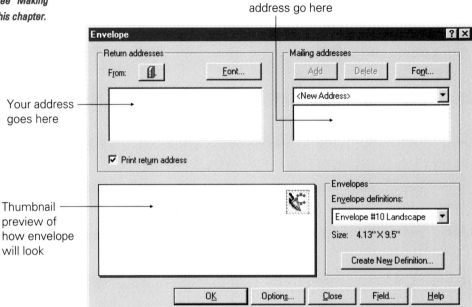

4. Click in the Mailing addresses text box to move your insertion point into that area.

5. Click the Field button to see a list of field names.

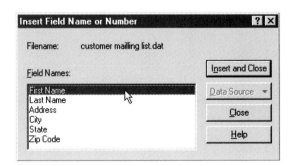

6. Double-click one of the field names to insert it in the Mailing addresses box.

7. Add a space or new line for the next field name.

8. Repeat steps 5-7 for all the field names you need in the mailing address.

Name fields separated by a space

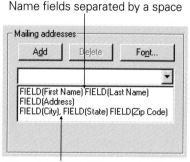

City, state, and ZIP separated by commas and spaces

9. If you're using envelopes with preprinted return addresses, skip to step 10. If you're using blank envelopes, select the Print return address checkbox, then type your address in the Return address box.

EXPERT ADVICE

If you don't want your return address or mailing address to appear in your printer default font, click their respective Font buttons and select different fonts. You have to set the return and mailing address fonts separately.

10. Click OK.

11. In the Perform Merge dialog box, click the Merge button. WordPerfect creates a customized letter for each address in your data file. A page break separates each letter; envelopes are at the bottom of the document and will print last.

12. Check your merged document. If everything looks good, go ahead and print it.

CAUTION

Check your document thoroughly. Merges usually result in a pretty big print job, and it's frustrating to find out—too late—that something went wrong in each of 150 letters. If something is wrong, close the merged document without saving. Fix the problem in the form file (a missing space before or after a field name is my guess), save your changes, then do the merge again.

Merge Tips and Tricks

Merge is one of WordPerfect's most powerful tools, and believe it or not, some of that power is actually *useful*. Go figure. The rest of this chapter shows you how to use the Merge options you're most likely to use.

Using the Address Book

WordPerfect's Address Book is the electronic equivalent of...well...an address book. You can get to it at any time—even when you're not in WordPerfect—so it's an easy-to-use, convenient tool you can use every day to keep track of business acquaintances, friends, vendors, and so forth. In addition, you can use the Address Book as your data source when you need to use the Merge feature.

SHORTCUT

One extremely cool thing about the Address Book is how easy it makes inserting addresses into any document, any time. Just move your insertion point to where you need an address, choose Tools | Address Book, then double-click the address you want to insert into your document.

EXPERT ADVICE

You can get to the Address Book when outside WordPerfect by clicking the Start button, then choosing Corel WordPerfect Suite 8 | Corel Address Book 8.

Create a New Address Book Tab

One of the nice things about the Address Book is that you can have more than one list of people. For example, you might want to have a Personal list, an Internal Company list, and a Business Contacts list. Once you've created these new lists (WordPerfect calls these lists "books," but I think it's too confusing to talk about "books" in the Address Book), you can switch between them easily, just by clicking a tab in the Address Book.

Click to switch to different lists of addresses

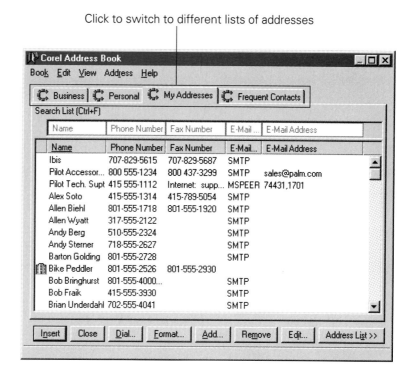

When you use the Address Book as a data source, you can choose which of these lists you want to merge with your form file—so you don't have to worry about all your friends and family getting your latest business letter.

To create a new list in your Address Book, follow these steps:

1. From the Address Book's menu bar, choose Book | New.

2. Type a name for your new list.

3. Click OK.

Adding People to the Address Book

Before the Address Book can do you any good, you need to type names and addresses into it.

EXPERT ADVICE

You can copy names from one list to another. Select the names you want to move (CTRL-click each name you want to select, or press CTRL-A to select all the names in a list), then choose Edit | Copy Names. A dialog box appears asking which list you want to move the names to. Select the one you want, then choose OK.

1. Click a tab in the Address Book to add a person to that list.
2. Click Add.
3. Click Person to add a person to your list, or click Organization to add a company.
4. Click OK.
5. Fill out the dialog box as completely as you can, then click OK.

EXPERT ADVICE

If you're entering several new people at the same time, finish filling out the dialog box, click New, and then click Yes to save your changes and add another person to the list.

Using the Address Book as a Data Source

Once you've started using the Address Book to keep track of your names and addresses, it's an easy step to use the Address Book instead of a data file in your merges. In fact, you can completely skip the process of building the data file, which is nice. After you've created a form file, just follow these steps:

1. Choose Tools | Merge, then click Create Document.

If you weren't in a new document window, a box appears asking whether you want to start in a new document. Select the New document window radio button and choose OK.

2. In the Associate Form and Data dialog box, select the Associate an address book radio button. Then, from the drop-down menu, select which Address Book list you want to use.

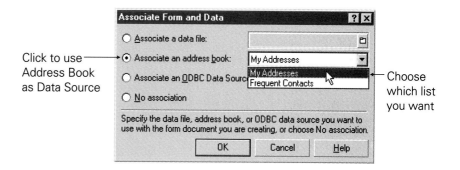

Click to use Address Book as Data Source

Choose which list you want

3. Click OK.

4. Create your form letter, as described in "Building the Form File," earlier in this chapter.

Note that since you followed *these* steps to start the Form File, you should skip the "Starting the Form File" section.

Making Labels

Not everybody wants envelopes to go with their form letters. Maybe you're mailing packages; maybe your printer doesn't handle envelopes very well (my printer, for example, has to be hand-fed envelopes one at a time, which is a total pain). Labels might work out better for you. Just print 'em and stick 'em.

Creating labels is a little different than creating envelopes with the Merge feature. There's no built-in "make labels to go along with my form letters" feature. Instead, if you're using a data file, you'll have to make a separate labels form file and merge the two. Or, if you're using the Address Book, you can make labels for your mailing list in just a few steps, without using Merge at all.

Making Labels with Merge

If you've got a data file and need mailing labels made for it, just follow these steps:

1. Follow all the steps from "Starting the Form File," earlier in this chapter.
2. In the blank document window, choose Format | Labels.
3. From the Labels list, find and select the type of labels you're going to print.

   The label numbers correspond to the numbers printed on most standard label packages.
4. Click Select.

CAUTION

If your font is 12 points or larger, some addresses may spill over onto a second label. It's a good idea to set a 10-point font right after you choose your label type.

5. Insert the field names for a single address (see "Adding Field Names in the Form File," earlier in this chapter), as shown in Figure 11.2.
6. Save the form file.
7. Click the Merge bar's Merge button.
8. In the Perform Merge dialog box, click the Merge button.

CAUTION

Check your labels carefully before printing—labels are expensive! If you notice that some addresses are spilling over onto a second label, close the merged document. Back in the form file, go to the top of the document and try setting a smaller font—maybe 10-point or even 9-point—then merge again.

EXPERT ADVICE

It's a good idea to print a single sheet of labels before printing the whole merged batch. That way you can make sure the addresses are lining up properly on the labels.

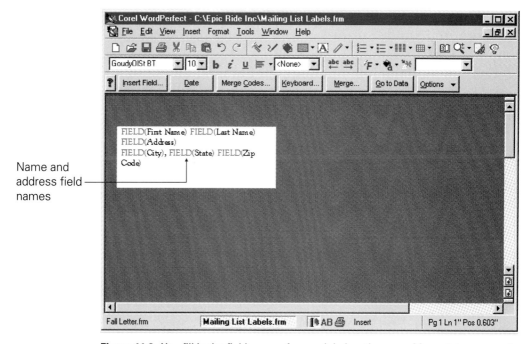

Name and address field names

FIELD(First Name) FIELD(Last Name)
FIELD(Address)
FIELD(City), FIELD(State) FIELD(Zip Code)

Figure 11.2 You fill in the field names for one label on the page; Merge takes care of the rest

Making Labels with the Address Book

You can make a batch of labels from the names in your Address Book in less than two minutes. Don't believe me? Start your stopwatch and follow along:

1. Click the New Document window to go to a blank document window.
2. Choose Format | Labels.

3. From the Labels list, find and select the type of labels you're going to print.
4. The label numbers correspond to the numbers printed on most standard label packages.
5. Click Select.

CAUTION

If your font is 12 points or larger, some addresses may spill over onto a second label. It's a good idea to set a 10-point font right after you choose your label type.

6. Choose Tools | Address Book, then click the tab for the list of names you want to put on labels.
7. Select the names you want labels for by holding down the CTRL key while you click them, or press CTRL-A to select all the names in the list.
8. Click Insert.

Your addresses appear on labels. (I clocked in at one minute, ten seconds. How'd you do?)

Making Web Pages with WordPerfect

FAST FORWARD

Build or Convert a Web Document ➤ pp. 283-285

1. Open a document or go to a blank document window.
2. Click the Change View icon.
3. If you get the "This document will be formatted as a Web document ..." message, click OK.
4. Write, edit, and format the document.

Preview Web Documents ➤ p. 286

1. Click the View in Web Browser icon.
2. View document in Web browser, noting any changes to make to the document.
3. Close Web browser and edit the document in WordPerfect.

Publish an HTML Version of Your Document ➤ pp. 286-287

1. Click the Toolbar's Publish to HTML icon.
2. Type a path and filename for your document.
3. Click OK.
4. Close the document normally.

Set the Document Title ➤ p. 289

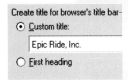

1. Click the HTML Document Properties button on the Internet Publisher Property Bar.
2. Click the Title tab.
3. Select the Custom title radio button.
4. Type your title.
5. Click OK.

Change Text and Background Colors ➤ *p. 289*

1. Click the Text/Background Colors tab.
2. Choose colors from palettes.
3. Click OK.

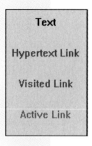

Create Links ➤ *p. 290*

1. Type the link text.
2. Select the link text.
3. Click the Toolbar's Hyperlink drop-down menu, then click Create Link.
4. If necessary, select the text in the Document: text box.
5. Type the URL you want to link to.
6. Click OK.

Set Headings ➤ *p. 291*

1. Move to where you want the heading.
2. Click the Toolbar's Font/Size drop-down menu, then click one of the headings.
3. If you haven't typed the heading, type it now.

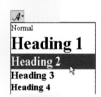

Change Font Attributes ➤ *pp. 291-292*

1. Move your insertion point to where you want the attribute to begin, or select the existing text to which you want to apply the attribute.
2. Click the Toolbar's Font Attributes drop-down menu.
3. Click the checkbox for any of the attributes you want.

Place a Graphic ➤ pp. 293-294

globe01.wpg

1. Move to where you want the graphic—by a character or paragraph.
2. Click the Toolbar's Image button.
3. In the Scrapbook, find the image you want, click it and drag it into the document window.
4. Close the Scrapbook.

Anchor a Graphic to a Paragraph ➤ p. 294

1. Right-click the graphic and choose Position.
2. From the Attach box to drop-down list, choose Paragraph.
3. From the Horizontal drop-down list, choose Left Margin, Right Margin, or Center of Paragraph.
4. Click OK, then click outside the graphic.

Create Barista-Format Documents ➤ pp. 299-300

1. Create, edit, and format a document as you normally would.
2. With the document open, choose File | Send to | Corel Barista.
3. Select either Send all pages in a single file or Send each page in a separate file.
4. **If you're sending all pages in a single file:** In the Folder and filename text box, set a location and filename for the Barista file. Be sure the filename ends with an .htm or .html extension.

   or

   If you're sending each page as a separate file: In the Folder only text box, type a new folder name where you want the files to be put.
5. Click Send.
6. Upload the resulting file or the contents of the directory you created to the location on the Web server where your Barista Java Class files are located.

The World Wide Web has brought mass communications to the masses. Armed with nothing but a computer, a phone line, and an Internet service provider, you can place anything you can think of—who your company is, what you do, what you have to sell—on the Internet. In this chapter, you'll learn how you can use WordPerfect to build documents for this exciting medium without using a shred of that arcane HTML language.

You'll be able to create traditional Web pages or use Corel's Java-based *Barista* publishing system to make Web documents that retain all their graphics and formatting with no more difficulty than if you had just printed a document on paper.

By necessity, this chapter will cover only the tip of WordPerfect's iceberg full of Internet capabilities. The fact is, the Corel WordPerfect 8 Suite has enough Internet tools to fill an entire book. And indeed, Osborne/McGraw-Hill has just such a book, *Web Publishing with Corel WordPerfect Suite,* by Jeff Hadfield (Osborne/McGraw-Hill, 1997). If you really want to learn more about using the WordPerfect suites to create Web documents and take advantage of the information on the Net, pick up a copy of this book.

Building Web Documents

Corel has made a big deal over WordPerfect's Internet Publishing capabilities, and justly so. Using "Internet Publisher," a catch-all term Corel uses for all of WordPerfect's Web-publishing tools, you'll have a fairly easy time creating Web pages from scratch or taking documents you've already created in WordPerfect and moving them over to the Web.

Turning on the Internet Publisher

You use WordPerfect's Internet Publisher to format documents for use on the Web. And turning on the Internet Publisher is as easy as the click of a button. Just follow these steps:

1. Open the document as you normally would.

CAUTION

When you create or convert Web documents, you'll discover that a number of formatting features disappear. Some of the most obvious are page numbering, margins, headers and footers, fonts, drop caps, paragraph and page borders and fills, watermarks, and vertical lines. As you can see, Web publishing has a ways to go before it can completely replace paper. If you really need to keep your formatting intact, see "Internet Publishing with Corel Barista," later in this chapter.

If you're creating a Web document from scratch, just go to a blank document window.

2. Click the Toolbar's Change View—switch between Web and page view icon.

3. If you get the "This document will be formatted as a Web document ..." message, click OK.

EXPERT ADVICE

This dialog box explains what I was just saying a moment ago—not every WordPerfect feature is available on the Web, so if you've got a highly formatted document and switch to the Web page view, some of that formatting is going to get lost—and it won't come back even if you switch back to the normal WordPerfect view. You can avoid getting this message box in the future by clicking the Do not show me this message next time I choose Web View checkbox.

4. Write, edit, and format the document, making any changes you like.

CAUTION

Formatting the document for the Web isn't the last step you need to take to use a document on the Internet. You also need to publish the document for use on the Web—that is, convert it into HTML format. See "Publish Your Document to HTML," later in this chapter, for information on how to do this.

If you're using the PerfectExpert, you can also click its View in Browser button.

Previewing Web Documents

WordPerfect ain't no Web browser, so the fact that your Web document looks good in WordPerfect doesn't mean that it's going to look good to people viewing it on the Internet. You need to check out your document in your Web browser to see how it will *really* look on the World Wide Web.

To preview your document, just click the Toolbar's View in Web Browser button.

EXPERT ADVICE

If you don't have a Web browser on your computer, this, of course, won't work. You're not out of luck, though. The Corel WordPerfect 8 Suite CD-ROM comes with Netscape Navigator 3.01—a popular Web browser.

Your browser pops up, showing how your document will look on the Web.

If you notice changes that need to be made, close the browser, go back to WordPerfect and make any modifications you want, then click the View in Web Browser button again.

Publish Your Document to HTML

When you're ready for the whole world (World Wide Web, that is) to see your work, it's time to publish your document to HTML. To do this, follow these steps:

1. Click the Toolbar's Publish to HTML button.

If you're using the PerfectExpert, you can also click its Publish to HTML button.

Publish to HTML	? X
Publish to:	OK
c:\webpages\springtrip.html	Cancel
Save new images and sound clips in:	Help
c:\webpages\	
Location of graphics on Web Server (optional):	

2. In the Publish to: text box, type a path and filename for your
   document, such as **c:\Webpages\springtrip.html**.

CAUTION

*It's important that you use an .htm or .html extension, since that's how many
Internet servers (as well as Windows 95's own Explorer) recognize Web
documents. Be sure to use one of these extensions even if you normally
don't use extensions with your documents.*

3. If you have graphics in the Web page you're creating, specify the
   directory where you want to store those graphics in the Save new
   images and sound clips in: text box. Or, if the graphics already exist on
   the Web server, type their location in the Location of graphics on Web
   Server text box.
4. Click OK.

CAUTION

*Note that you now have two copies of your document. First, there's your
WordPerfect version, which has the name you see in the title bar. Second,
there's the HTML version, which you just created when you "published" to
HTML. So, if you want to make changes, which copy do you work on? The
WordPerfect version. Then, after you make changes, publish to HTML
again, overwriting the old HTML version.*

5. Close the document normally.

EXPERT ADVICE

*When you send your files to the Internet, be sure to send the HTML file you
just published and the graphics associated with the HTML file. Otherwise,
your graphics won't appear on the Web page.*

Web Formatting Features

I've already said that working on a Web document is a lot like working on any WordPerfect document. Well, I was *mostly* telling the truth. The fact is, there are a few new formatting tricks you need to know when you're using WordPerfect to create Web documents.

EXPERT ADVICE

Your Web documents are really just WordPerfect files and should be saved as WordPerfect documents, not as HTML. (WordPerfect creates the HTML-format version when you use the "Publish to HTML" feature.) Be sure to save often!

Web Formatting Essentials

Many things you never have to think about with regular documents—the background color or the name of the document—are important formatting tools when you're working on a Web document. Web browsers show the document's title in the program's title bar, so your readers have an easy way of finding the contents of the current document.

The Step-By-Step instructions on the next page show how to set these important Web document elements.

EXPERT ADVICE

If someone adds your document to a bookmark list, it's your document's title which appears on that list, so be sure to use a title that will remind people what's in the document.

Working with Hypertext Links

If you've spent any time browsing the Web (and if you haven't, you probably should before you begin creating documents for the Web—otherwise it's like trying to speak Spanish before you've ever heard it), you've no doubt noticed that

STEP BY STEP   Changing Colors and the Document Title

① **Choose Format | Text/Background Colors.**

④ **Click here, then type document title.**

② **Click to see color palette.**

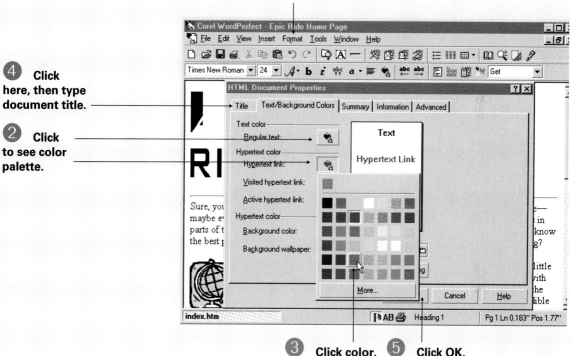

③ **Click color.**   **⑤** **Click OK.**

practically *every* Web page has links—they're what make the World Wide Web so convenient and powerful to use.

The most common type of link is clickable text (usually blue and underlined) that takes you to a different document on the Web.

EXPERT ADVICE

By default, documents on the Web have a boring, light gray background. Your readers will appreciate a white background, which provides maximum contrast to the text.

Creating Hypertext Links

It's not too difficult to create links in your own documents. Just follow these steps:

1. Type the text you want people to click, then select that text.

<u>Tours Coming Soon</u> No matter what the time of year, we've always got some incredible rides lined up. Check the calendar to see where we'll be going within the next couple of months.

What's an Epic Ride Tour Like? If you're not sure you're the touring type, browse through this virtual tour, complete with photos, quotes from our customers, and an itinerary of a typical tour.

2. Click the Toolbar's Hyperlink icon, then click Create Link.
3. If necessary, select any text in the Document: text box (<current document> should already be selected) and type the Web page address (often called a "URL") to which you want to link.

EXPERT ADVICE

Sometimes you won't be sure what the URL is. In that case, click the Browse Web button to start your Web browser, find the document to which you want to link, and close the browser.

4. Click OK.

Editing Hypertext Links

Ordinarily, after you've created a link, WordPerfect makes it "active"—that is, if you click your mouse pointer in a word that's part of a link, WordPerfect tries to launch your Web browser and go to that link. If you want to edit the text of the link or where that link points to, you need to deactivate hypertext links in WordPerfect. Here's how:

1. Choose Tools | Hyperlink to bring up the Hyperlink Properties dialog box.
2. Deselect the Activate Hyperlinks checkbox.
3. Choose OK.

With that out of the way, you can now click in that blue, underlined text and edit away.

But what if you want to change where the link points to? First, click in the link text. This makes the Hyperlink Property bar appear. Next, click the Hyperlink edit icon to bring up the Hyperlink Properties dialog box. In the Document text box, change the location to which you want the link to point, and click OK.

Finally, if you want to make hypertext links active so that clicking them opens up your Web browser and takes you to that link, choose Tools | Hyperlink, select the Activate Hyperlinks checkbox, and choose OK.

Fonts and Headings

Usually, WordPerfect gives you almost unlimited control over how your text looks in a document. When you're working on Web documents, though, practically all that power is stripped—the HTML format is pretty restrictive on how fonts and headings ought to look. You have to choose between a few preset heading styles. And although you *can* choose a font, it's a bad idea to do so, because unless the person reading your document *also* has that font, it won't show up as you intended it on the browser. Sheesh.

Setting Headings

Web pages are generally highly structured, with lots of levels of headings. Why? To compensate for the lack of control you have over design, I suppose. To create a heading for a section, follow these steps:

1. Move your insertion point to where you want the heading.

   It can be a blank line or a line where you've already typed the heading.

2. Click the Toolbar's Font/Size drop-down menu, then click one of the heading styles.

3. If you haven't typed the heading, type it now.

Changing Font Attributes

I'd love to be able to title this section, "Changing Fonts," but that would be misleading. You can control your text *size* and *attributes* like bold, italic, and so forth, but you don't have reliable control over the font itself. Hey, don't blame

WordPerfect—if it let you change fonts, the changes wouldn't show up on other people's browsers, anyway.

SHORTCUT

As usual, you can press CTRL-B for bold and CTRL-I for italics or press their buttons on the Toolbar.

To type text with a size or emphasis attribute, follow these steps:

1. Move your insertion point to where you want the attribute to begin.
2. Click the Toolbar's Font Attributes drop-down menu.
3. Click the checkbox for any of the attributes you want.

    Note that after you click a checkbox, the menu snaps shut, so if you want to select more than one attribute, you'll have to pull down the menu more than once.

    Unless you were working with selected text, after you're finished typing, bring up the menu again and click the Normal checkbox to turn off all attributes.

You can also select text and apply attributes.

EXPERT ADVICE

If you do want to try changing the font itself, choose Format | Font, or click the PerfectExpert's Change Font Attributes button. This brings you to the Font dialog box, where you can change the font face, attributes (bold, italic, monospaced, and blink), size, and styles (such as headers, bulleted and numbered lists, definition lists, and so forth). You can even change the font size. Bear in mind, though, that the font change will only work on your audience's browsers if they have the same font—so you're best off selecting very common fonts, like Times New Roman, Helvetica (or Arial), and Courier.

See Chapter 9 for more information about using graphics in documents.

Placing Graphics

Graphics are an important part of Web documents. Like text, however, you're more restricted with your use of graphics in Web documents than in other WordPerfect files.

First, you can't use the "Drag to Create" method of placing graphics. Instead, follow these steps:

1. Move the insertion point to where you want the graphic to go—next to a character or paragraph.
2. Click the Toolbar's Image button.
3. Browse through the Scrapbook until you've found the image you want.
4. Click the image and drag it into the document window.
5. Close the Scrapbook.
6. Click the Toolbar's Paste icon to insert the graphic into the document.

SHORTCUT

You can skip steps 4-6 by clicking the graphic you want and dragging it into your document window.

Other options you have when using graphics:

• Normally, a graphic is treated as a character. That is, if you type text in front of it, the graphic moves to the right.

Character-based graphic flows with text

If you're interested in some of the "epic" trails in around the globe, but are a little nervous about the travel arrangements and logistics, you're ready for a tour with Epic Ride, Inc. We'll tell you how to prepare yourself. We'll take care of all the food, travel, and gear arrangements. Then we'll guide you on the most incredible ride of your life.

- You can also have graphics set at the left or right side of a paragraph, or centered. Right-click the graphic and choose Position from the QuickMenu. In the Attach box to drop-down list, choose Paragraph. From the Horizontal drop-down list, you can now choose Left Margin, Right Margin, or Center of Paragraph—whichever you prefer. Click OK. When back in the document, click outside the graphic to deselect it.

Text flows around paragraph-based graphics

If you're interested in some of the "epic" trails in around the globe, but are a little nervous about the travel arrangements and logistics, you're ready for a tour with Epic Ride, Inc. We'll tell you how to prepare yourself. We'll take care of all the food, travel, and gear arrangements. Then we'll guide you on the most incredible ride of your life.

- It's a good idea to provide "alternate text"—a description of your graphic— for browsers that don't support graphics or have graphic display turned off. Click the graphic, then click the Property Bar's Box HTML properties icon. In the Alternate text box, describe the graphic (be brief), then choose OK.
- Often, people use graphics as links to other Web pages. To do this in WordPerfect, first create the graphic and place it where you want. Next, click the graphic, then click the Property Bar's Box HTML properties icon. Under Define mouse click action, select Link. Now, at the top of the dialog box, click the Link tab and type where the link ought to lead in the Document/URL text box. Click OK.

Internet Publishing with Corel Barista

Even with the help WordPerfect gives you, creating a nice-looking HTML-format document can be a chore. Why? HTML was originally designed to be a very basic, text-and-simple-graphics-only format. Even now, it still has limitations that frustrate those of us used to being able to put text and graphics anywhere we want.

Corel has come up with an interesting solution, called "Barista." The idea behind Barista is that you create your WordPerfect document the way you normally would, in a regular document window. Use all the formatting and graphics you want, placing them wherever you want. Then, when you want to put that document on the Internet, you use Barista to convert the document into a file that gets read by a Java program, with the end result being that Web browsers show your document just as you created it, as shown in Figure 12.1.

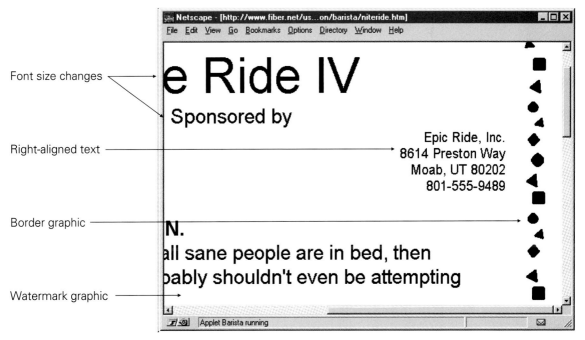

Figure 12.1 Web documents published by Barista retain graphics, formatting, and font size. Note that the fonts themselves are not retained

Barista Pros and Cons

When people see how easy it is to use Barista to create fully-formatted Web documents, they sometimes want to jump right in and use it for everything. I don't want to discourage you, but there are some good reasons to use Barista in some situations, and some equally good reasons *not* to use Barista for everything. Consider some of these facts before you decide whether (or when) Barista documents belong on your Web site.

- **Pro**: Barista is easy. Once you've set up your Web site to use Barista documents, creating new documents for your Web site is practically as easy as printing on a piece of paper.

- **Con**: Barista is big, and big is slow. In addition to the documents they view, your readers will need to download the accompanying Java applets. For many people, the wait just isn't worth it.

- **Pro**: Barista looks great. People just don't expect to see documents so fully, effortlessly formatted on the Web.

- **Con**: Barista documents don't show up on all browsers. As explained earlier, Barista documents use Java applets to show off all that formatting. The problem is, not all Web browsers support Java. People using Mosaic, for example, or an early version of *any* browser, won't be able to see your documents.

- **Pro**: Barista doesn't require reformatting. If you've created a document that relies on formatting to deliver its message (a flyer, or brochure, maybe a newsletter), it can be very disappointing to have all that formatting get changed and mangled when you try to convert the document into HTML. If you publish it to Barista, you don't have that problem.

- **Con**: Barista has some important limitations.

  1. Barista documents you create must be in the same directory as the Barista applets you upload. If you want your documents to be in a hierarchy of directories—not just in a single folder—be aware that Barista won't work with that type of structure.
  2. Barista documents can't easily be saved or printed from the browser. If you want people to be able to reuse the documents you put on the Web, Barista is not a good choice.
  3. Barista documents don't retain their fonts. Everything gets converted to Times Roman, Arial, or Courier.

In short, the best time to use Barista to create documents for the Web is when formatting is an important part of the document and when you're confident your readers have fast connections and up-to-date browsers.

Setting Your Web Site Up to Use Barista

You can't just create Web pages with Barista and then put them up on your Web site. If you do, nobody will be able to view them. First, you need to copy a large batch of files and directories from your Corel WordPerfect 8 Suite CD-ROM up to your Web site.

CAUTION

There are a number of different ways of copying files and folders to a Web site, so I'm afraid I won't be able to be too specific in some of the following steps. If you don't know how to copy files and directories to your Web server, you should talk with your Internet service provider, Webmaster, or Intranet manager for information on how this is done and what tools (such as WS_FTP Limited Edition) they have available to help.

Follow these steps to copy these Barista Java class files up to your Web site:

CAUTION

In order to be able to copy these files and directories properly, your Internet/Intranet server must support long file names (i.e., be able to have more than eight characters for filenames and more than three characters for filename extensions). You must also have rights to create directories on the server.

WS_FTP is a well-known, easy-to-use, Windows-based file transfer program— and the Limited Edition is freeware to private parties! Download a copy at http://www.ipswitch.com/ index.html

1. While holding down the SHIFT key, place your Corel WordPerfect 8 Suite CD-ROM in the CD-ROM drive. Hold down the SHIFT key at least ten seconds—until there is no further activity on your CD-ROM drive.

   Holding down the SHIFT key prevents the Setup program from running. If the Setup screen appears anyway (sometimes it's easy to think you've held down the key long enough, and it turns out you haven't), click the Close button at the bottom-right corner of the screen.

2. Log in to your Internet Service Provider, if you use one.

3. Start the tool or application you use to transfer files to your Web site (such as WS_FTP).

4. Using this tool, browse the CD to the following folder: \Corel\Suite8\Shared\Barista.

5. Select all the files and subfolders in the Barista folder.

6. Copy these files and folders (some of which contain subfolders of their own) to the directory on your Internet/Intranet server in which you plan to put your Barista documents.

CAUTION

Remember, Barista documents will only work from the single directory in which you copy the Barista class files.

7. You can now exit the file transfer tool and log out of the Internet server.

Creating Barista Documents

Once you've got the Barista Java class files up on your Internet server, you're over the hump. Creating Barista files from your WordPerfect documents is a snap. Just follow these steps:

EXPERT ADVICE

You can also create Barista documents from Presentations and Quattro Pro, not to mention Corel Ventura. The steps are very similar to the steps shown in this section.

1. Create, edit, and format a WordPerfect 8 document as you normally would.

CAUTION

There are a couple of caveats to look out for. If you're using numerous fonts, bear in mind that people who view your document will only see Arial, Times Roman, and Courier. Also, Barista documents don't handle curly quotes, apostrophes, or other non-standard characters very well.

2. Save your document, updating any changes.
3. With the document open, choose File | Send to | Corel Barista.
   You now have the option of making the entire document a single file, or of making each page in the document a separate file. The "single file" approach is easier to post on the Web server; the "separate files" approach doesn't demand as much time up front from people viewing the document on their browsers.
4. Select either Send all pages in a single file or Send each page in a separate file.

5. Depending on what you chose in step 4, do one of the following:

- **If you're sending all pages in a single file:** In the Folder and filename text box, set a location and filename for the Barista file. Be sure the document filename ends with an .htm or .html extension so that it will be treated as a Web document by your server. (If the document you're sending to Barista already has a filename, that same path and filename, with an .htm extension, will be used by default.) Click Send.

- **If you're sending each page as a separate file:** In the Folder only text box, set a folder where you want the files to be put. You should type a new folder name for this batch of Barista files, to make it easier to know what files to upload later (that folder doesn't need to exist; when you click Send, WordPerfect will ask if you want to create the folder). Click Send.

After the Barista files have been created, a message box appears letting you know they're ready to be uploaded. Click OK.

You can now log back on to your Internet server and upload your Barista document. If you created all the pages as a single file, you just need to upload the file you specified earlier in the Folder and filename textbox. If you created each page as a separate file, you'll need to upload the file and subfolder that appear in the folder you named in the Folder only text box.

Be *certain* that when you upload the Barista files, they go into the exact same directory as the one where you put the Barista Java class files, as described in "Setting Your Web Site Up to Use Barista," earlier in this chapter.

Special Tools for Law Offices

INCLUDES

- Tables of Authorities

- Paragraph numbering

- Outlines

- Cross-Referencing

- Legal templates

- Comparing different versions of the same document

WordPerfect is far and away the leading word processor in the legal market, and it's no wonder. The program is full of features designed for lawyers. Let's take a look at some of the most useful tools.

Bring Up the Legal Toolbar

Before we get started, you should have the Legal Toolbar up and running. Why? Because many of the features discussed in this appendix are available with a click of the mouse from the Legal Toolbar. To bring up this Toolbar, right-click on the Toolbar and choose Legal from the QuickMenu that appears.

Normal Toolbar

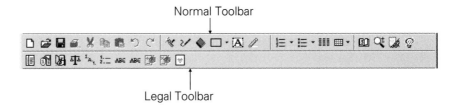

Legal Toolbar

If, at any time, you want to turn off the Legal Toolbar, right-click over the regular or Legal toolbar. From the QuickMenu that appears, click Legal to deselect it.

Tables of Authorities

Remember writing appellate briefs in the days before word processors? Once you *finally* completed all of the rewrites and editing and changes, you had to read through the brief *again*, find all the citations, note the page numbers, note every page where the citations were discussed, alphabetize the list, and type it manually—and heaven help you if you decided to change the brief after the list was finished! All the page numbers had to be rechecked and updated manually.

How many offices still work this way? If yours does, you need to discover the Table of Authorities feature of WordPerfect. This feature will help you maintain a listing of all of the cases, statutes, rules, or other authorities you cite in your briefs, and it can automatically generate an accurate listing of where each authority is cited in the brief at the click of a button.

Table of Authorities Terms

The quickest way to learn to use the Table of Authorities is to understand some of the terms it uses. Let's define them:

- **Table of Authorities Definition**. (Yes, we have to define the "definition" since it isn't what you might think it is!) This refers to a special code that marks the location on a special page where the program will insert one section of the final Table of Authorities. Note that you will need a separate Table of Authorities Definition for each type of authority you want to list!
- **Section**. A group of citations of the same kind. You may have sections for Constitutional citations, case citations, statutory citations, rules and regulations, etc.
- **Full Form**. The full name of the case, statute, or other authority, as it will appear in the final Table of Authorities.
- **Short Form**. This is a shorthand "code" assigned to each case, statute, or other authority. You use these to mark every spot in your brief where the authority is discussed, so that every page will appear in the final Table.
- **Generate**. WordPerfect reads your brief, gathers up all of the citations and the page references, and puts everything in its proper section. This is called "generating" the Table of Authorities.

Defining a Table of Authorities

The first step in creating your Table of Authorities is to "define" it, which is not as easy as it may seem at first. Here's what to do:

1. Put the insertion point at the spot in your document where you want the Table of Authorities to appear.

2. Display the Table of Authorities Feature Bar by clicking the Legal Toolbar's Table of Authorities icon.

3. Insert a new page by choosing Insert | New Page (or pressing CTRL-ENTER) to ensure that the Table starts on its own page.
4. Type **Table of Authorities** at the top of the page, formatted in the way you want this to appear.
5. Move down a line or two and type in the name of the first section of your table (for example, **Constitutional References**), formatted according to your preferences.
6. Move down another line and click the Table of Authorities Feature Bar's Define button.
7. In the Define Table of Authorities dialog box, click Create.
8. Type in the name of the section you are creating in the Name box and click OK.
9. Repeat steps 5–8 for each section you need to set up.
10. End the Table of Authorities with another new page, by choosing Insert | New Page or pressing CTRL-ENTER.

Marking the Authorities

Now that you've told WordPerfect *where* to put the Table of Authorities, you need to tell it *what* to put in the Table. You do this by marking two things: the *full form* of the citation (usually the first place in the brief where the authority is cited) and any subsequent places (if any) in the brief where you discuss that authority.

To mark the full form citations, follow these steps:

1. Find and select the citation in your brief that you want to include in the Table.
2. Click the Table of Authorities Feature Bar's Create Full Form button.

3. In the Create Full Form dialog box, choose the appropriate Section from the drop-down list (the list will include all of the sections you defined earlier).

4. In the Short Form entry field, you can either accept the default short name (there is nothing short about it though—it's the first 40 or so characters of what you selected!) or type in your own shorthand name for this citation.

5. Click OK.

6. You are now taken to a special document window, where your selected text appears. You can edit the case name or citation here (i.e., correct any typographical errors, delete "pinpoint citations" to specific pages, etc.). Remember that whatever appears in this window is exactly how the case citation will finally appear in your Table of Authorities.

7. Click Close to insert a [ToA:Full Form] code into your document. (You can see this code in Reveal Codes; be careful not to delete it, since this is the mark that the Generate feature will look for in order to create the final Table.)

8. Repeat steps 1–7 for each new citation you want to include.

Adding Additional References

Once you have marked all of the full form citations, you can go back and mark additional references in your brief to any of the authorities you've identified. Just follow these steps:

1. Find the additional reference in the brief that you want to make note of in your final Table of Authorities and place the insertion point just in front of it.

2. In the Table of Authorities Feature Bar, find the correct Short Form marker on the drop-down list at the left edge of the bar.

3. With the correct marker displayed as the Short Form, just click Mark on the Table of Authorities Feature Bar.

That's it! A [ToA] short form code is placed at the insertion point. Repeat these steps for every reference you want to include in your Table of Authorities.

Generating the Table of Authorities

With WordPerfect, this step, which is the hardest part to do manually, is now the easiest. Just click the Table of Authorities Feature Bar's Generate button, then click OK in the Generate dialog box, and the Table of Authorities will appear, finished and ready to print.

Cross-Referencing and Paragraph Numbering

Lawyers are forever cross-referencing their documents. Wills, contracts, and other documents need to be internally consistent, and cross-references from one paragraph to another within a legal document help achieve this.

However, it can be a nightmare to keep all the paragraph numbers and cross-references straight when documents go through many drafts, cspccially contracts which may be negotiated and passed back and forth between different parties many times before the final version is settled on. How many hours have you wasted rereading a final contract to be sure that all of the cross-references are correct?

WordPerfect includes a wonderful Cross-Reference feature that can do all of this for you automatically and save you hours of time in the preparation of any complex contract. But before you can use this feature, you must also learn to use automatic paragraph numbers, since the Cross-Reference feature will look for those codes in order to display the correct number. Automatic paragraph numbers have many uses even aside from the Cross-Reference feature, though. And we'll also take a little frolic and detour through the Outline feature before finishing up our study of the Cross-Reference feature.

This feature is described in more detail in Chapter 10 in the "Numbered and Bulleted Lists" section.

Automatic Paragraph Numbers

The basic Paragraph Number feature is very simple.

1. Move your insertion point to the line where you want the paragraph number.
2. Click the Toolbar's Numbering palette, and choose the Paragraph Numbering option.

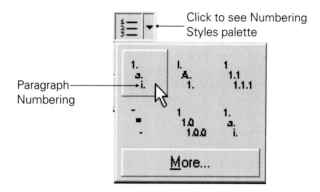

Just for practice, type some text after the number you just inserted and press ENTER. Another paragraph number appears, this time incremented up to 2.

To complete the exercise, go back and delete the first number. Notice that the second paragraph number changes from a 2 to a 1; all other codes below it would adjust themselves too, if they were there. You can see how this will help you immensely in keeping paragraphs of pleadings or other lists in sequential order as you edit and revise your documents.

This simple little feature actually has a lot of power lying under the hood. Try this: insert a paragraph number, then press the TAB key. The number turns into the letter "a"! What is going on here?

Paragraph numbers, like some other features, have "levels." You can go eight levels deep using automatic paragraph numbers, like this:

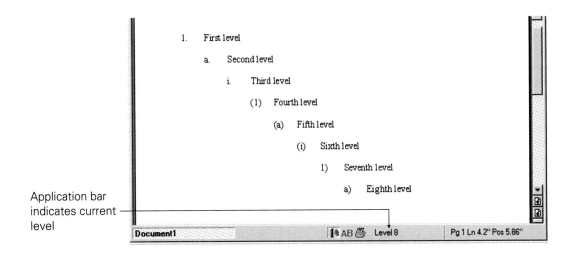

Application bar indicates current level

Each level of numbering is subordinate to all higher levels. That is, after you insert paragraphs "a" through "g" as Level 2 paragraphs under a Level 1 paragraph number, the next set of Level 2 numbers will start over beginning with "a."

To move back up a level, after inserting a Paragraph Number just press SHIFT-TAB.

EXPERT ADVICE

If you want a regular tab to follow a Paragraph Number, just press CTRL-TAB to insert it.

Using Outlines

Many lawyers may think of "outlines" as something they learned in grade school, and they don't apply them to standard legal drafting. But the WordPerfect Outline feature is a very powerful tool that can make drafting complex documents a breeze...and it will also enable you to use the Cross-Reference feature (we still haven't lost sight of the goal line here).

Turn on the Outline Feature by clicking the Legal Toolbar's Outline icon.

WordPerfect defaults to Paragraph numbers as the style of the Outline, which may be what you want if you are drafting a court pleading or some other sort of document with numbered paragraphs. But if you want a different style of numbering, you can easily switch to another option, such as Legal or Legal 2; both are excellent choices for contracts, agreements, and similar documents. To switch to a different numbering style, click the drop-down arrow by the Toolbar's Numbering icon, then click the numbering style you want.

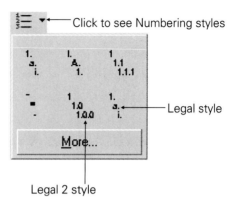

Click to see Numbering styles

Legal style

Legal 2 style

EXPERT ADVICE

The Paragraph style outline defaults to putting the first level paragraph number at the left margin. If you want it indented, you can just edit the style associated with that level. The easiest way to do this is to turn on Reveal Codes by pressing ALT-F3, double-click the Style code that appears at the beginning of your paragraph, and insert an indent by pressing F7 immediately before the Paragraph Number code in the Styles Editor. You may also wish to delete the left indent after the paragraph number and replace it with spaces or tabs to "finish" the look of your paragraphs. Click OK when you're finished, and press ALT-F3 to turn Reveal Codes off again.

As long as you are in Outline mode, pressing ENTER will bring up the next paragraph number. You can also move down a level in your outline by pressing TAB immediately after a paragraph number; you can move back up a level by pressing SHIFT-TAB.

When you're ready to turn off outlining, just backspace over a line number and keep typing.

Cross-References

If you have used the Paragraph Numbering or Outline features to create your document, you will now be able to use one of the most powerful features of WordPerfect for law offices: Cross-Reference.

The Cross-Reference feature works by inserting two codes into your document called the *target* and the *reference* codes. Pay attention here, because lots of people get these two codes mixed up. You put the target code at the location of the material you want to refer back to, and you put the reference code at the place where you make reference to the other material. Think of the target as the bulls-eye at an archery range; where you are standing is the point of reference, and the target is what you point your arrow at.

One nice thing about the Cross-Reference feature is that you can make multiple references to the same target. Thus, if you want to refer to the powers and duties of a fiduciary at several places in a trust instrument, you can just put one target code at the beginning of the section dealing with this topic and put as many references to that target as you need to throughout the rest of the document.

Let's do a simple Cross-Reference to see how this works in practice. Open up (or create) any document that uses Automatic Paragraph Numbers or the Outline feature, then follow these steps:

1. Turn on the Cross-Reference Feature bar by choosing Tools | Reference | Cross-Reference.

2. Click on the Reference drop-down button at the left side of the Feature Bar and choose Paragraph/Outline.

EXPERT ADVICE

Note that you can also make Cross-References to pages, footnote/endnote numbers, counters, and other objects.

3. Now place the insertion point within the paragraph you wish to refer to (remember: this is the *target*).

CAUTION

Be sure the insertion point appears after the paragraph number code you want to refer to, or the reference will be inaccurate.

4. In the Target window of the Cross-Reference Feature Bar, type a word that briefly describes the subject matter of the target material (for example, **powers**).
5. Click the Mark Target button on the Cross-Reference Feature Bar to insert that Target code at that location.
6. Now move to the spot in your document where you want to make reference to the targeted material.
7. With the correct target name still showing in the Target window, just click Mark Reference on the Feature Bar to insert a Reference code at that location.

You can also generate these Cross-References, along with any Tables of Contents or Authorities, at any time by choosing Tools | Reference | Generate.

Note that a question mark now appears where the paragraph number should go. To turn that question mark into the correct paragraph number, click Generate. Then, in the dialog box that appears, click OK. Or you can wait until your document is completed and Generate all of the Cross-References at one time.

Make a Pleading Paper

For you non-lawyers, a pleading paper is *not* a kind of paper that begs for mercy. It is paper with vertical ruled lines down one or both sides, and numbers running down the left margin.

To start a document using Pleading Paper, just follow these steps:

1. Click the New document icon to create a new pleading paper. Skip this step if you want to format the current document as a pleading paper.
2. Click the Legal Toolbar's Pleading icon.

3. In the Pleading Paper dialog box which appears, choose your margin, line, font, numbering, and other options as you prefer, then click OK.

WordPerfect will then generate a sheet of pleading paper, as shown in Figure A.1, and you can begin typing away.

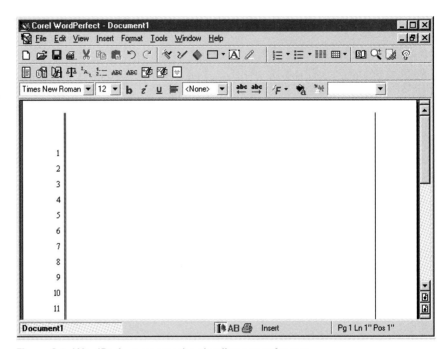

Figure A.1 WordPerfect creates the pleading paper for you

The line numbering that you will see on the paper cannot be seen if you are working in Draft view, but it will be visible in Page view. These numbers and the vertical lines are actually stored in a Watermark. This is done intentionally to make it practically impossible to accidentally delete—but it also makes it practically impossible to edit the darn thing if you want to change its appearance or add your firm's name to the paper.

CAUTION

The line numbers stored in the Watermark are automatically stored at double spacing for the font you choose, so you should use Format | Line | Spacing on the Menu bar to set double spacing in the document. If you use a different font for the body of the document or anything other than double spacing, the lines of text will not line up properly with the line numbers printed in the margin of the page.

Comparing Different Versions of the Same Document

One more feature of WordPerfect deserves mention as well. Many lawyers need to keep track of revisions to documents as they are passed back and forth between offices or between attorneys in the same office. One way to display quickly what has changed from draft to draft is by using the Compare Document feature that's built into WordPerfect. Using this feature, material added to the new version will appear as highlighted, or "redlined," text, while material deleted from the old document will appear with a line through it as "strikeout" text.

New material is redlined

This is the ~~old~~new version of a document.

Deleted text has a strikeout line

To use this feature, be sure that both the original version and the revised version of your document are stored to different filenames on your disk. Follow these steps:

1. Locate and note the filenames of the two documents you wish to compare.

2. Open the newer (more recently revised) version of the document.

3. From the File menu, choose Document | Add Compare Markings.

4. In the Add Compare Markings dialog box, specify the filename of the original (older) version of the document in the Compare Current Document to: entry field.

5. Specify the level of detail you want compared by selecting one of the radio buttons under Compare by.

Compare by
- ⦿ Word   ○ Sentence
- ○ Phrase   ○ Paragraph

6. Click OK.

That's it! The two documents will be compared and the redline and strikeout markings will be added in the appropriate places. You can either save the marked-up document to the same filename as the new version or (as is usually preferred) save it to a third filename so that both the original and the revised versions remain on your disk.

EXPERT ADVICE

If you save the marked-up version to the same filename as the revised document, you can easily restore the revised version to its original condition by choosing File | Compare Document | Remove Compare Markings.

Index